T0354965

CULTURAL GENE

OF THE INSTITUTION

CULTURAL GENE

OF THE INSTITUTION

JIAMING SUN

Archway Publishing books may be ordered through booksellers or by contacting:

Archway Publishing
1663 Liberty Drive
Bloomington, IN 47403
www.archwaypublishing.com
844-669-3957

Cover design by Michelle Fogg
Cover images @Texas A&M University-Commerce, @Adobe Stock Images

ISBN: 978-1-6657-5338-8 (sc)
ISBN: 978-1-6657-5339-5 (e)

Library of Congress Control Number: 2023922061

Print information available on the last page.

Archway Publishing rev. date: 11/30/2023

CONTENTS

FOREWORD

Jiaming Sun's *Cultural Gene of the Institution* offers a close-up of American university life based on the author's intimate, first-hand experience across various institutions. Through "American Campus Observation," the author investigates the characteristics of Western cultural attributes by utilizing sociological methods, including field observation and comparative analysis. The book elucidates the underlying reason behind specific cases and common phenomena, particularly the distinctions rooted in Western and Eastern cultural backgrounds. In *Cultural Gene of the Institution*, Dr. Sun shares a revealing look at the operations and fundamental systems in higher education. He sociologically examines and explains the unique environment of the American and Chinese university system.

His book provides pertinent information about the Western and Eastern university systems that are frequently overlooked or misunderstood by the average layperson or those who are often critical of how a university system operates. *Cultural Gene of the Institution* clarifies how the classroom operates as faculty members follow the class syllabus while covering the hiring process and faculty evaluations once hired. He elaborates on the campus ecology regarding student organizations and the transformation of students who are integrated into a diverse society with employable skills and knowledge that assist them in becoming successful citizens regardless of their specific culture. This book addresses the professor's environment and activities while also describing the attention given to the students, such as special groups that emphasize individualism yet describe the development of the whole person. A special chapter shares information on the preparation and integration of the student into professional society. Also included is a stirring chapter that compares graduate research writing in China and America.

In the first chapter, Dr. Sun describes in detail the development of the class syllabus, especially in American universities. This document becomes the contract between the professor and the student. He explains how important this document is in terms of representing the university. It is sort of a pledge to the students that most state government educational commissions require. Every class must have a syllabus, and it is published for public consumption. In addition to describing such details in the classroom, there are several chapters relating to the training and preparation of university professors, their hiring (recruitment) process, and their promotion (tenure). It is here where the Chinese and American systems may differ somewhat. The training in the Chinese system is more standardized, while the American system is more individualized with flexibility. Dr. Sun's experience in both systems has made him familiar with how promotion is conducted; he elaborates on how research productivity is essential in both systems, but with the American system giving research productivity and scholarly contributions more weight in the promotion process. There is a very clear, detailed chapter on salary. He described the Chinese as having a "more centralized and standardized salary structure" than the American university system.

In Chapter Seven, Dr. Sun presents an area addressing "multicultural ecology" in the American university. He highlights that American colleges and universities emphasize a curriculum of diversity and a global perspective. Such an idea supports the Quality Enhancement Plan (QEP), a program where Dr. Sun is employed. The QEP focuses on the interconnected world, assisting students in developing a global perspective through international travel and creating projects that expose students to new cultures. This global perspective, although appearing to be the opposite of individualism, as discussed in Chapter 12, "The Individualized Campus Ecology of American College Students and its Social Consequences," allowed Dr. Sun to share information on how American culture and universities practice individualism in terms of projects and assignments while encouraging independence. This contrasts with Chinese culture, which he describes as valuing "harmony and collective well-being."

Culture Gene of the Institution has several chapters that address the development of the whole person, student organizations, students with disabilities, students as workers after school, students identifying and finding an ideal partner, and the growth of virtual course work. In presenting these chapters, Dr. Sun compares the similarities and differences between the American and Chinese university systems. His chapter on China and America's graduate research proved to be an interesting and informative viewpoint. In this chapter, he compares how the Eastern and Western cultures, respectively, promote a macro and micro perspective regarding research conducted by graduate students.

Dr. Sun's book is a collection of several articles he has written that describe some of the basic and highly dynamic areas of the Chinese and American university system. His book is a clear indication of how the two university systems are similar yet different. The enclosed information provides valuable insight into the operation of two of the world's superpower higher educational systems.

Willie J. Edwards, Ph.D.
Professor – Department Head
Department of Sociology & Criminal Justice
Texas A&M University-Commerce

PREFACE AND ACKNOWLEDGMENT

I have lived in the United States for over twenty years, spending most of my time on campus. In 1997, my first stop upon arriving in the United States was at the Institute of Global Affairs at Syracuse University in New York. A year later, I was invited to visit the Department of Sociology at the University of Illinois in Chicago and participated in research projects related to globalization. Subsequently, I was granted permission to pursue a doctoral degree. I completed my doctoral dissertation in 2005 and obtained my Ph.D. At the same time, I was hired as a faculty member at Texas A&M University in Texas. Looking back, I have spent almost all of these twenty-plus years on campus and have personally experienced the characteristics of Western culture in university campus life and institutional development.

However, I also had nearly twenty years of campus life in my home country. As early as 1971, I attended a high school in the bustling streets of Shanghai. During the Cultural Revolution, students became Red Guards, and senior intellectuals were targeted for criticism. Campus life was filled with an atmosphere of ideological struggle. I graduated in 1975, during the height of the "Up to the Mountains and Down to the Countryside" movement. As a student leader at the time, I actively signed up to work in the Shanghai Huangshan Tea Plantation in Anhui Province, where I served in grassroots units for over six years. After the resumption of the national college entrance examination, I was admitted to Fudan University's branch campus with a sociology major in 1981. After graduating in 1985, I was assigned to Fudan University and taught in both the Department of International Politics and the Department of Sociology until I went abroad in 1997. Therefore, if we add it all up, including the years during high school, I spent a total of 20 years in campus life. Since youth is a crucial stage in life, these twenty years of campus life fundamentally shaped my worldview and perspective on life. However, at the time, I did not perceive the distinctiveness of Eastern culture in campus life and institutional aspects, nor did I contrast it significantly with Western culture.

After comparing twenty years of life in Western and Eastern campuses, I began to perceive the differences between them and the significant importance of cultural genes in institutional development. Discussions about Western culture can be found in various publications; however, there seem to be relatively few articles that approach the topic from the perspective of cultural genes, focusing on campus life and institutional development.

In the course of human societal development, two major cultural development models emerged: Eastern culture and Western culture. The fundamental difference between these two cultures lies in their philosophical ideologies of collectivism and individualism. Individualism is closely associated with Western culture, while collectivism is intertwined with Eastern culture. For instance, in China, from the collectivism of feudal society to the collectivism of socialism, there has been an emphasis on the interests of society, the state, and the collective. A society-centric value system is the mainstream in Chinese society. On the other hand, Western market economies have brought about individualism, emphasizing individualism and inherent rights and freedoms.

As the renowned contemporary sociologist Peter L. Berger stated in his book *The Capitalist Revolution*, the individualistic genes within Western culture are a prerequisite for the formation of modern capitalist economies in Europe and America. The individualistic genes rooted in Western traditional culture were first articulated as cultural ideals of personal liberation, individual autonomy, and personal freedom through the Enlightenment and religious reforms. Subsequently, these cultural ideals provided the foundation for forming contractual relationships among individuals. Because contractual relationships clearly defined individual rights and obligations, this marked a crucial step towards the institutionalization of the modern market economy order.

From this perspective, the formation of the individualism concept in Western culture has historical and cultural roots. As a result, it has had a substantial impact on the design and operation of social systems. In the process of modern Western societal development, alongside the active market economy, individualism, which is a cultural gene that aligns with the functioning of the market economy, has displayed significant social influence, ultimately contributing to the establishment of institutionalized market economies and the regulation of the order in Western societies in modern history.

Similarly, within the cultural genes of socialism, collectivism undeniably constitutes the core of socialist cultural genes, aiming to spread and replicate itself as extensively as possible among its members. It places greater emphasis on individual subordination to the collective, with collective interests taking precedence over individual interests. Within the collective, there is an emphasis on hierarchical and orderly relationships, with a clear "hierarchy pattern." Simultaneously, the cultural genes of collectivism seek to monitor, identify, and criticize various non-socialist cultural ideologies, resisting and limiting their potential harm to socialist systems and ideological frameworks. They are vigilant and critical of so-called "universal values" touted by the West, such as "human rights" and "freedom." They resist capitalist cultural views centered around individualism and materialism, and they address and refute various erroneous notions that criticize, attack, or seek to subvert socialist ideology.

It is evident that market economies originate within the framework of individualistic culture and carry distinct individualistic cultural genes. However, transplanting Western market economies into a socialist system in China is not only an unprecedented creative endeavor but also a massive and intricate "genetic engineering" project. This "genetic engineering" project involves the initial separation of the capitalist economic system from its capitalist institutional context. Subsequently, it entails the recombination and integration of this capitalist economic system with the cultural genes of socialism. The end goal is to create a market economy that combines Western market competitiveness with socialist characteristics, ultimately integrating it into the socialist system, achieving a perfect synergy with socialism, and unveiling an unprecedented historical chapter known as the "socialist market economy." The complexity and magnitude of this project become apparent, considering the numerous formidable challenges that arise during this transformation process. The fundamental reason for these challenges lies in the fact that the institutional transition has not been aligned with the accompanying cultural transition, and culture is constrained by its core "genetic" components.

Institutions and culture complement each other. Having institutions without culture makes it difficult for institutions to be effectively implemented. Institutions must be supplemented by culture to manifest their positive functions and effects. Cultural genes and institutional outcomes are mutually causal. In this sense, transforming the face of a society doesn't just involve changing its laws and institutions but also altering its overall culture and the many individuals who carry this culture. Completing this endeavor may require several generations.

"Institutions" are also the "yardstick" of civilization. Or, one could say that "institutions," as a subset of the cultural concept, represent the benchmarking dimension, serving as the "technical indicators" that gauge whether a culture is civilized. Institutions are the "tangible" aspect, while culture is the "soul." Once institutions are established, culture can be revealed. Therefore, issues related to institutions are essentially issues related to culture. The uniqueness of culture determines the uniqueness of institutions. So, when we talk about exploring the "characteristics of institutions," we are essentially delving into the "features of culture."

This book is a collection of several articles I have published on my WeChat public account regarding "Observations of Overseas Campuses." It aims to provide insights into the characteristics of Western cultural genes through observations of life at American universities and investigations into various institutional aspects. These articles are based on my firsthand experiences and interactions in different cultural environments in the East and the West. By using a comparative approach, they showcase the real-life aspects of campus life at American universities. The book consists of 19 independent articles written in an accessible and straightforward style, suitable for readers from diverse cultural backgrounds and professional fields. I welcome readers' feedback and comments.

Acknowledgments

At the impending publication of this book, I would like to express gratitude to the head of the Department, Dr. Willie Edwards, for writing the foreword to this book. For the past several decades, he has served as the department head for consecutive terms. When I applied for this position and was invited for a campus interview 18 years ago, he was the department head. He drove to the airport to pick me up, leaving a deep impression on me.

I want to thank my research assistant, Rilla Cox, who started preliminary editing and revisions for this book a year ago. Despite completing her graduate studies thereafter, she voluntarily continued the unfinished editing. During the summer, despite the scorching heat, she persisted in completing all the editing work according to the schedule. Her dedication is commendable.

I want to express gratitude to my research assistant, Michelle Fogg, who took over Rilla's editing work and conducted the final proofreading review and editing of the entire book. She contributed to the layout of the book and the design of the book cover. Under her efforts, she maintained communication with the publishing house and submitted the final version of the book as required.

I also want to thank Richard Tecson and Aimee Reff at the publishing house for their utmost efforts in this book's final printing and publication.

Jiaming Sun in Oak Village, TX

CHAPTER 1

The System Design and Concept of the Course Syllabus in the American University

I n American colleges and universities, a well-crafted syllabus is an instructor's signature creation, encapsulating their teaching approach, subject expertise, and overall course quality. From the perspective of students, who act as consumers of this educational product, they make course selections based on factors such as its unique features, cost, instructional approach, and anticipated intellectual benefits – all of which can be readily gleaned from the syllabus.

In this context, instructors are akin to entrepreneurs, meticulously shaping and refining their educational offerings. This level of care and preparation elevates them beyond mere street vendors. Consequently, it is commonplace for American academic institutions to request applicants to submit their existing syllabi when applying for teaching positions. This practice is valuable for assessing an applicant's teaching philosophy, pedagogical style, professional competence, and alignment with student needs. Thus, the syllabus emerges as another significant product of college and university instructors, complementing their contributions to scientific research.

The most basic work in college teaching management is the formulation of a syllabus, the system design and concept of which directly affect the level of teaching quality. The syllabus is a document that specifies the content of a course in the form of an outline according to the lesson plan and includes the purpose, scope, depth, structure of the educational content, progress, and basic requirements for students. The syllabus is the primary basis for instructors to teach and is an important standard for checking and evaluating students' academic performance and measuring the quality of teachers' progress.

Colleges and universities in the United States, especially state universities, clearly stipulate that the formulation of the syllabus is the primary responsibility of instructors, and the public release of the syllabus is mandated by state law and must be addressed. More specifically, instructors must submit the syllabus after clarifying the teaching courses they agree to undertake. This must be made public at least one month before the start of each semester so that students have enough time to select classes. Some colleges and universities also publish the instructors' academic resumes (CVs) while publishing the syllabus on the relevant school websites so that students can easily check the information about the instructors and choose the courses of their preferred instructors. Generally speaking, the design of the American college syllabus system has the following characteristics:

Institutionalized

The syllabus of almost all American universities' related courses can be found online. This is due to the formulation and publication of the syllabus as a basic regulation of the university teaching system and the basic code of conduct for instructors. The syllabus makes it easy for students to select courses and enables them to understand the entire course expectations and layout before the semester starts. Instructors have a relatively clear arrangement of courses and lesson plans to be offered in the upcoming semester, including textbooks, reading materials, discussion questions, examination methods, and scoring matrixes. Therefore, the syllabus design is essential for completing a successful course.

Figure 1.1 – Sample Syllabus Introduction

COURSE INFORMATION

Lectures (Web-Enhanced): MWF 10:00a-10:50a
Classroom: SS309 **meet:** 1/14/2019 through 5/10/2019

This syllabus intends to help you clearly understand the course goals, expectations, testing methods and topics we are going through so you may maximize your performance. It should also help you avoid mistakes and misunderstandings that may affect your grade adversely.

Text W. Lawrence Neuman. *Social Research Methods: Qualitative and Quantitative Approaches.* 7th Ed. Publisher: Pearson, 2009 ISBN-10: 0205615961; ISBN-13: 978-0205615964. (required). It can be purchased through Amazon for the 7th edition.

Institutions have a zero-tolerance policy for missing syllabuses on the first day of class. Therefore, formulating a teaching syllabus in advance, publishing it publicly on the Internet, and downloading it at will are all standard practices in American colleges and universities. For example, in the spring semester, the department head begins to speak with instructors to collect feedback on the courses the university will be able to offer in the fall. After the department is fully balanced according to the education requirements, the courses to be offered in the fall are determined, and the syllabus submission deadline is set. When the deadline nears, the department secretary will provide reminders, including that the submission of the syllabus is mandated by the school and must be upheld. Failure to submit it on time is a serious dereliction of duty.

Personalized

There are a wide variety of courses offered in American colleges and universities. Even when the same courses are available, different instructors' teaching materials and methods will vary. Instructors have absolute autonomy over what textbooks to use in their courses, how to arrange courseware content, and how to gauge students' knowledge. Therefore, individualization of the syllabus is logical and necessary. In various universities in the United States, different instructors have favored textbooks and preferred task assignments that they prefer to utilize. This leads to individual and unique ways in which they formulate their syllabuses. It is impossible to see a similar situation in China, where the Ministry of Education formulated the teaching syllabus uniformly in the 1950s and 1960s. In the 1980s, the teaching and research office set the same teaching syllabus for the same course. For example, the teaching objectives stipulated in the Research Methods class I took are as follows:

Figure 1.2 – Sample Teaching Objectives

Student Learning Outcomes/Objectives

This course provides an introduction to research methods and focuses particularly on the application ⟨ social research, developing fundamental, conceptual and empirical research skills in both quantitative and qualitative research methods. The course will provide students with tools to be able to apply in their own research and to understand scholarly work produced by others. The main goals of the cours are (upon successful completion of the course the student will):

- Understand the relationship between theory and research as they apply to social science as well as to public policy;
- Demonstrate a wide variety of research techniques and design issues that are utilized in soci. science research;
- Describe survey instrumentation and be able to develop a quality survey questionnaire;
- Enable to use appropriate techniques to answer research questions;
- Identify the components of and be able to construct a research proposal;

At the same U.S. institution, another professor in the same department set up a research methods course with different teaching objectives, showing its characteristics as follows:

Figure 1.3 – Differing Teaching Objectives

Student Learning Outcomes:
1. Students will demonstrate their comprehension of major concepts and methodological techniques through scores on objective quizzes.
2. Students will demonstrate their comprehension of using the library databases to gain access to peer reviewed literature
3. Students will demonstrate their comprehension of citing peer-reviewed literature according to APA format Sociology 331.01W Syllabus Spring 2014 2
4. Students will synthesize peer-review literature by writing a literature review
5. Students will demonstrate their ability to critique the literature in written assignments
6. Student will demonstrate the ability to assess and evaluate the merits of particular methodological techniques in written assignments
7. Students will show their ability to apply social scientific logic, reasoning and

Strictly speaking, each instructor's syllabus is his personal quasi-intellectual property and cannot be copied without permission.

Normalized

Although the syllabus of each course and each instructor is different, the structure of the content and format need to be relatively uniform and standardized. The relevant policies stipulated by the Academic Affairs Office of the university, including federal and state laws and regulations, must be reflected in each syllabus. For example, the policy on student cheating and plagiarism (Cheating & Plagiarism), the special policy on students with disabilities (Students with Disabilities), and the nondiscrimination policy (Nondiscrimination Notice) are all required to be mentioned in the syllabus.

Figure 1.4 – Sample Disability Policy

ADA Statement
Students with Disabilities
The Americans with Disabilities Act (ADA) is a federal anti-discrimination statute that provides comprehensive civil rights protection for persons with disabilities. Among other things, this legislation requires that all students with disabilities be guaranteed a learning environment that provides for reasonable accommodation of their disabilities. If you have a disability requiring an accommodation, please contact:
Office of Student Disability Resources and Services

In addition, the handling methods (Policies on Enrollment, "X," "DP," "DF," and Withdrawal) for students' course selection, withdrawal, failure, etc., should also be mentioned in the syllabus. These are all part of the normalized content. The department secretary will review each syllabus and submit it to the university's Academic Affairs Office for the unified announcement. Some universities also stipulate that all university syllabuses must be affixed with the school's logo to reflect a specific recognition of the school. Therefore, this part of the content in the syllabus can be used without modification (unless the policy changes). What needs to be modified is the update of teaching materials, the arrangement of each semester, and any adjustments to course content. The syllabus usually has at least four to six pages; some more detailed ones can reach ten or even a dozen pages. I have never seen a one or 2-page syllabus.

Figure 1.5 – Sample Course Schedule

The course schedule is tentative and somewhat subject to change. Although this course will follow the schedule, it is possible that some adjustments will be made as we progress through the semester.

Week	Dates (T, R)	Topic	Readings
1	Aug.28, 30	Introduction to the course outline and syllabus. Science and research.	Ch. 1
2	Sep.4, 6	Dimensions of research	Ch. 2
3	Sep.11, 13	Theory and research.	Ch. 3
4	Sep. 18, 20	How to Write a Research Proposal.	Ch. 4
5	Sep.25, 27	The Literature Review and Ethical Concerns	Ch. 5
6	Oct. 2, 4	Qualitative and Quantitative research designs.	Ch. 6
7	Oct. 9, 11	**Review,**	Ch. 1-6
8	Oct. 16, 18	***** Mid term exam*****	
9	Oct. 23, 25	Qualitative and Quantitative, Measurement.	Ch. 7

Detailed

The syllabus should be detailed in content, and the teaching materials should also be updated at the time of publication. At the same time, some basic course information must be clearly announced, including course name, instructor name, phone number, email, and office hours. In addition to those details, the syllabus should also include the basic requirements of the course (Course Requirements), including attendance, online activities (Online Activity), homework, quizzes (Assignment/Quiz), writing and discussion presentations, term report (Writing and Presentation Term Project), basic mid-term requirements for exams and final exams (Exams), scoring methods (Grading Policy), basic requirements for students' classroom performance (Student Performance Expectations), etc.

Figure 1.6 – Sample Grading Policy

Grading Policy

Attendance	80
Homework/Reading	70
Proposal/Presentation	80
Quizzes	60
Midterm Exam	80
Final Exam	90
Overall performance	40
Total	**500**

Overall performance points (40 points) based primarily on a ranking percentile in the class will be added on a student's total points by the end of the semester. For instance, a student who is at the 80th percentile will receive 36 points, and a student who is at the 60th percentile will receive 28 points and so on (See the detail at Stimulative Grading Scheme in D2L).

Final letter grade: A: 450-500
B: 400-449
C: 350-399
D: 300-349
F: below 299

Students' computer operating requirements are also listed in detail, such as the requirement of specific software, the method of communicating with teachers, the email address (Email Correspondence), etc. If it is an online course, it is also necessary to clarify the network's support department and telephone number so that the student can contact relevant parties in time if errors or interruptions with the Internet are experienced. Finally, detailed topics, reading materials, course scenarios, and so on must also be included in the weekly course schedule. Usually, on the first class day of my courses, I always need to spend at least half of the time explaining the syllabus so that each student can understand the content, requirements, grading rules, expectations, etc. of the course. At the same time, the syllabus quiz can be arranged for fully online courses or for courses with intermittent face-to-face interactions to ensure that students fully understand it.

Testable

The syllabus serves as a two-way contract. It reflects a contract between instructors and institutions and between instructors and students and is a binding document. Teachers should strive to complete the tasks stipulated in the contract in a timely manner, and they will be assessed accordingly. Students must also complete the coursework according to the requirements and regulations of the syllabus contract. If students cannot or will not accept the syllabus requirements, they may choose another course within the first two weeks of the start of the semester. Once a student decides to remain in a course, it translates as an acceptance of the syllabus contract.

The student learning effect (Student Learning Outcome) listed in the syllabus serves as a criterion at the end of each semester. The school requests that students evaluate the teaching situation of the instructor each semester. The assessment includes whether the relevant courses are carried out according to the syllabus requirements. At the same time, instructors must conduct a self-evaluation. For example, Student Learning Outcome Measures estimate the effect of students' learning and whether they reached the standard. The Academic Affairs Office of the university, such as the Teaching Effectiveness Supervision Department (Institutional Effectiveness), will also check and evaluate students' learning outcomes according to the syllabus, obtain evidence and statistics, and accountability to promote the teaching quality of the institution as well as maintain and improve the university's reputation.

Teaching syllabi hold a position of great significance in American colleges and universities. Their deeper significance lies in encapsulating a sense of contractual commitment that places responsibility upon the instructor while simultaneously affording a degree of freedom and individualized recognition of teaching style and content. The syllabus serves as a critical resource for students, offering information and the ability to make informed choices—a manifestation of the market-oriented concept emphasizing student-driven freedom of choice.

The efficacy of teaching within higher education institutions hinges upon the quality of instruction, with the syllabus of each instructor's courses playing a pivotal role. An instructor lacking a well-structured syllabus is deemed unqualified, as it is through a proficient syllabus that a high level of teaching effectiveness is achievable. Therefore, the distinction between a first-class university and others often lies in the quality of its instructors, exemplified by the excellence of their syllabi.

Relevant Information for Reference

The curriculum syllabus design and teaching systems in Chinese and American colleges and universities exhibit similarities and differences. Here's a comparison of some key aspects:

Curriculum Design

1. Similarities: Chinese and American institutions strive to provide a well-rounded education that includes general education requirements and specialized courses. They aim to develop critical thinking, problem-solving skills, and subject expertise.
2. Differences: Chinese universities often have a more structured and prescriptive curriculum, with fewer elective

options than American universities. American institutions typically emphasize flexibility and allow students to choose a broader range of courses based on their interests and academic goals.

Course Content

1. Similarities: Both Chinese and American universities offer courses that cover various disciplines, such as sciences, humanities, social sciences, and professional fields. Core subjects in majors are typically similar, focusing on foundational knowledge and skills.
2. Differences: Chinese universities often emphasize theoretical knowledge and mastery of foundational concepts. American universities tend to provide a broader range of elective courses, allowing students to explore interdisciplinary topics and personalize their educational experience.

Teaching Methods

1. Similarities: Chinese and American institutions employ lectures, discussions, laboratory work, and group projects as standard teaching methods. They aim to promote active learning, critical thinking, and collaborative skills.
2. Differences: Chinese universities often have larger class sizes, leading to more lecture-based teaching. American universities often encourage student engagement through smaller class sizes, interactive discussions, and a greater emphasis on student participation.

Assessment and Evaluation

1. Similarities: Chinese and American universities use a combination of exams, projects, presentations, and

assignments to assess student learning. They both aim to
evaluate students' knowledge, skills, and understanding
of the subject matter.

2. Differences: Chinese universities typically emphasize
high-stakes exams and standardized testing, which heavily influence students' grades. American universities often adopt a more diversified assessment approach, including continuous evaluation throughout the semester and a
focus on student engagement and participation.

Educational Philosophy

1. Similarities: Chinese and American institutions value
pursuing knowledge, academic excellence, and developing
critical thinking skills. They strive to prepare students for
future careers and lifelong learning.

2. Differences: Chinese universities often prioritize
discipline-specific knowledge and rote learning, while
American universities emphasize interdisciplinary
approaches, critical inquiry, and the development of
problem-solving and analytical skills.

It's important to note that the educational systems in China and
the United States can vary across institutions, and these comparisons provide general observations. Curriculum syllabus design
and teaching systems can also evolve based on various factors,
including cultural, societal, and economic influences.

CHAPTER 2

The Ideas, Forms, and Indicators of Students' Course Evaluations in the American University

Almost all universities in the United States have a Course Evaluation for each class offered, which is made available to students before the end of the semester. This is sometimes also called a routine teaching evaluation. Its purpose is to examine whether the semester's instruction has been carried out according to the syllabus. It also acts to gain students' feedback about how satisfied they are with the course and so on. Generally speaking, American colleges and universities' course evaluation is multi-level and multi-faceted. Students' course evaluations are only one type of teaching evaluation. Other examples include peer evaluation, self-evaluation, and institutional evaluation. Teaching evaluations are of great significance for strengthening college instructors in lesson preparation, teaching strategies, overall presentation and quality of lessons, and as a gauge of student satisfaction with the course. This chapter introduces the students' course evaluation.

The student's course evaluation in American colleges and universities has long been a practice and is a basic routine in college teaching management. Each school has its own approach to conducting its students' course evaluations. Usually, within one or two weeks before the final exam of each semester, the school will send teaching evaluation materials to each department, and the department secretary will distribute them to the instructor's mailbox as required. The instructor is required to arrange time for students to receive and complete the course evaluation in terms of the current semester. The course evaluation results often become the basis for gauging the teaching effectiveness of the course, which is an important indicator of the level of instruction and quality of the professor and can affect the professor's annual merit increase (similar to a performance award, the merit increase is an increase in base salary as opposed to a one-time remittance), as well as renewals, promotions, and awards of tenure. Therefore, the school's administration at all levels, including the provost, deans, department heads, and instructors, attaches great importance to student course evaluations. The characteristics of the student course evaluation in American colleges and universities are reflected in three aspects:

"Demand-side": Concept of Course Evaluations

The concept of the "demand-side" in education regards students as active consumers of knowledge, with their satisfaction as the primary basis for course evaluations. Consequently, student course evaluations can be likened to the practice of leaving feedback after using a product, where the voice of the student-consumer holds significant weight.

This perspective has shifted the traditional view of students as passive entities managed within the administrative structure of educational institutions. Instead, students are recognized as consumers whose input is integral to maintaining a balanced teaching ecology. In this context, student course evaluations are not just a procedure but a right—a choice that students can exercise. They are free to decide whether to participate in these evaluations. This freedom extends to the absence of administrative coercion; students cannot be compelled to partake in course evaluations. Furthermore, evaluations are not only anonymous but also voluntary. As a result, participation rates in course evaluations can vary widely, and students who choose not to participate do not face any adverse consequences regarding course selection, scholarships, graduation, or other aspects of their academic journey.

The "demand-side" concept also aligns with contemporary educational thought's emphasis on activating and nurturing students' sense of agency. It champions a student-centered constructivist teaching approach and underscores students' positive role in shaping and upholding the teaching ecology. In American colleges and universities, this "demand-side" concept in student course evaluations finds expression in the form and criteria used for teaching evaluations.

"Student-led": Form of Course Evaluation

Student course evaluations use two different methods: on paper and online. Course evaluations on paper require students to complete them in class. After the teacher announces the school's course evaluation in class, a volunteer student must be selected to distribute the forms and supervise the entire evaluation process. At this time, the teacher must leave the classroom until after the evaluation. In the process of student course evaluations, students cannot discuss with each other or fill in on another's behalf, as the evaluations must be completed independently. After students complete the course evaluation form, the volunteer student is responsible for sealing all the course evaluation forms and sending these materials to the department office, as the instructor cannot handle them. On the other hand, online evaluations are relatively flexible. Students may choose to complete the evaluation at any time prior to the final exam. All of these student reviews are anonymous. Student participation in the paper evaluations conducted in the classroom is much greater than in the online evaluations. Students in the classroom on the day of the paper evaluation can participate, and a student rarely abandons the evaluation and leaves without submitting it.

The scores given by most students in the teaching evaluation are relatively fair. Still, it does not rule out that individual students deliberately give low scores to their instructors for various reasons, including the idea that their final grades are estimated to have fallen below the expected passing scores. This, however, is relatively rare. The scoring has multiple choice and short answer questions, a mixture of quantitative and qualitative. Since each student's evaluation of the teacher will be different, it is rare to see an absolute high or absolute low score on quantitative questions. If a professor's teaching effect is generally good, the average score will be around four (if 1-5 is the scale, with five being the best).

Figure 2.1 – Sample Teaching Evaluation Quantitative Questions

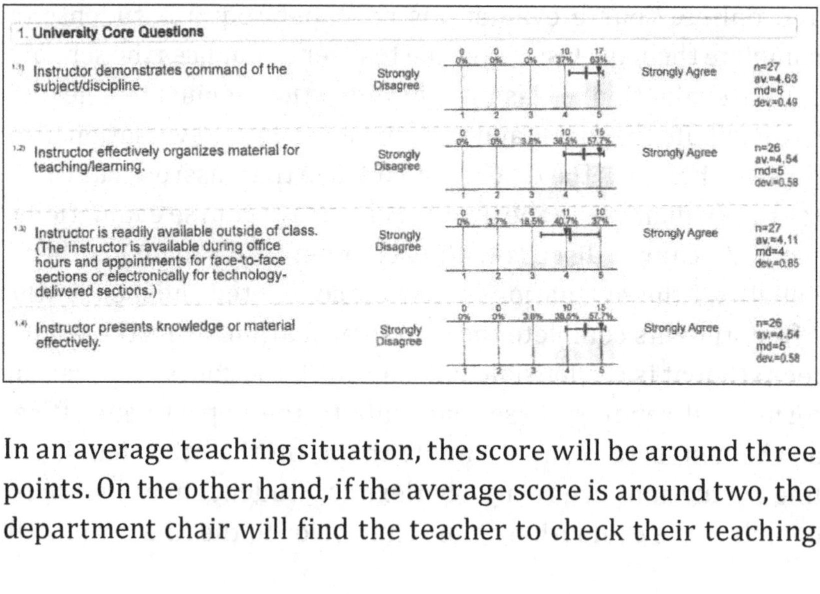

In an average teaching situation, the score will be around three points. On the other hand, if the average score is around two, the department chair will find the teacher to check their teaching

content and method and request that it be improved. If there is no progress after a few semesters, the professor will have no choice but to leave. Qualitative questions reflect students' opinions on the teacher's teaching effectiveness, including both praise and complaints. Because of the anonymous evaluation, students can express their feelings without fear of reprisal. Usually, qualitative questions can reflect the teaching style characteristics of teachers, but it is difficult to find them in quantitative questions.

Figure 2.2 – Sample Teaching Evaluation Qualitative Questions

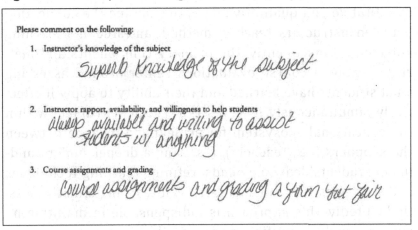

Teaching evaluations in American colleges and universities are multi-level and multi-faceted. Student course evaluations are just one type of teaching evaluation. Therefore, its score can only be used as a reference for the quality of teachers' level of instruction. Even if the student evaluation score is used to evaluate perfor-mance (merit), its weight is not so great.

Operationalization: Evaluation and Teaching Indicators

In the realm of student course evaluations, most American colleges and universities have progressively embraced the concept of "Learning Outcomes," viewing it as the central focus of these assessments, commonly known as "student learning effect evaluations" or Student Learning Outcome Assessment (SLOA). The primary objective behind this approach is to harness students' perspectives as valuable input to gather and analyze feedback on the efficacy of instruction. This evaluation process employs various assessment tools, including quantitative and qualitative data, to examine the connection between instructors' teaching methods and students' learning outcomes. Consequently, the primary components and metrics of student course evaluations center around assessing what students have learned and their ability to apply it effectively. Simultaneously, it serves as a crucial instrument within the educational ecosystem for achieving a balance between the suppliers (i.e., teachers), fostering a deeper understanding of students' learning needs, refining teaching techniques and strategies, and enhancing overall teaching effectiveness. Undoubtedly, this approach is indispensable in maintaining rigorous quality certification standards.

Figure 2.3 – Sample Course Evaluation Survey

Course Evaluation Survey

College	Humanities Social Sci & Arts
CourseTitle	Intro to Social Research
Instructor	███████████
Campus	Main

CourseName	SOC-351
DeptCode	SOC
Section	01E
CRN	80592

To complete the following course evaluation, please clearly mark *only within the answer box*.

Q1 What is your expected grade in this course?
A ☐ B ☐ C ☐ D ☐ F ☐

Q2 What is your current rank in school?
Fr ☐ So ☐ Jn ☐ Sn ☐ Gr ☐

Questions 3 through 19 are on a 5 point scale. From left to right response boxes indicate "Strongly Agree," "Agree," "Neutral," "Disagree," and "Strongly Disagree." "Neutral" is the center response box.

Q3 The instructor demonstrated knowledge of course materials
Strongly Agree ☐ ☐ ☐ ☐ ☐ Strongly Disagree

Q4 The instructor was prepared for class
Strongly Agree ☐ ☐ ☐ ☐ ☐ Strongly Disagree

Q5 The instructor was available outside of class
Strongly Agree ☐ ☐ ☐ ☐ ☐ Strongly Disagree

Q6 The instructor stimulated interest in the course.
Strongly Agree ☐ ☐ ☐ ☐ ☐ Strongly Disagree

Q8 The instructor set high standards that challenged me in this course.
Strongly Agree ☐ ☐ ☐ ☐ ☐ Strongly Disagree

Q9 I was provided with timely comments, responses and positive constructive feedback.
Strongly Agree ☐ ☐ ☐ ☐ ☐ Strongly Disagree

Q10 I would recommend this instructor to another student.
Strongly Agree ☐ ☐ ☐ ☐ ☐ Strongly Disagree

Q11 The course description accurately reflected the content of the course.
Strongly Agree ☐ ☐ ☐ ☐ ☐ Strongly Disagree

Q12 Expectations were clearly outlined in the syllabus.
Strongly Agree ☐ ☐ ☐ ☐ ☐ Strongly Disagree

Q13 Reading assignments were of reasonable length and level.
Strongly Agree ☐ ☐ ☐ ☐ ☐ Strongly Disagree

Although the indicators of student course evaluations in American colleges and universities differ, they are all indicators at the school level (University Core Questions) and department level, reflecting its consistency and considering the differences between disciplines. As far as my state university is concerned, its operational teaching evaluation indicators include three major parts: Student Learning Outcomes, Methods of Teaching and Grading, and the general concern of American colleges and universities, which has translated, in recent years, to Preparing Students for an Interconnected World assessment.

1. Questions related to Student Learning Outcomes, such as:
   - This course allowed me to accumulate knowledge in this field (facts, vocabulary, processes, basic skills, competencies)
   - In this course, I was able to get timely guidance, answers, and constructive feedback, which enriched my learning experience
   - This course provides me with appropriate learning activities and opportunities to be successful
   - The content in this course is meaningful and valuable to me
   - The teacher in the class set a challenging high standard for me in this class

2. Questions related to the methods of teaching and grading of teachers, such as:
   - Whether the course materials are adequately prepared
   - Whether the course adequately follows the syllabus
   - Whether feedback on exam papers/assignments is valuable
   - Whether the method of evaluating student work is fair and appropriate
   - Whether the exam/homework covers the course content that the teacher emphasizes
   - Marked materials for exams/homework are returned to students in a timely manner
   - Whether extra-curricular readings and homework help to understand course topics
   - Whether the teacher's explanation of the assignment is clear
   - Whether the course develops critical thinking
   - Does the teacher's class time catch my interest
   - Are teachers easily accessible during office hours
   - Whether the teacher encourages students to participate in class discussions

3. Questions related to the assessment of Preparing Students
    for an Interconnected World, such as:
    *   This course prepared me for an interconnected world
    *   This course improves my understanding of the inter-
        connected knowledge (issues, processes, trends, sys-
        tems) of global dynamics
    *   This course enhances my ability to apply knowledge
        of global dynamic interconnections (problems, pro-
        cesses, trends, systems)
    *   This course inspired me to see myself as a citizen in
        an interconnected and diverse world

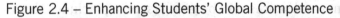

Figure 2.4 – Enhancing Students' Global Competence

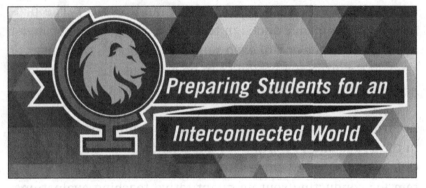

When comparing "student learning effect evaluation" to traditional methods of assessing higher education, it becomes evident
that it represents a significant shift in the perspective of those on
the receiving end of education. Traditional higher education evaluation places schools and teachers at the center, primarily focusing on achieving teaching objectives. In contrast, student learning
effect evaluation prioritizes a student-centered approach and
strongly emphasizes the actual attainment of learning outcomes.
Both teaching objectives and learning effects are connected
to educational expectations, but their emphasis differs markedly. Teaching objectives encompass the broader educational

aspirations of institutions, educators, and disciplines, making them relatively intricate and challenging to evaluate. Conversely, learning effects concentrate on students' specific, measurable, and more attainable learning expectations.

The results of the student course evaluations in American colleges and universities are usually provided to the teaching professor. The professor must summarize the results independently and attach relevant materials to the annual self-evaluation. According to the professor's self-assessment and combined with peer evaluation, institutional evaluation, and other materials, a review and examination will be made, and comments and scores will be given (scoring includes three items of scientific research, teaching, and service). The professor must approve and sign this score as the basis for merit awards. After the end of each semester, although the scores of student's course evaluations can be checked, they are usually not explicitly announced.

According to my experience teaching at a university in China in the 1980s and 1990s and my experience in the United States, Chinese colleges and universities had little to no established system for conducting routine quantitative teaching evaluations. Typically, teaching evaluations were limited to teacher-student symposiums or end-of-term meetings, with very few assessments employing standardized scales. However, in recent years, particularly in national key universities, student evaluations of teaching have gained popularity. These institutions have introduced online teaching evaluation platforms and statistical analysis of the results. Teachers now have access to student reviews for the courses they teach.

Despite this progress, there are certain challenges in Chinese Universities. The school's Academic Affairs Office administers these student course evaluations, and participation is mandatory for all students. Failure to participate affects a student's course selection for the next semester, resulting in a high participation rate but often compromising the rating's reliability. For instance, if the overall weighted average score for a school's course teaching in the spring semester is 4.825 out of five points, it becomes challenging to accurately distinguish the quality of teaching. In some cases, evaluations are completed after students receive their course grades, which can be perceived as unfair.

There is room for improvement in the specific methods of teaching evaluation and the design of evaluation scales in Chinese universities. Moreover, many colleges and universities overly emphasize the public dissemination of students' course evaluation scores, believing that if the results are not made public, there has been no teaching evaluation. This places undue pressure on teachers, leading to concerns about receiving negative evaluations if they are perceived as strict. Additionally, teaching evaluation criteria often lack specificity and clarity. Questions such as whether "the teacher loves teaching," "the teaching method is appropriate," or "the teacher adapts to students' needs" may be seen as vague or unintelligible by students, leaving them unanswered. As a result, student course evaluations have not yet fully fulfilled their potential in prioritizing teaching, enhancing teaching quality, or rectifying the tendency of instructors to prioritize research over teaching. This trend persists in many colleges and universities.

In essence, the effectiveness of teaching evaluations hinges on the accuracy of the underlying concept. Without a sound conceptual foundation, the evaluation process becomes a mere ritual, rendering students' assessments of their teachers inconsequential. The challenges faced by student course evaluations in Chinese colleges and universities represent a pervasive issue, reflecting an imbalance in the educational ecosystem. While the educational systems of Chinese and American universities differ, there are shared aspects worth considering. The consumer-oriented approach to student course evaluations in American higher education, characterized by student-driven evaluations and practical assessment criteria, offers valuable insights that can inform improvements in the Chinese context.

Relevant Information for Reference

The forms and indicators of "students' evaluation of courses" can vary between Chinese and American colleges and universities. While there are similarities, there are also notable differences that can impact the teaching process. Let's compare these aspects in both systems:

Forms of Evaluation

1. Chinese System: In Chinese universities, students' evaluation of courses often takes the form of standardized questionnaires. These questionnaires are typically distributed towards the end of the semester and include multiple-choice and open-ended questions. They cover various aspects of the course, such as teaching effectiveness, course content, workload, and organization.

2. American System: In American colleges and universities, students' evaluation of courses can take multiple forms. Commonly, institutions use online surveys or evaluation platforms where students provide feedback on their learning experiences. Additionally, some institutions may employ in-class evaluations, giving students paper forms to share their opinions on the course and teaching quality.

Indicators of Evaluation

1. Chinese System: Chinese universities often emphasize indicators such as teaching methods, course content, knowledge transfer, and overall organization. Students may be asked to rate the instructor's lecturing skills, clarity of explanations, interaction with students, and ability to stimulate critical thinking. Course-related factors like syllabus design, assignments, and assessment methods may also be evaluated.

2. American System: American universities typically focus on indicators similar to their Chinese counterparts but may include additional elements. Instructors are evaluated based on their teaching effectiveness, communication skills, accessibility, responsiveness to student needs, and ability to create an engaging learning environment. Course-related factors are also important, including content relevance, assignment quality, and grading fairness.

Impact on Teaching

1. Chinese System: In Chinese universities, student evaluations of courses play a significant role in assessing teaching effectiveness. The feedback obtained from these evaluations is often used for faculty performance evaluations, promotions, and rewards. However, there is a concern that relying solely on student evaluations may lead to a greater emphasis on pleasing students rather than focusing on pedagogical excellence.

2. American System: In American colleges and universities, student evaluations are essential for assessing teaching quality. However, they are usually just one component of a broader evaluation process, considering other factors such as peer reviews, self-assessment, and teaching

portfolios. The aim is to provide a more comprehensive and balanced assessment of teaching effectiveness.

It's important to note that the impact of student evaluations on teaching can vary between institutions and even among individual instructors within the same system. While these evaluations provide valuable feedback, they should be used in conjunction with other assessment methods to ensure a fair and accurate evaluation of teaching quality.

CHAPTER 3

The System and Operation of Full-Scale Teacher's Training in American Universities

Although there is no unified college teacher training material or college teacher training network system in the United States, each college and campus system (referring to the group of universities with headquarters and branch campuses) conducts training for teachers in their schools or systems. Regular, normative, all-round, full-staff training aims to ensure the quality of the teaching staff, strengthen ethics, promote scientific research, and improve teaching skills.

Taking myself as a case, here I only intercepted the training file records of the five years after 2005 (i.e., 2005-2010): I participated in the training 30 times in total; the average training time was 40 minutes per session. Among them are ten mandatory trainings, four on-the-job trainings, ten scientific research trainings, and six teaching skills trainings. These trainings do not include undocumented, ad hoc training. The vast majority of training is free, and since it is done online, you can take the training course online at any time, such as weekends or evenings, either at home or on campus. There are quizzes at the end of the training, and you must gain full marks to pass. If you fail to get full marks, you can repeat the quiz several times until you succeed. After passing the full score, you will be notified by email, and some training will also issue certificates, which will be sent to you by mail.

The all-round teacher training system is reflected in the training concept, legislation, and set of school mechanisms. The idea is that the training of all teaching staff is the basic function of a formal institution, which is mainly reflected in four aspects (-tions): Attention, Education, Retention, and Function, reminding you that you need to pay attention and providing you with various continuing education opportunities; trying to keep you on the job; and performing a weed-out function for non-compliance. The School's Office of Training and Development oversees all faculty and staff training programs authorized by the university or campus system; various other training opportunities are also available to meet the requirements of individual departments, specialized content, and various team-building needs to improve work efficiency and help to improve employee competencies and skills.

Figure 3.1 – Training Webpage Welcome

WELCOME

The Office of Training and Development oversees mandated university and systems training for all faculty and staff members. We offer other training opportunities to meet departmental requirements, and customer service and team building sessions to enhance working relationships and help improve the abilities and skills of employees. We are in place and here for the faculty and staff of the university to help them plan and implement their own training events. Our own faculty and staff members facilitate our courses, whether it be a required training with a subject matter expert or training for personal and professional enrichment.

Our goal is to maintain a 100% university wide compliance rating within our university system. We appreciate the continuing support of managers, supervisors, department heads,

Figure 3.2 – Training & Development Menu

TRAINING & **DEVELOPMENT**
Training & Development
Resources
Staff
Self-Paced Online Business Skills Training
2020 Training and Development Calendar
Center for Professional Development
Staff & Faculty Professional Development Day

All-round training can be roughly divided into five categories: normative, post-related, scientific, teaching, and welfare:

Normative Training

The school's personnel office usually arranges normative training and is a part of Human Resource (HR) training, that is, training on local and state regulations and national laws. Most of these trainings are mandatory, such as Ethics, Information Security Training, and Sexual Harassment Compliance. For training on ethics, all faculty (some including staff) are required to complete the training program within 30 days of their official employment and every two years after that. A course on information security requires faculty members to participate within 30 days of accepting the position and every year thereafter. The requirements for these types of training are very strict.

Ethics training covers a wide variety of subtopics, generally including teachers' code of conduct, such as teaching guidelines, teacher-student relationship (avoidance of teacher-student intimate relationships), job responsibilities, and so on, and even small business trip reimbursements, the receiving of gifts, etc. For example, there is a clear limit set that the cost of any gift received cannot be more than $50 USD, and there are special regulations on how to deal with violations. Since there is a great deal of specialized content, the Code of Conduct for Teachers in American Colleges and Universities will be presented in a special article, omitted here for space.

Figure 3.3 - Screenshot of the Receipt of Gifts Policy from the Ethics online training

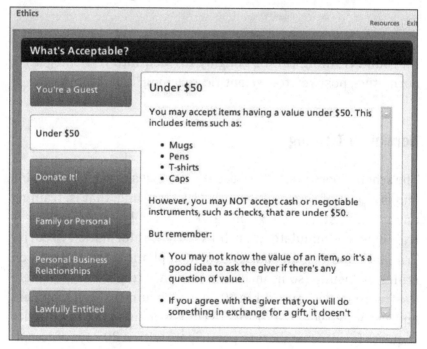

Figure 3.4 - Screenshot of the Public Expenses Reimbursement
Rules from the Ethics online training

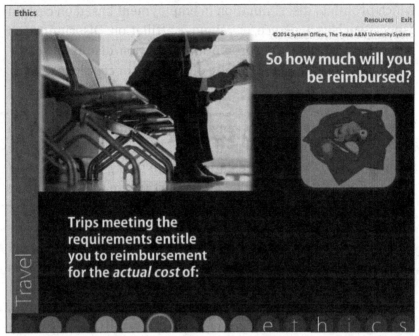

On-the-job Training

Job training is mainly the responsibility of the department to
which the corresponding position belongs. For example, suppose
you are the head of a department. In that case, there are certain
training programs that you must complete in correspondence
to your position, including training on Civil Rights Compliance,
which focuses on ensuring freedom from all forms of discrimination in employment and education and creating an environment
of non-retaliation at work. If anyone determines they have been
discriminated against or subjected to some form of retaliation,
the victim may resort to informal or formal complaint procedures. The department chair must understand and comply with
these policies and regulations.

Other trainings are related to national legislative provisions, such as Equal Opportunity and Affirmative Action training, which prohibits discrimination in employment based on certain aspects such as age, race, or religious affiliation. Discrimination in recruitment, selection, promotion, demotion, dismissal, termination, transfer, training, or any other form of compensation or payment is prohibited.

The graduate school will arrange basic training programs if you are the department's graduate director. This training may include using the relevant graduate database and filling in the data and year-end forms. For example, if you participate in a committee that involves a strong policy, you must be trained in that policy. One year, my sociology department needed to recruit a new lecturer, and the department arranged for me to sit on the Search Committee for Faculty Recruitment. Once a training roster list is reported to the school, the trainee will receive an email reminder: "If you have not obtained the relevant recruitment and selection training course certificate, you must complete the training within one week before you can officially participate in this work." No matter what position you hold within the university system, you must obtain relevant training before taking the job.

Scientific Research Training

Scientific research training is primarily the responsibility of the school's Office of Research and Sponsored Programs. The purpose of this office is to guide and promote the participation of teachers and researchers in various scientific research activities, to provide friendly services, and various other academic research opportunities. Therefore, the content of this training includes how to obtain scientific research funding projects from the federal government and other channels, how to comply with the norms of the research field, and how to use various online information platforms to develop research and funding project topics. Specifically included in this training are Research Compliance Training, Protection of Human Subjects, Time and Effort Reporting Training, Academic Integrity Training, Biosafety Training, and so on. All participating researchers must complete the required compliance training before formally participating.

There are also trainings on the use of online resources such as How to Find Research Funding and How to Use the Global Research Council (GRC) and Pivot Funding Opportunities Database (PIVOT). The GRC is an online platform for finding federally funded research grants. Initiated by 11 institutions, including the National Science Foundation of the United States, the German Science Foundation, and the Chinese Academy of Sciences, it was established in 2012 to explore and seek scientific development strategies that the international scientific and technological community can accept and to promote and achieve more and better international Technology cooperation. PIVOT is designed to help applicants find global research projects with a database of up to 30 billion resources. It provides a variety of literature indexes and abstracts, full text, and image databases and uses a variety of language interfaces. Fourteen language interfaces are available and can be changed at any time during retrieval. It can realize cross-database and specific database searches and provide a global scholar information database (COS Scholar Universe) and global funding database (COS Funding). Researchers can use PIVOT's excellent research assistance resources to immediately obtain the most comprehensive and up-to-date information on scientific research funds, academic conferences, and scholars.

For the investigation and research projects related to the social sciences and humanities, schools set up a special Institutional Review Board (IRB) to be responsible for the review. The IRB, also called an independent ethics committee, is formally designated in the United States to monitor and review biomedical and behavioral research involving humans. The IRB is located at all universities and research institutions and conducts some risk-benefit analysis to determine whether such research should or is permitted. The IRB aims to ensure that appropriate steps are taken to protect the welfare and rights of those who participate as research subjects and is responsible for reviewing the Protection of Human Subjects. Therefore, any person in charge of or involved in a research project involving human subjects must participate in relevant training to obtain approval and conduct relevant research.

Teaching and Technical Training

The teaching technology training is mainly responsible for the school's Center for Faculty Excellence and Innovation, which largely provides applied training, computer skills, technology, online courses, and other training. Its goal is to provide timely and effective support for teaching reform and optimization and to provide opportunities for teacher development and teaching research.

American colleges and universities generally have educational technology training centers that attach great importance to teaching skills training and are open to all school instructors. Teachers can voluntarily go to the teaching skills training center to help improve their teaching level and gain new skills and understandings. All relevant training programs and courses can be viewed online, and training registration can be done immediately. Such training can include Teaching Strategies, The Teaching Professor Blog, Websites for Instructional Use, and Accessibility of Electronic Information Resources training. Suppose you cannot find the particular project you want additional training in. In that case, you can send a request (Faculty Training Request), and the training department can conduct relevant training for you individually. As long as it relates to the teaching theme, it benefits curriculum development and teacher development. Most of these trainings are free, although a few are paid trainings, including Microsoft Outlook 2013 - Essentials, The 7 Habits of Highly Effective People, etc.

Welfare Training

Other training available are welfare training, mostly paid classes such as Wellness Programs, Fitness Course Training, and Yoga Courses.

American colleges and universities attach great importance to the recruitment and selection of teachers and their on-the-job training, and they strive to reflect their coherence and effectiveness in terms of systems and institutions. If any non-compliance is found, or if a report is filed, once it is determined to be valid, changes must be implemented in accordance with institutional regulations.

Comprehensive faculty training is a standard practice in American colleges and universities. Its primary aim is to ensure that every faculty member seeking a position continually maintains a solid understanding of the fundamental expectations, essential criteria, and skills pertaining to both scientific research and teaching. It is imperative for each faculty member to comprehend their role's expectations and the consequences of violating institutional policies. Analogous to adhering to family rules and national laws, violations must be understood, justified, guided by corrective actions, and subject to appropriate consequences.

Unlike some educational systems, American colleges and universities lack a dedicated propaganda department. Instead, they acknowledge and reward outstanding educators but refrain from extravagant promotion of exemplary figures, as such practices can often lead to inaccuracies. This phenomenon is attributable to the fact that individuals considered typical often behave differently when they become the center of attention. Psychological studies, such as the famous Hawthorne test, have substantiated that when people are aware of being observed for research purposes, they may consciously or unconsciously alter their normal behavior to align with researchers' expectations. This parallels the Observer Expectancy Effect in social research, where investigators tend to behave in ways that align with the researcher's preferences, potentially compromising the research's credibility.

Given these considerations, fostering ethical conduct and compliance is not accomplished solely through creating role models or attempting to influence individuals through promotional campaigns. Instead, it relies on comprehensive training and the design and implementation of effective systems. This approach enables institutions to better understand the rationale behind desired behaviors, guide individuals in their actions, and apply appropriate consequences when needed.

While the concept of comprehensive training for college instructors in the United States is both reasonable and practical, it is not without its imperfections in practice. Mandatory training is generally enforced, but participation in additional scientific research or teaching technology training often allows for more flexibility, leading to varying levels of engagement among faculty members.

Prior to the 1980s, Chinese colleges and universities typically prioritized political studies, cadre training, and party school programs over teacher training. In the 1990s, various study sessions and training courses emerged, predominantly focusing on ideological and political education, with occasional forays into business training. However, a systematic, standardized, and institution-wide approach to teacher training has yet to be fully implemented. Consequently, some college educators tarnished the reputation and integrity of the teaching profession, resulting in regrettable instances of unethical conduct and misconduct.

As an illustrative anecdote, at an annual meeting of the American Sociology Society a decade ago, a professor and doctoral supervisor from a Mainland Chinese university openly admitted to receiving an expensive electronic camera as a gift from one of his doctoral students. It was customary for each doctoral student to present a gift to their supervisor, and there was even a competitive element among students regarding who could offer the most impressive gift. In contrast, the acceptance of high-value gifts by professors from students is considered a form of bribery in the United States, subject to potential legal prosecution and criminal penalties. Consequently, such situations are exceedingly rare in American colleges and universities.

In recent years, China's domestic colleges and universities have made notable reforms, with increasing attention directed toward the training of college-level educators. However, following the reformation of administrative systems and the transformation of colleges and departments into autonomous entities in many academic institutions, several university-level responsibilities have been delegated to these individual units. To avoid any perception of overreach, university-level administration has entrusted colleges and departments with important training initiatives, which, unfortunately, have sometimes been neglected or treated as mere formalities.

Conversely, when tasked with training responsibilities, the colleges and departments have occasionally faced challenges executing them effectively, often due to resource constraints and a need for concerted effort. It's worth emphasizing that comprehensive teacher training is a prolonged, meticulous, and recurring process, necessitating substantial investment. It is not an optional or secondary undertaking; rather, it demands the commitment and coordination of university-level administrative bodies. If faculty members exhibit behaviors that deviate from professional norms, it can often be attributed to the university's shortcomings in providing adequate training and education.

In traditional Chinese culture, there is a saying that "lack of education is the fault of the father," suggesting that children's disregard for rules often reflects poorly on their parents' upbringing. Likewise, educators serve as role models, and their conduct significantly mirrors the institution's commitment to training, knowledge dissemination, ethical conduct, and accountability. It is a national tragedy when college professors transition from dignified educators to individuals whose conduct may be perceived as lacking integrity. Professors in universities play a pivotal role in nurturing the next generation of talent, making their professional development an utmost priority that must not be taken lightly or treated with indifference.

Relevant Information for Reference

The mechanisms, forms, and content of faculty training in Chinese and American universities can exhibit similarities and differences. Let's explore these aspects:

Similarities in Mechanism

1. Professional Development: Chinese and American universities recognize the importance of faculty professional development. They strive to enhance teaching and research skills, promote pedagogical innovation, and support continuous learning.

2. Workshops and Seminars: Both systems often organize workshops, seminars, and conferences to facilitate faculty training. These events provide opportunities for faculty members to share best practices, engage in discussions, and stay updated with the latest developments in their respective fields.

Differences in Mechanism

1. Institutional Support: American universities typically have dedicated centers or offices of teaching and learning, instructional design, or faculty development. These entities provide centralized support for faculty training and offer resources, consultation services, and expertise. In Chinese universities, such dedicated units are less common, and faculty training may be integrated within existing administrative structures.

2. Flexibility and Autonomy: American universities often grant faculty members more autonomy in selecting training opportunities that align with their professional goals. They may have the freedom to choose from a variety of workshops, conferences, and programs. In Chinese universities, faculty training may be more standardized and coordinated at the institutional level.

Similarities in Form

1. Workshops and Short-Term Programs: Both Chinese and American universities commonly offer workshops and short-term programs as a form of faculty training. These can be focused on teaching methodologies, technology integration, research skills, grant writing, and other relevant topics.

2. Peer Observation and Feedback: Peer observation and feedback are valued in both systems. Faculty members

may have opportunities to observe their colleagues' teaching, provide constructive feedback, and engage in collaborative discussions to enhance their instructional practices.

Differences in Form

1. Mentoring Programs: In American universities, formal mentoring programs are often established to support junior faculty members. Senior faculty members provide guidance and support in various aspects of their careers, including teaching, research, and professional development. In Chinese universities, mentoring programs may be less structured or formalized.

2. Teaching Portfolios: American universities frequently encourage faculty members to develop teaching portfolios, which are comprehensive collections of their teaching philosophy, instructional materials, student feedback, and evidence of their teaching effectiveness. While some Chinese universities also adopt teaching portfolios, they may not be as widespread or standardized.

Content Differences

1. Cultural and Contextual Considerations: Faculty training in American universities may address specific cultural and contextual aspects of teaching, such as promoting inclusivity, diversity, and intercultural competence in the classroom. Chinese universities may focus more on pedagogical approaches, curriculum design, and assessment methods relevant to their educational context.

2. Research and Funding: American universities often provide training on research methodologies, grant writing, and securing external funding for research projects.

While research training is also important in Chinese universities, there may be greater emphasis on securing national or provincial-level grants and conducting research aligned with national priorities.

It's worth noting that the mechanisms, forms, and content of faculty training can vary widely within both Chinese and American universities, as institutional practices, resources, and priorities may differ. These comparisons provide a general overview, but individual universities may have unique approaches to faculty training.

CHAPTER 4

The Process and Characteristics of Faculty Recruitment and Selection in the American University

A round two decades ago, as I was nearing the completion of my doctoral degree (All But Dissertation (ABD)) at the University of Illinois at Chicago, I stumbled upon a job posting for a sociology professor position on the department's bulletin board. I promptly submitted my application, including all the requisite documents. This marked my inaugural attempt at securing a faculty position in a United States university. Given my circumstances as a Chinese student without an established network in American higher education and being in my middle-aged years, one might wonder how it would be possible to secure such a position, especially in a field like sociology, which was relatively niche. Perhaps fate led to a phone interview a few months later, followed by an on-campus interview. Subsequently, everything unfolded according to plan, culminating in my appointment as an assistant professor of Sociology. Was this a fortuitous accident or the result of some intricacies within the higher education recruitment system?

More than a decade later, I found myself actively engaged in faculty recruitment, serving as a member of the department's Faculty Recruitment and Selection Committee. Reflecting upon my own journey, I revisited the skepticism that had colored my initial application submission and the complex emotions I experienced upon receiving that job offer. My sentiments were a blend of enthusiasm and yearning, a recognition that destiny had realigned itself for me. Although I had already held a faculty position at a reputable university in China for over a decade before relocating to the United States, my new beginning here entailed starting from square one, embarking on an uncertain path. As I look back on my personal voyage and critically assess the entire recruitment and selection process, I now find myself able to discern certain elements of serendipity and uncover the cultural underpinnings and core social values that underscore the American higher education recruitment system.

It is safe to say that the college recruitment system I have introduced here is representative of both public and private universities in the United States. Considering that the article's content is "quasi-confidential," some details of this article are omitted, and the specific figures are approximate, but that will not affect the overall picture presented.

Faculty recruitment and selection is an important part of human resource management in American universities. In particular, the recruitment of tenure-track faculty is a serious task that the department committee must carry out under the guidance of the framework of the faculty division of the University's personnel office. The department's working committee which is generally called the Search Committee, drafts plans, writes and publishes advertisements according to the department's requirements for additional faculty, and conducts first-round screening based on applicants' materials. It also arranges for telephone interviews, if needed, and campus visits for top-ranked candidates interviews. Formal appointment of candidates falls to the department head and dean. The reason why so much importance is attached to recruitment and selection is the drive to recruit the best scholars, ensure the teaching and research ability of the recruits, and maintain the reputation and status of the university.

Figure 4.1 – Snapshot of City University of New York (CUNY) Search Committee Guide

The purpose of this Guide is to help Search Committees:

✓ Attract a broad range of qualified applicants

✓ Identify the most highly qualified candidate(s)

✓ Complete searches efficiently and effectively

✓ Provide fair and equitable treatment in search and selection.

There are several reasons why conducting effective searches is a CUNY priority.

Recruiting and selecting employees is critical. The skills, expertise, and dedication of our faculty and staff are key to CUNY's success and there are negative consequences if a newly-selected colleague is a poor fit, lacks necessary qualifications, or resigns early in his/her employment.

As was the case with my participation in the faculty recruitment and selection process, it is described as follows:

Preparation Stage

Due to a professor's retirement, the department needed a new faculty member at the beginning of that year. According to the regulations, the selection committee comprised four senior professors, one of whom was a professor from a different department. The professional fields of the selection committee members should be sufficient to cover the professional areas of the proposed faculty member. The committee then discussed the content and wording of the recruitment advertisement. We were recruiting an assistant professor for the tenure track at that time. Therefore, the proposed job title, job responsibilities, requirements and expectations for the applicant's professional fields and qualifications, the range of remuneration and benefits, and the application termination date were clearly stated in the advertisement. Ads were delivered across the United States and worldwide through job recruitment websites. It was primarily sent to commonly used college faculty recruitment websites, such as The Chronicle of Higher Education, HigherEd Jobs, Workplace Diversity, Higher Education Recruitment Consortium (HERC), Job Fair, and GettingHired.com.

The Initial Selection Stage

Fifty applications were received within two months of posting the job opening, and, at this point, the primary selection began. Once the primary selection begins, no more application material can be accepted. After reading and scoring the applicant's materials online, committee members made the primary selection according to the criteria formulated through discussion. The four committee members met once or twice weekly to discuss specific concerns and adjust and unify their scoring standards. Grading criteria covers questions such as:

- Have you previously taught courses related to sociology?
- Have you taken part in an undergraduate or graduate program?
- How would you rate your research ability?
- Do you have experience with online courses?

Figure 4.2 – Applicant Scoring Standards

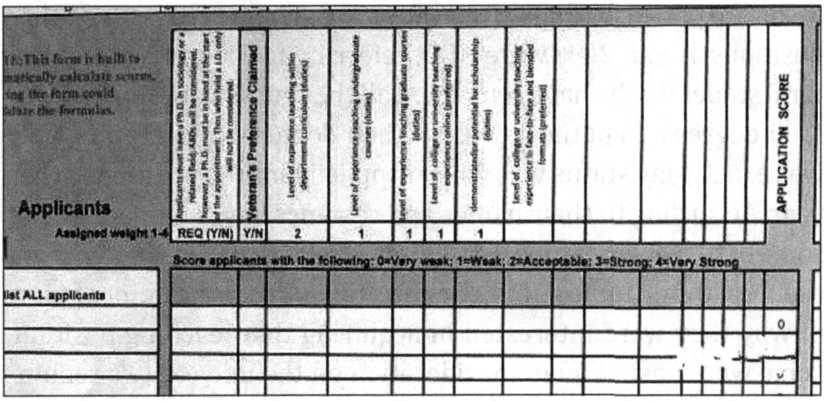

Applicants upload application materials (Required Documents) on the prescribed website, typically an application letter or cover letter, resume or curriculum vitae, proof of academic qualification certification or transcript, and a letter of recommendation. The job applicants come from all over the United States and worldwide.

From the applicant's general information, you can check a variety of things:

- Is the applicant currently employed?
- If they are employed, where do they work?
- Are they a U.S. Citizen or an overseas immigrant?
- What is their immigration status?
- Are they a veteran? (Veterans have priority hiring rights under federal law.)
- What is their education and work experience?

In this particular situation, all fifty applicants were doctoral degree recipients, of which nearly 8% were foreign applicants. About half were full-time or part-time teachers who were teaching at other universities or working in non-educational sectors or research institutions. These included applicants who had been awarded associate professorships or served as department chairs and other positions. About 20% were ABD, referring to the graduating doctoral students who have completed all the coursework required for their degree except the defense of their doctoral dissertation. This was exactly my status was when I applied for a job position earlier year. According to their names and resumes, it was apparent that some of them were Chinese students who had just graduated from their doctoral studies in the United States. From the point of view of why they were interested in acquiring that teaching position, some were basing their consideration on the university's reputation and were thinking of changing their immigration status. Some were looking for a position in the United States for family relocation reasons, and some were coming from research institutions and wanted to change careers to become professors.

Telephone Interviews

After scoring the results of the initial selection stage, the candidates are summarized and ranked, and the top ten highest scorers from the fifty are selected for telephone interviews. For the telephone interviews, the committee director generally confirms the time with the interviewees by e-mail in advance and prepares a set of interview questions according to the unified regulations of the university. At the designated interview time, all committee members are required to be present and ask questions, one by one, according to the pre-determined interview questions. Based on the answers provided by the respondents, the scores are calculated on the spot. The committee then selected those with the highest scores. It eliminated those who did not meet the requirements during the interview, such as those with poor verbal skills or those who failed to answer relevant questions adequately. Six applicants were ultimately identified for follow-up telephone interviews and reference checks.

Figure 4.3 – Telephone Interview Questions

Candidate' Name _____   **Rater's Name** _____

Sociology Search Committee 2016
Telephone Interview Questions

Ratings: 4 = Outstanding; 3 = Highly satisfactory; 2 = Satisfactory; 0 = Unsatisfactory

1. What about our position announcement motivated you to apply?

2. If you have not completed the Ph.D., what is your timeline for completion?

3. Please describe your teaching philosophy and teaching style.

4. Have you taught both undergraduate and graduate courses? If so, which ones?

The telephone interviews were based on the applicant's three or four academic professional references in their application materials, two of whom were randomly selected to receive phone calls. The main questions of the phone reference interviews are:

- How long have you known the applicant?
- How would you rate their teaching style and research ability?
- How do they get along with their colleagues?
- What are their main strengths and weaknesses?
- Do you think we should hire them? Why or why not?

Campus Interviews

After phone interviews with references, three application finalists were selected for campus interviews. The committee director notified the three selected candidates and arranged times for them to visit the campus separately. The university provided round-trip air tickets and accommodation. On their day of arrival, the applicants visited the campus. They gave a lecture similar to what would be expected of them in a classroom situation, which was scored by the committee members and the students attending the lecture. Arrangements were also made for the applicant to meet with the head of the department and the dean. This visit usually lasted for one or two days. During that time, the applicant could meet with faculty members in the department over informal lunches or dinners, explore the campus more fully, and better understand the university itself. This is a short testing phase to assess whether the applicant can fit in with the present instructional groups, to judge their personality characteristics separately as well as within the larger group, and so on. At the end of the campus interview process, the committee synthesized the opinions of all available aspects to produce the most desirable candidate for the assistant professor recruitment and submitted it to the department head to report it to the university for official approval and appointment.

It is not an exaggeration to see parallels in the process of applying for a professor position in American colleges and universities with the Chinese folktale of "to pass five gates and kill six generals." (The phrase "to pass five gates and kill six generals" is often used to describe how strong competitors continually defeat stronger rivals, thereby upgrading their levels or becoming champions. It originated from legends about the famous Chinese general Guan Yu, sometimes regarded as the "god of martial arts or war." This story is part of the famous Chinese classic novel The Three Kingdoms, one of the four greatest works of Chinese literature.) After careful review and summary, the characteristics of this process are:

1. Openness and fairness —Recruitment advertisements are publicly posted on major college teacher recruitment websites. Because tenure-track recruiting involves federal anti-discrimination laws, it is important to also include a statement about anti-discrimination laws in the ad

to avoid legal trouble. Therefore, the personal information in the applicant's materials only has their name, address, phone number, and email, and no information related to their gender, age, race, etcetera is allowed. This ensures a more fair and equitable recruitment process. Professors in American colleges and universities are almost always openly recruited, and they rarely stay on the same campus directly after their time as postdocs, adjunct lecturers, or researchers. Even if the university wants to keep particular individuals, it must go through the recruitment channels and follow the procedures. The school will never approve a professor who is not admitted through open recruitment.

2. Procedure Specifications —All aspects of the recruitment and selection process are stipulated in documents, and the university's personnel department instructs a particular liaison person to act as a guide at the department selection committee meeting. The department's selection committee is merely executive. According to the university's rules, any situation or conflict must be immediately reported to the university personnel department. The original data of all committee members' scores must be kept and documented. These have been formed into institutional provisions and can be accessed anytime. In this way, the entire selection process is standardized, and black-box operations are prohibited.

3. Checks and Balances Mechanism — The selection committee is usually composed of full professors in the department, without the participation of the dean and department head. Throughout the recruitment and selection process, exercisers of executive power are excluded to ensure protection from undue interference. When the committee is done, it must report to the department head and the dean, the final decision-makers. As a result, the final

determination of candidates for hire is at the managers' discretion, and the hiring committee is excluded now.

4. Professionalism — The selection committee members guide the recruitment and selection process with strict professionalism. The members of the committee are professionally self-disciplined and guided by integrity. They work to qualify candidates from a professional standpoint. Moreover, the committee members are scored according to their standards and are not influenced by others; the criteria for controversial candidates are determined through discussion, and no private agreement is allowed. In the actual selection, even if I were to give high marks to a student I favor, it would be useless because, in the end, the total average score of the committee members is considered.

5. Market Concept —It is the responsibility of the university to make reasonable arrangements for the finalists of the recruitment interviews in order to reflect the humanization of the institution. The campus interview committee not only arranges all required air travel and accommodations but also provides airport pick-up services. Candidates typically present their expectations regarding working conditions, salary packages, spousal employment considerations, and relocation assistance. The institution, in turn, assesses these demands in light of the candidate's qualifications and desirability. This negotiation process is both rational and customary, aligning with market principles. Occasionally, negotiations may reach an impasse, in which case the institution may explore the possibility of extending an offer to the next most qualified candidate.

The recruitment and selection of faculty in American universities adhere firmly to principles of openness, fairness, standardized procedures, checks and balances, professionalism, and market-driven concepts. These principles have consistently attracted exceptional talent worldwide to American academia. Additionally, American college professors enjoy a substantial degree of autonomy and independence in their work. Throughout the teaching process, professors wield absolute authority, free from external interference in matters such as the choice of teaching materials, grading of assessments, and determining students' grades. This autonomy is partly a result of the rigorous scrutiny applied during the recruitment and selection phase.

While occasional imperfections may emerge in the implementation process, such as the rare instance of new faculty members being dismissed shortly after their appointment, these cases remain outliers. The principles of openness, fairness, procedural standards, checks and balances, professionalism, and market-driven concepts underpin the recruitment and selection procedures of American colleges and universities and represent shared values within American society as a whole.

Prior to the 1980s, the recruitment process in Chinese colleges and universities rarely involved open and transparent procedures. Many applicants were recommended by higher-level leaders or professors. Consequently, particularly in prestigious and well-established institutions, there was an overrepresentation of individuals with influential connections, leading to a perception of nepotism. A substantial number of university professors came from privileged backgrounds. However, with the advent of reform and opening up, there was a noticeable shift towards strengthening the academic ranks in higher education institutions.

This transformation involved a greater focus on selecting high-achieving graduate students to remain within the university as educators. As a result, the proportion of faculty members with master's and doctoral degrees increased, elevating the overall quality of the academic staff and positively impacting scientific research and the overall advancement of universities. In recent years, faculty recruitment has actively sought to mitigate "inbreeding" by reducing the number of internal graduate students who continue to teach at the same institution. Instead, there has been a shift towards recruiting new faculty members from outside the university, domestically and internationally. Consequently, email notifications and online job postings have become more common, marking a positive development in the reform of China's higher education recruitment system offering greater procedural transparency.

While on the surface, the recruitment process in Chinese colleges and universities appears to draw inspiration from American practices, with several similarities, there remains room for improvement in the finer details. Notably, removing age restrictions for candidates, implementing a system of checks and balances, avoiding direct involvement of department heads in recruitment, and promoting a culture of "professionalism" are areas that could be enhanced. Some institutions have substituted the concept of a search committee with a professorial assembly or an academic committee, leading to superficial processes that lack thoroughness, often merely going through the motions in an attempt to appear more regulated.

China and the United States possess markedly distinct national conditions, particularly within their cultural ecosystems. Consequently, colleges and universities' recruitment and selection procedures cannot be simply transplanted from one context to another. Nevertheless, as Chinese universities aspire to attain world-class status, it becomes imperative for them to break away from traditional faculty recruitment models. Instead, they should endeavor to standardize, institutionalize, and rationalize their recruitment processes in pursuit of excellence.

Relevant Information for Reference

The teacher recruitment and selection process in Chinese and American colleges and universities can exhibit several characteristics that highlight both similarities and differences. Let's explore these aspects:

Similarities in Recruitment and Selection

1. Job Postings: In Chinese and American institutions, vacancies for teaching positions are typically advertised through job postings. These postings include information about the position, qualifications required, application process, and deadlines. They may be displayed on university websites, job portals, or academic job boards.

2. Application Materials: Prospective teachers in both systems are generally required to submit application materials, such as a cover letter, curriculum vitae (CV), academic transcripts, and letters of recommendation. These materials are used to assess candidates' qualifications, educational background, research experience, and teaching capabilities.

Differences in Recruitment and Selection

1. Hiring Process: The hiring process can vary significantly between Chinese and American institutions. In Chinese universities, it is common for the process to be more centralized and involve multiple stages, including written exams, interviews, and sometimes teaching demonstrations or research presentations. American universities often have a more decentralized process, with individual departments or committees responsible for their own hiring decisions.

2. Emphasis on Research: In American universities, research accomplishments and potential are often given significant weight during recruitment and selection, particularly for tenure-track positions or those with research expectations. Candidates' publication records, research grants, and scholarly contributions are closely evaluated. In Chinese universities, while research achievements are also valued, there may be a relatively greater emphasis on teaching qualifications and pedagogical skills.

3. Teaching Philosophy and Experience: American universities frequently place importance on candidates' teaching philosophy, experience, and evidence of teaching effectiveness. They may require teaching statements, sample syllabi, and evaluations from students or peers. Chinese universities also value teaching qualifications, but the emphasis may be more on subject knowledge, teaching methods, and the ability to engage students effectively.

4. Interview Process: Interviews in American universities often include a combination of phone or video interviews and on-campus interviews, where candidates meet with faculty members, administrators, and sometimes students. The interviews may involve discussions on teaching philosophy, research agenda, and fit with the institution's culture. In Chinese universities, interviews may include panels of faculty members and administrators, focusing on candidates' qualifications, teaching experience, research plans, and their potential contributions to the university.

5. Language Proficiency: For teaching positions conducted in English, American universities generally require candidates to demonstrate a high level of proficiency in English, particularly for non-native speakers. Chinese universities may also have language proficiency requirements, but the expectations may vary depending on the specific institution and position.

It's important to note that the recruitment and selection processes can vary between Chinese and American universities and different institutions and departments within each system. The specific characteristics and priorities may depend on factors such as the type of institution, the level of the position (e.g., assistant professor, lecturer), and the field of study.

CHAPTER 5

The Experience of Faculty's Promotion & Tenure in the American University

Approximately three decades ago, I received a promotion to the rank of associate professor at a renowned Chinese university. Several years later, I embarked on a journey to the United States for academic exploration and further study---teaching and research career. In this remarkable crossroads of time and space, I found myself experiencing the process of promotion anew, progressing from associate professor to full professor, albeit on American soil. Despite the fundamental similarity in the act of obtaining a higher academic title, the contrasting academic landscapes of China and the United States infused the experiences with distinct nuances.

Drawing from my personal experiences and reflections on the faculty promotion systems in both Chinese and American universities, this chapter offers a concise overview of the promotion framework in American higher education. It encompasses aspects such as the eligible candidates for promotion, the prerequisites, the evaluation criteria, the procedural intricacies, and the defining attributes of this process. The aim is to provide insights into creating a healthy academic ecosystem and designing a sound mechanism for advancing professional titles. Given the constraints of space, this article serves as a broad introduction to the topic. For those eager to delve deeper into the specifics, I welcome readers to reach out to the author for more comprehensive information and detailed insights.

The experience of promotion in an American university is simple: submit all the required materials according to the schedule and then wait for the final approval. It is a bit of an overstatement to say it is a complicated procedure. The entire review process takes about six months, all the way through the three-level review of the department, the college, and the university. During this period, no "behind the scenes" is allowed on the applicant's part. In this atmosphere, there is no "acquaintance relationship" to be used, no favors to be sent, and no small notes to be delivered secretly. The emphasis here is professionalism and academic influence rather than acquiring faculty member seniority incentives or benefits. The promotion of university professor titles ensures their teaching and research level and maintains the university's quality and reputation. Most universities in the United States have a complete and rigorous system of professor promotion, including promotion and tenure. Since promotion is often accompanied by the evaluation of the tenure track, this article mainly introduces promotion as the main line. In addition, American universities are divided into "research universities," "research and teaching (or teaching and research) universities," and "teaching universities," so the promotion criteria are also significantly different. The universities described in this article are mainly "research-teaching universities." Most state universities and many private universities fall into this category.

Promotion Objective

An important distinction among U.S. college or university professors is the difference between the tenure track and the non-tenure track. The tenure track professors generally include full, associate, and assistant professors. The non-tenure track professors include adjunct professors, lecturers and general faculty, postdoctoral fellows and researchers, etc. The main difference between the tenure track and non-tenure track is that the former undertakes the three basic tasks of teaching, research, and service and is the core of the university's teaching and scientific research strength. At the same time, the latter only engages in teaching or less scientific research and performs little to no service work.

Another regulation of American universities is the difference between full-time and part-time professors. Professors cannot be called full-time faculty if they also hold administrative positions or can only be calculated as a percentage of part-time jobs. A professor is considered a full-time professor if their workload exceeds 75% of their overall work expectations, and a part-time professor is considered such if their workload falls below 75%. Most tenure-track faculty and some non-tenure-track faculty have full-time positions. The main difference between full-time and part-time faculty is that full-time faculty have greater job security, enjoy basic university benefits, including academic conferences and research funding, and qualify for academic leave applications. In contrast, part-time faculty have no job security, do not enjoy school benefits or university assistance with scientific research, and lack eligibility for funding. Part-time faculty usually carry a bag to class, leave after class, and are paid according to the number of classes they teach. In Chinese terminology, they are merely "temporary workers" among college professors.

Only those who belong to both the tenure track and full-time faculty are eligible to participate in promotions. Therefore, these professors are limited relative to the total number of faculty in colleges and universities. In recent decades, the faculty structure of American colleges and universities has undergone significant changes. According to some data, the proportion of tenure-track (including those who have obtained tenure and those still on the tenure track) in American universities has dropped from 57% in 1975 to 31% in 2007. That is to say, a large number of professors specializing in teaching only have emerged in American universities, and the number has exceeded two-thirds of the total number of professors. Most non-tenure-track professors are part-time professors.

For example, the tenured/tenure track category of professors at my state university is 38.7%, while the non-tenure track, or part-time instructors, is 61.2%. The proportion of professors on the non-tenure track has exceeded half of the total. The usual way to gain a promotion is by assistant professors on the tenure track accumulating extensive teaching and research experience, obtaining tenure after the application and review of the tenure track, and being promoted to associate professor at the same time. The most senior title of professors in American colleges and universities is Full Professor.

Promotion Conditions

Usually, American colleges and universities confirm whether they have tenure-track positions available when recruiting professors. The bottom line for promotion is the applicant's teaching and research experience, that is, the number of years they have been on the job. A newly graduated doctor (or one with two or three years of post-doctoral experience) is usually given the position of an assistant professor if hired; six years of assistant professor experience can allow for promotion to associate professor and onto the tenure track; five years of associate professor experience can allow for promotion to full professor. This promotion time sequence is not something that everyone can achieve smoothly. Although many associate professors have obtained tenure-track positions, they are still only associate professors after many years, sometimes even decades, until they retire.

There are quite a few such examples. Chinese-style "helicopter" or "leap-forward" promotions to an up-level position; opportunities for exceptional promotions such as "fighting-in-the-ring" (competition) for young faculty members are rare and almost unheard of in the United States.

Newly appointed assistant professors go through a critical review after three years to decide whether they can continue to teach in the sixth year based on their performance, achievements, and contributions over the past three years. Passing this level allows eligibility to apply for tenure after the sixth year and be promoted to associate professor simultaneously. Usually, there are two opportunities to apply for a position as tenure-track faculty (the sixth year of being hired and the following year); if the two applications fail, you must leave the university to find another way at the end of the seventh year.

The basic conditions for gaining an assistant professor position from a postdoctoral fellow are that the applicant must have scientific research ability in the professional field and competency in classroom teaching. The essential condition for promotion from assistant professor to associate professor and obtaining a tenure-track position is to have sufficient academic research ability (academic capability), to have made considerable scientific research achievements in their professional field, and to have been recognized by their domestic counterparts. The essential condition for promotion from associate professor to full professor is to have considerable academic impact, be recognized by peers worldwide, and be an academic leader. Although the promotion criteria for each level are different, the basic procedures for approval are the same.

Figure 5.1 – Example of Outstanding Accomplishments Required for Promotion

Research, Scholarships, and/or Creative Work

Candidates for promotion to professor shall demonstrate outstanding accomplishments in Research, Scholarship, and/or Creative Work. Some departments or disciplines will expect significant funded grants in this area .The definition of outstanding accomplishments require for promotion to professors will be defined by the individual department or programs, but will be based on elaboration of the following list. Invited work is considered equivalent to peer-reviewed.

1. Peer-reviewed journal article will be the standard for many disciplines
2. Monographs in scholarly publications
3. Book chapters in scholarly publications
4. Peer-reviewed conference presentations at national/international conferences
5. Encyclopedia Entries
6. Peer-reviewed conference presentations at regional conference
7. Editorships of scholarly journals/publication or curating exhibitions
8. Performances, exhibitions, installations, and workshops that meet criteria determined by the department
9. Other work

Promotion Criteria

There is no uniform standard for promotion in American colleges and universities. Due to the different requirements of each university and each major, the standards are also different. Usually, the departments, colleges, and universities where professors are located have their own corresponding promotion standards, which can include teaching, research, and service. As an old president of my university once said, the teaching, scientific research, and service of colleges and universities each have their own application and scope of evaluation. Teaching is mainly on campus, research is typically off-campus and on a larger scale that has an impact on academia (worldwide), and service is a bridge between on-campus and off-campus professional focus. However, an easy way to find exactly how professorships in different disciplines and levels in U.S. universities are awarded and the actual judging criteria for tenure-track grants is to look at professors' resumes. Most colleges and universities in the United States require professors' resumes to be online and kept up to date. By looking at the resumes of these professors, you can find the tenure-track positions implemented by various universities and departments and the assessment standards for various professional titles.

Taking the evaluation of associate professor positions as an example, the most common evaluation criteria for the promotion of associate professors in social science fields in the current research and teaching universities in the United States (and tenure-track positions) are an academic monograph published by a university press and with the publication of three to five papers in major journals of their discipline. Of course, this evaluation standard should vary from time to time. For example, the evaluation standard for promotion in the social sciences has been slowly improving in the past few decades. Thirty or forty years ago, only two to three papers published in journals, and an academically published monograph was required. This standard has the ability and expectation to improve, requiring more high-level papers or a second monograph.

In my department, the evaluation criteria are divided into three categories, A, B, and C, and are calculated with different scores for category A (highest score), category B (middle score), and category C (lowest score), and the total score is a combination of the three categories as follows:

Figure 5.2 – Evaluation Criteria

CATEGORY A	CATEGORY B	CATEGORY C
The emphasis on publications in Category A is on major publications involving peer-reviewed, original research that contributes to the existing literature in the discipline in novel ways. • Full-length academic book or monograph (cannot be self-published, or published in a vanity press) • Peer-reviewed article published in a scholarly journal • Chapter in a scholarly book • Externally-funded Research Grant • Editor of a scholarly, peer-reviewed journal • Agency or research Report contributing original knowledge for a grant-funded agency	Items in Category B are smaller in scope and impact; they also may or may not involve both peer-review and/or serve as original research. • Textbook • Book review • Encyclopedia entry • Edited book • Research note • Agency report • Articles in non-refereed scholarly journals • Published proceedings • Applied scholarship (oral history, local impact studies) • Unfunded major research grant proposal (only one of these may be counted)	Items in Category C demonstrate active engagement in the discipline, but may not involve written publication • Conference presentation • (Funded) Mini Grant through Graduate School • Manuscript reviewer • Professional development of research skills (i.e. attendance at NIH workshop) • Organizer of panel or discussant in roundtable at academic conference • Invited professional and academic speeches

Although there are quantitative indicators for promotion standards, the emphasis is on academic quality. If a teacher has published more than ten articles, but they are all published in journals with a relatively low academic status, they cannot be counted in the score. The same goes for books and their publishers, which can have very different academic statuses and academic influences. At the time, I had a monograph published by University Press of America and another published by Routledge, Taylor & Francis Group. The evaluation weights were completely different when the review committee reviewed the two books. Books published by prestigious and senior publishers, whose worldwide academic influence is recognized in the evaluation system of American college professors, hold more weight than lesser-known publishing houses.

Promotion Procedure

The promotion process of American colleges and universities is rigorous, and the timetable is fixed. For example, the time procedure for any type of promotion review at my university is a consistent, step-by-step, strict process that follows unfluctuating timelines.

Figure 5.3 – Sample Tenure and Promotion Timeline

Sixth Year Tenure & Promotion

Dates*	Action Needed
Sept 30	Deans will conduct an annual election of College Tenure and Promotion Advisory Committee prior to September 30.
Sept 15	Candidates for tenure and promotion should submit their portfolios to their respective department heads on or before this date.
Oct 5	Provost office distributes tenure advisory forms (ballots) for 6th year probationary faculty to department heads by this date. (Ballots are distributed for tenure only.)
Oct 15	Department heads must submit tenured advisory forms (ballots), vita, faculty service reports and departmental recommendations to respective deans by this date.
Nov 15	Deans must submit the recommendations of the College Tenure & Promotion Committee along with his/her recomendations to the Provost by this date.
Dec 3	Deans Council begins review and votes on Tenure and Promotion.
Jan 10	Provost submits his/her tenure and promotion recommendations to the President by this date.
Feb 22	Agenda Item for tenure due to TAMUS for May Board of Regents meeting. (Promotions are submitted to the Chancellor.)

*If the due date falls on the weekend, the due date will be the following Monday.

As the timetable stipulates, September 15 is the deadline for submitting all application materials. Faculty members applying for promotion must submit all materials according to the prescribed timeframe, and they will be reviewed in an orderly manner from the bottom to the top through the departments, colleges, and the university. Each tier has a set date that must be completed by that time. If the due date falls on a weekend, the due date will be the following Monday. The specific promotion evaluation process is illustrated by applying for a tenure-track position (and promotion to associate professor) as an example:

1. Submit a Personal Summary Report (Portfolio) — Applicants must submit a portfolio reflecting their achievements in teaching and research for the past six years. Materials must be informative and specific, and various originals and supporting texts can be attached to convince all reviewers that the applicant is eligible for this promotion. The content of the portfolio usually includes the following:

    a. Personal academic resume and employment history.

    b. Teaching achievements with detailed results of classroom teaching, new courses, and student evaluations, including raw materials such as student comments and scores.

    c. Scientific research results include academic works that can highlight the applicant's achievements of the past five or six years and a listing of recently published books, authored book chapters, articles published in official journals, patents applied for, if any, invited scholarly presentations, and conference presentations.

    d. Any scientific research funds with a list of the names of scientific research projects at the applicant's disposal for the past six years, the amount of funds, the source of funds, and the start and end dates.

e. Service work with a list of the service work that has contributed to the department, college, university, and even the community and off-campus in the past six years; lists of the work that has made outstanding contributions to participation in professional societies and academic leadership.

f. A list of any awards granted in the past six years.

g. Applicants must spend sufficient time preparing these materials because they are out of the applicant's hands once submitted.

2. Deliberation by the Department Evaluation Committee — Upon the proposal of the department head, a Promotion and Tenure Committee will be formed with five to eight professors or associate professors who have been awarded tenure-track positions. If the number of professors in the department is limited, all tenure-track professors should be review committee members. However, the department head cannot participate in the committee himself. According to the materials provided by the applicant, members of the committee will write an honest evaluation of the applicant's performance and existence in various aspects after reviewing them separately (they can now be scanned and sent to the e-mail addresses of the committees in electronic form and read directly online). The committee members can then attach their own ballots expressly agreeing, disagreeing, or abstaining. The voting results are reported to the head of the department after the final summary.

3. External Expert Review—Based on the summary report and corresponding materials provided by the applicant,

the head of the department will email these materials (or electronic versions) to well-known scholars in related fields at external domestic universities and abroad, asking them to write their comments on the applicant's academic level and contribution, known as evaluation letters. Generally, at least two or more letters are required (depending on the situation of each university). Its purpose is to determine the applicant's reputation of academic or international influence. Usually, the applicant's doctoral supervisor cannot serve as an external reviewer.

4. Recommendation Letters and Comments from the Head of the Department —The head of the department will give a summary of the applicant's work achievements and existing concerns in the unit according to the report of the review committee and write comments on the applicant's academic quality and academic influence as well as the applicant's teaching evaluation results, teaching quality, etc. If the department head approves, they must write a letter of recommendation to the college, which will be kept on file. However, if the department head disagrees with the results of the committee votes, they are required to provide a full explanation. Whether expressing approval or disapproval, the department head needs to have a copy of the letter sent to the applicant.

5. Opinions of the Faculty Evaluation Committee — According to the recommendation of the department head, the Faculty Evaluation Committee comprises eight to ten professors from departments across the college. However, the dean cannot participate in the committee. Committee members review the applicant's materials and give their independent review opinions. The committee will also balance all applicants for promotion

across the university to avoid biases and mistakes caused by department-level reviews. Upon completion of the review by the committee, a written report will be given to the dean of the college. Based on all the above review materials, the college dean submits a written report of his decision to the president. The dean also needs to send a copy to the applicant.

6. Opinions of the University Academic Committee (Dean Council) —The university academic committee, composed of the deans or representatives of each college, will synthesize all the materials and make a decision on the applicant to the provost. The purpose of this committee is to maintain balance among the various colleges. After approval by the provost, it will be reported to the president. At the same time, the provost will also notify the applicant of their comments, usually in writing.

Figure 5.4 – Provost Personal Notification

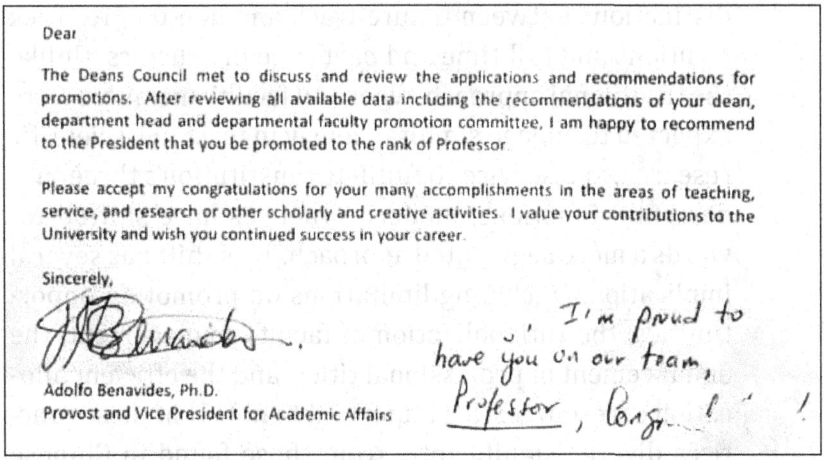

Dear

The Deans Council met to discuss and review the applications and recommendations for promotions. After reviewing all available data including the recommendations of your dean, department head and departmental faculty promotion committee, I am happy to recommend to the President that you be promoted to the rank of Professor

Please accept my congratulations for your many accomplishments in the areas of teaching, service, and research or other scholarly and creative activities. I value your contributions to the University and wish you continued success in your career.

Sincerely,

Adolfo Benavides, Ph.D.
Provost and Vice President for Academic Affairs

I'm proud to have you on our team, Professor, Congr.!

7. President's Final Decision — The president makes the final decision based on all the comments. In the case of a private university, the president's decision is the final

decision. For public schools, the president's decision is reported to the State Board of Regency for final approval, which will be the final approval result. At this point, the entire approval process is over.

Characteristics of Faculty Promotion in American Colleges and Universities

The American professor promotion system is quite standardized and has strict procedures. The above is just an introduction to American colleges and universities' promotion objectives, conditions, standards, and practices. It is meant to give you a rough understanding of their operation. The following is a comparison of its main characteristics and the differences in promotion within universities in the United States and China.

1. Faculty Classification – In American higher education, faculty classification is a nuanced and dynamic aspect, with distinctions between tenure track and non-tenure track positions and full-time and part-time instructors. Unlike the traditional approach, where all faculty members were expected to engage simultaneously in teaching, scientific research, and service to fulfill the institution's three fundamental functions, modern practices have shifted towards a more segmented approach. This shift has several implications, including limitations on promotion opportunities, the rationalization of faculty management, the enhancement of professional titles, and the efficient allocation of resources. It's important to note that these practices diverge significantly from those found in Chinese colleges and universities. Chinese colleges and universities historically favored a more holistic approach, where faculty members were expected to fulfill multiple roles

simultaneously. While this approach has its merits, the American system's segmentation offers a more targeted and efficient allocation of human resources.

2. Procedure Specification – The promotion process is standardized, the timetable is fixed, and the procedure is the same for multiple levels of professional titles and all applicants. Once the promotion process begins, each link has corresponding steps, and even if a veto is raised, the process will still be completed. Only the applicant himself has the right to withdraw from the approval process at any level, and no Chief Executive or any committee member has the right to block or interrupt the promotion process. However, suppose the applicant withdraws after submitting the official application for promotion report. In that case, the applicant will receive a document to terminate the renewal contract after the end of the current academic year (this only applies to the applicant in the final year of the application for tenure) or the withdrawal will be kept on file. Therefore, applicants must be very aware before applying for any promotion and carefully measure whether they meet the standards.

3. Independent Review – The Chief Executive does not participate in the work of the committee. Each committee member conducts independent reviews with professional vision, honesty, and dignity, submits review reports and votes, and avoids small-scale private discussions. All audit reports and raw voting results are transferred to the next level and kept on file for future review. Although the department head is not allowed to participate in the review and voting process, the department head's comprehensive comments and recommendation letters still play an important role in the process. The upper level will carefully consider the opinions of the lower level,

and the department head can overrule the committee's vote but must present sufficient persuasive evidence. In addition, third-party opinions are highly valued. This is due to American management culture's assumption that direct stakeholders are biased by interests. Therefore, expert opinions on behalf of a neutral third party should be more reliable and related to general professionalism in the American academic community. However, colleges and universities in China over-strengthen administrative power at all levels, and managers infiltrate too much professional title evaluation. As a result, the academic evaluation of promoted faculty members is more unrealistic, ultimately damaging the university's professionalism and academic development.

4. Feedback from all Academic Levels – The promotion system of American colleges and universities stipulates that applicants must be notified in writing of the relevant evaluation decisions during the evaluation process at each level. Applicants who receive a negative opinion on promotion at any level and are dissatisfied can submit a petition of no more than three pages within five days. After receiving the appeal, the person in charge at this level must review the applicant's file, arrange a meeting with the complainant, and respond to the appeal requirements within five working days. If the complainant is still unsatisfied with the decision, he can appeal to the next level. The upper tier must also respond within five working days. This hierarchical feedback mechanism allows applicants to express their dissatisfaction when they learn of negative results so that potential conflicts can be resolved in a timely manner.

Figure 5.5 – Appeal Process Snapshot

8 APPEAL PROCESS FOR PROMOTION AND/OR TENURE

8.1 Any candidate for promotion and/or tenure may appeal a negative decision if the negative decision is reached at any level in the university promotion and tenure process. There is no appeal of a decision by the Board of Regents.

8.2 After receiving notice of a negative decision, a candidate may appeal the decision by submitting a letter of appeal. Unless a candidate withdraws from consideration for promotion and/or tenure (see § 7), a candidate for promotion and/or tenure shall receive consideration at all levels of the university promotion and tenure process.

8.3 The letter of appeal, which may not exceed three pages in length, must describe the basis for the appeal and must be submitted within five business days of the date ⁿ the notice of a negative decision.

5. Academic Supremacy – In the American higher education system, promoting academic titles strongly emphasizes professionalism, with evaluation standards grounded in professional and academic criteria. This approach does not factor in elements like a faculty member's seniority or on-campus service as voting criteria; instead, it centers on assessing academic ability and influence. In contrast, the evaluation process for professorial titles in Chinese colleges and universities often considers seniority. The primary reason behind this practice is the direct link between professional titles and salary and benefits in the Chinese system. In American universities, the annual salary increase, often called a "merit increase," is not contingent on changes in professorial titles. Consequently, it is not uncommon to encounter situations where an individual holds the title of an associate professor yet boasts longer seniority and a higher annual salary than someone with the title of full professor. Such occurrences are not infrequent in the American context and are a testament to the focus on merit-based compensation. In addition to the differences in title evaluation, the two systems have significant variations in the academic environment. Chinese faculty members often find themselves compelled

to publish articles prolifically in pursuit of promotions. Magazines and publishing houses, aware of this demand, usually charge publication fees, generating additional income. Unfortunately, this practice has accumulated academic output, with both high-quality and low-quality work often indistinguishable. Consequently, the academic ecology in Chinese institutions has suffered a decline in quality.

Having personally experienced the promotion of professor titles in universities in China and the United States, I sincerely feel that the reason why professional title evaluations in China are frequently criticized is legitimate and that there is room for improvement. In the early 1980s, the promotion of faculty in the universities of China was mainly based on seniority. Since salary is directly linked to professional titles, professors with higher seniority are often taken care of first, and the applicant's scientific research achievements can be relatively low, which is related to the overall quality of the faculty at that time. Due to the administrative orientation of colleges and universities in China, there is no way to talk about academic ecology. In the late 1980s and early 1990s, due to a large number of graduate students who stayed to become faculty members in the university where they were students, they began to focus on the so-called fighting arena for the promotion of young faculty. And many young faculty members in their 30s were directly promoted to professors or associate professors. Because the policy is tilted to favor young faculty, the promotion of middle-aged faculty has been neglected. As a result, middle-aged faculty members "do not touch the sky above, but do not touch the ground below: both ends fail."

To make up for the shortcomings of such a system, a "nominal associate professor" or "nominal professor" title has been designed; that is, for those who have met the professional title standards but are unable to be promoted, applicants are awarded nominal titles that are not related to salary. Since the late 1990s, due to "not much gruel and many monks" (which means there are few things but many people, and there is not enough distribution), the continuous updating and improvement of the standards in the evaluation of professional titles in colleges and universities in China, it has become more and more challenging to promote professional titles. Some colleges and universities require applicants for associate professor positions to complete nationwide, provincial, and ministerial-level research projects. As a result, the so-called "project-based survival" ecology has sprung up on campus.

The faculty's academic life is tied to research projects; therefore, teaching is generally despised. However, funded research projects are limited, and there is no reasonable mechanism to allocate resources, so scandals such as robbing projects, plagiarism, and bribery emerge on campus. This tendency further leads to academic "power rent-seeking," which forces some scholars to fight for various so-called academic interests and honors. Because of this, there are often reports and complaints about the evaluation and promotion of professional titles in the universities of China. During the evaluation process for professional titles, professors who were usually polite and courteous would often become disrespectful and even attack and abuse each other because of the unfair behavior in the evaluation procedures. Rumors were endless. During the university's professional title review season, relevant reports would become a social hotspot in the local newspaper. There were reports of "hand-to-hand combat" in which departments compete for indicators and review and approval; there were reports of "treats and gifts" to promotion committee members for a professional title and research projects, which became some of the most common scandals in colleges and universities in China at that time. The reason may not have been simply the quality of faculty but also the defects in the design and operation of the faculty promotion system altogether, as well as the unhealthy academic ecology as a whole.

Generally speaking, the faculty members of universities in China are composed of a group of academics with high levels of self-esteem who advocate science and pursue the perfection of their personalities. They regard their jobs as an important part of academic life. In the promotion of professional titles, professionalism is ignored, and the tendency of administrative orientation can mean contempt or even blasphemy for faculty members who advocate scientific careers, and to a certain extent, it is also an insult to their personalities. In recent years, these issues in evaluating faculty promotion in colleges and universities in China have gradually gained attention. However, cultivating an excellent academic ecology can not be expected to be achieved overnight and requires synchronizing the entire ecological environment of the institution. If the overall environment remains unchanged, any improvement is useless. The personal experiences of the promotion of professor titles in both Chinese and American universities can be seen as differences in the academic ecologies largely determine the survival of any individual in this ecology, their circumstances, and their growth trajectories. It is urgent to create a benign and beneficial academic ecology and a health promotion system of faculty's professional titles in all colleges and universities in China.

Relevant Information for Reference

The promotion conditions and processes for teachers' professional titles in Chinese and American colleges and universities can exhibit similarities and differences. Let's explore these aspects:

Similarities in Promotion Conditions and Process

1. Academic Qualifications: In Chinese and American institutions, academic qualifications play a significant role in promotion. Teachers are typically required to meet specific educational requirements, such as holding advanced degrees (master's or doctoral) in relevant fields.
2. Years of Experience: Both systems consider years of teaching experience as an important factor for promotion. Teachers are often expected to have accumulated several years of teaching or research experience before they become eligible for higher professional titles.

Differences in Promotion Conditions and Process

1. Research Productivity: In American universities, research productivity and scholarly contributions are often given significant weight in the promotion process. Faculty members are expected to demonstrate a strong record of research, including publications in reputable journals, presentations at conferences, and securing research grants. Chinese universities value research productivity, but the emphasis may vary depending on the institution and the specific requirements of the professional title being sought.
2. Teaching Effectiveness: While teaching effectiveness is considered important in both systems, the weight assigned to it may differ. In American universities, the promotion process often includes evaluations of teaching effectiveness, such as student feedback, peer evaluations, and teaching portfolios. Chinese universities also assess teaching effectiveness, but the emphasis may be more on teaching methods, pedagogical innovation, and student outcomes.

3. Service and Engagement: American universities typically place importance on service and engagement activities when considering promotions. This can include participation in departmental committees, academic advising, community outreach, and involvement in professional organizations. Chinese universities also value service contributions, such as administrative roles, student mentorship, and engagement in academic societies, but the weight assigned to them may differ depending on the institution and the specific requirements.

4. Evaluation Process: The promotion evaluation processes can differ between Chinese and American universities. In Chinese universities, promotions are often subject to a rigorous review process conducted by internal evaluation committees. These committees assess candidates' qualifications, research outputs, teaching effectiveness, and contributions to the university. American universities may have similar review committees, but the process may be more decentralized, with individual departments or promotion committees making recommendations.

5. Professional Title System: Chinese universities typically have a hierarchical professional title system with specific criteria and requirements for each title, such as lecturer, associate professor, and professor. The promotion process follows a step-by-step progression through these titles. The professional title system in American universities may be less structured, and the titles may vary between institutions. The criteria for promotion may also differ, with some institutions using a tenure-track system where faculty undergo a comprehensive review for tenure and promotion simultaneously.

It's important to note that the promotion conditions and processes can vary between Chinese and American universities and within different institutions, disciplines, and even individual departments. These comparisons provide a general overview, but the specific requirements and processes can differ based on institutional policies, disciplinary norms, and academic culture.

CHAPTER 6

The Salary System of Faculty & Staff in the American University

American colleges and universities lack a standardized federal salary system, with each institution shaping its compensation structure based on its unique financial resources. When examining the financial foundations of these higher education establishments, public universities primarily rely on state government funding, followed by revenue from university operations, tuition fees, and income generated from school property taxes. In contrast, private universities heavily depend on tuition and miscellaneous fees, supplemented by alumni donations, university operational income, and some government grants. Furthermore, private universities can seek research and teaching funding from various government levels. Consequently, colleges and universities, as employers, naturally assume a dominant role in shaping salary systems. They possess the autonomy to tailor these systems to meet their development needs, utilize salaries as indicators for resource allocation in line with the human resource market, and operate within a market-driven framework.

As the adage goes, "water flows down, and people go up." The considerable salary disparities among colleges and universities have given rise to a talent resources market and the creation of talent hubs. Undoubtedly, this market-oriented compensation system, coupled with internal promotion mechanisms within these institutions, has played a significant role in the rational distribution of highly skilled and qualified individuals. It has facilitated greater mobility among faculty members across different regions and universities of varying levels, contributing significantly to the advancement of colleges and universities.

The salary of American college and university faculty is generally above the national median household salary. According to the September 2014 U.S. Census Bureau, the median household income in the United States is $51,939. These include disparities in household income across racial and ethnic groups. Trends in the distribution of median household income (1967-2014) by race and minority status can be seen in the chart below.

Figure 6.1 – Average Wage Index

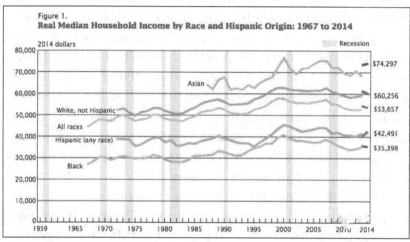

Figure 1.
Real Median Household Income by Race and Hispanic Origin: 1967 to 2014

Another indicator that reflects per capita income is the average wage index. The national average wage index in 2014 was $46,481. The wage index offsets the effect of inflation on consumption for the year and is, therefore, more reflective of actual income levels. The average wage index is established by the U.S. Social Security Administration (SSA) as a measure of federal income tax collection and is also used in U.S. retirement and insurance benefit plans (https://www.ssa.gov/oact/cola/AWI.html)

In addition, in the United States, the effect of education level on income is quite significant. As the graph below shows, the higher the education level, the higher the income. Annual salaries for Ph.D. and professionals tend to be much higher than those for master's and bachelor's degrees; high school degrees are significantly lower, and those below high school are even lower. Because college and university professors in the United States generally possess higher levels of education, their salaries are more often higher than those of the general public.

Figure 6.2 – Annual Salary Based on Education

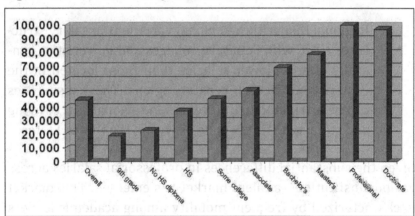

While the overall salary levels within American colleges and universities are generally high, the compensation for professors varies significantly. This discrepancy is primarily evident in four key areas:

1. Disciplinary Differences: Professors' salaries vary based on their academic disciplines. Applied disciplines tend to command higher salaries, while basic disciplines typically offer lower compensation. Additionally, salaries in liberal

arts fields are generally lower compared to those in science and engineering.

2. Institutional Popularity: The prestige and popularity of an academic institution are closely tied to its academic standing. Renowned universities, such as Ivy League schools, offer significantly higher salaries than lesser-known institutions.

3. Institutional Nature: The public or private status of an academic institution plays a pivotal role in determining salaries. Private colleges, often funded by higher tuition fees, typically provide better compensation for professors compared to public colleges.

4. Regional Disparities: Regional variations in salary structures exist, with Southern colleges and universities generally offering lower salaries than those located in the eastern and western coastal regions. These disparities can be attributed to differences in regional cost of living and state-specific tax policies within the United States.

Given the substantial differences in professorial salaries across various institutions, a talent market has emerged. This market is characterized by frequent mobility among academic leaders and faculty members in colleges and universities. Department heads, deans, and even university presidents are often openly recruited, and cross-institutional mobility is common. Faculty mobility typically involves salary negotiations, wherein universities seeking to attract senior professors are willing to offer higher compensation, while institutions striving to retain these professors are willing to address any salary disparities to ensure their retention.

The nature of American college and university faculty work is relatively open, and the annual salary is usually calculated by nine months. Three months are unpaid free time (during the summer vacation). Many professors can use this time to do scientific research, during which time they extract labor fees from scientific research funds, which then allows them to be paid according to the salary standard. In addition, many American colleges and universities offer summer courses, which provide professors with the option of teaching during the summer break. During this period, the income from teaching is also considerable (equivalent to about 20%-30% of the annual salary), and it is figured as an additional income (that is, not included in the annual salary, but it is taxed).

Figure 6.3 – Income Schedule Example

TERM	SCH	SALARY
May Mini – 5/16-6/1/2016		
Summer I – 6/6-7/7/2016	6	$ 9,108
Summer II – 7/11-8/11/2016	6	$ 9,108
August Mini – 8/12-8/26/2016		
TOTAL		**$18,216**

Compared to the overall salary landscape in the United States, the income of college and university professors typically provides a comfortable standard of living conducive to a middle-class lifestyle, including the ability to secure suitable housing. When considering expenses related to food and housing, daily food costs typically represent only a small fraction, around one-tenth, of the total salary. While housing prices exhibit significant variation, the entirety of a general college or university faculty member's salary over three to five years often equates to purchasing a home that exceeds the local median housing price.

Compared to highly skilled professions such as doctors and lawyers in the United States, the salaries of college and university professors may not rank among the highest. However, what makes American professors desirable is not solely the level of their salaries but rather the considerable degree of professional freedom they enjoy, the opportunity for extended annual vacations, and the ability to secure nearly a thousand dollars in annual travel expenses for attending conferences. These factors align closely with the aspirations of many PhD graduates seeking a fulfilling career.

In order to gain a more detailed understanding of the salary situation of faculty and staff in American universities, let's first look at the results of the four-year college faculty salary survey conducted by The College and University Professional Association for Human Resources (CUPA-HR). The 2013 data show that the average annual salary of professors of all majors in all colleges and universities in the United States is $95,224, the average annual salary of associate professors is $74,473, and the average annual salary of assistant professors is $64,414 (this data is based on 184,924 tenured/tenure-track full-time faculty in 794 colleges and universities in the United States and the analysis of a sample of 31 discipline-specific salary packages).

Figure 6.4 – 2012-13 Faculty in Higher Education Salary Survey by Discipline, Rank, and Tenure Status in Four-Year Colleges and Universities

All Disciplines Combined

Job Title	All Institutions
Professor	$95,224
Associate Professor	$74,473
Assistant Professor	$64,414
New Assistant Professor	$65,372

To gain insights into the structure and allocation of faculty compensation within colleges and universities, this paper predominantly employs the faculty compensation data from a state university as a case study. While this data is regarded as illustrative of state universities in the United States, it does not encompass branch campuses of state universities. It should not be extrapolated to draw conclusions about private universities or community colleges. It's essential to note that this article offers a broad overview rather than an exhaustive, intricate analysis and refrains from making value judgments. For those seeking more comprehensive information, please feel free to email the author for further inquiries.

According to the data of this case, it can be summarized that the main characteristics of the salary schemes of American colleges and universities have the following key aspects: significant differences, accurate payments, performance fluctuations, and public releases (for public universities).

Significant Differences

The salary differences between American university administrators and faculty members are quite large; professors' salaries across different disciplines are significant, and the difference between faculty and staff is also prominent. In this case, the president of the state university (public) was paid $1 million a year. What is unbelievable is that the salary of college athletics coaches is quite high, which is a jaw-dropping difference in this research. According to the data, the annual salary of coaches at the state university level is between $500,000 and $800,000 USD, and the annual salary of assistant coaches is between $300,000 and $500,000 (2015 public data). These ranges are significantly higher than the median annual salary of other university faculty and staff, which is $58,843 (this is most likely related to the American college sports culture and the resulting market effect). However, the highest level of pay is ten times the average pay. As can be seen from the distribution chart below, the total number of faculty and staff in the university is 7,644. The highest annual salary is $1 million, while the salary of most faculty and staff is concentrated on the left, less than $85,000 (5,393 people) and between $85,000 and $168,800 (1,845 people).

Figure 6.5 – University Faculty and Staff Case Study (circa 2010)

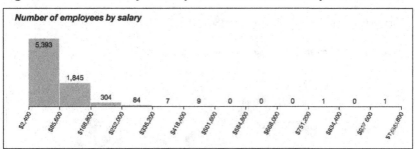

Statistics show that the annual salary of administrative officials at all levels of the university is generally the highest, with the annual salary of the provost and office management officials reaching $252,750; the dean and management officials of the college also reach $169,868.

Salaries vary across disciplines at state universities, and as mentioned earlier, non-basic and more practical professional salaries generally tend to be higher. For example, the average annual salary of the accounting department is $132,799, the economics department is $128,772, the finance department is $108,009, and the marketing department is $132,145. The average annual salary for social science majors is: $87,989 in sociology (the average annual salary for sociology faculty in the United States is $62,000, see below), $82,278 in psychology, $87,300 in political science, and $87,300 in anthropology. $72,108 and $88,204 for the faculty of Law.

Figure 6.6 – Average Annual Salary (circa 2010)

Sociologist Salary (United States)

A Sociologist earns an average salary of $61,825 per year.

$30K	$40K	$62K	$87K		$140K
	MEDIAN: $61,825				
10%	25%	50%	75%		

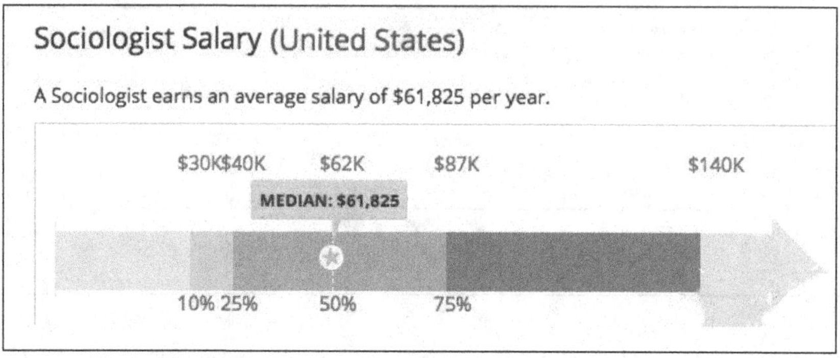

In Figure 6.7, as far as the sociology department is concerned, although the average annual salary is $87,989, the specific distribution shows that the average annual salary of professors is $121,338 (this is derived from a total of 13 people, of which the annual salary of the head of the department is 250,000 US dollars, and the annual salary of senior professors is nearly 200,000 US dollars), associate professors average $87,989 (out of 9) and assistant professors earned $73,253. Compensation for staff in the department is relatively low, with an assistant to the dean at $42,336 and office staff at $26,410.

Figure 6.7 – Average Annual Salary (circa 2010)

Positions with most employees in Sociology

Title	Employees	Median salary
Professor	13	$121,338
Associate Professor	9	$87,989
Instruct Assoc Prof	4	$73,439
Assistant Professor	4	$73,253
Bus Coordinator I	1	$43,332
Office Associate	1	$26,410
Instruct Asst Prof	1	$52,479
Asst To Dept Head	1	$42,336
Academic Advisor Ii	1	$35,640
Lecturer	1	$30,006

From the perspective of the entire university, the annual salary of faculty is two or three times that of the staff. Librarians averaged $49,956, Logistics services averaged $31,849, Admissions officers $27,688, Finance $31,901, International Student Services $35,445, Security Guards $33,065, and Campus Police averaged $45,861. In addition, many of the logistics management departments in American universities are outsourced projects and are not included in the university's salary distribution. For example, housekeepers, gardeners, etc., have lower incomes, generally around $20,000.

Precise Distribution

The salary of American university and college faculty generally refers to the annual salary before tax, which is the amount of money displayed on the payroll. Salary is calculated on a lump sum basis. Each year, a few months before the start of the new school year, the personnel department sends each faculty a confidential document specifying the total salary for the next year, and at the same time informs how much the merit increase that has been included in the salary is for that year. This total is calculated on a 9-month basis, and is transferred directly through the bank on a monthly basis. The take-home pay also deducts federal taxes, social security taxes (personal payment part), and individual medical insurance policies or other types of optional insurance. The federal tax deducted is tax withholding. This withholding tax can be submitted before April 15 (tax report deadline) of the following year and a partial refund may be provided. The tax report is based on the average salary index of the United States for the year after adding or subtracting other income and expenses during the year as well as various subsidies that can be combined according to federal policy and determines the amount of tax that individuals must pay, usually more refunds and less compensation (the U.S. tax system has its considerable advantages as a means of secondary distribution, but it is significantly more complicated. This is another research topic which will not be detailed here).

Fringe benefits are not included in the salaries paid to American university and college faculty and staff. Fringe benefits are included in the benefits paid by the university, these benefits include social security paid by the university each month, health insurance (health benefits for faculty and staff and their spouse/families), workers' compensation coverage, unemployment compensation insurance, retirement disability, survivor benefits, life insurance, etc. Fringe benefits must be included in the university and college budget on all faculty salary budgets but are not in the salary breakdown (not included in tax returns). Usually this benefit is one-third of the book salary. Therefore, if an associate professor earns more than $80,000 a year, the total compensation, including fringe benefits, will most likely exceed $100,000.

Performance Fluctuation

The "performance award," also known as a merit reward offered by American universities and colleges, represents a dynamic, performance-driven component of salary that undergoes annual adjustments. These adjustments primarily align with developments within the university and nationwide inflation rates. This merit-based compensation is primarily disbursed to full-time faculty and staff, and its distribution widens or narrows depending on individual work performance.

For instance, in the case of professors, merit evaluations encompass teaching effectiveness, research contributions, and service activities. Faculty members submit self-reports and department heads calculate a comprehensive score based on the faculty's performance and student evaluations of their courses. Once the professor endorses this assessment, it is filed within their records.

The merit pay for the year is contingent upon this evaluation and is incorporated into their total salary as a baseline component.

With the exception of years marked by economic downturns, there is typically a one to four percent increase in funding each year, designed to offset annual currency inflation. Consequently, faculty or staff members who fail to meet full-time workload requirements (defined as more than 75% of the workload) or who perform unsatisfactorily may receive lower total salaries compared to their colleagues. This disparity can accumulate over time and is a key contributing factor to variations in compensation among university and college faculty and staff.

The merit pay system in American universities and colleges originated in the 1980s and 1990s and has since evolved into a prominent feature of faculty salary structures in the United States and other Western nations. Merit-based compensation constitutes a variable component of salaries, designed to incentivize faculty members to remain committed to their roles and earn more through enhanced performance. This approach aims to boost faculty motivation, productivity, and, ultimately, elevate the overall quality of teaching and research within colleges and universities.

Public Release

After residing in the United States for an extended period, I've come to observe that the concept of personal privacy in this country is significantly different from what I have experienced elsewhere. Virtually all types of information, including the annual salaries of government officials, university presidents, and professors, are readily accessible online. The data mentioned in this article pertaining to state universities, for instance, can be freely obtained from publicly accessible sources on the internet. This accessibility is largely attributed to the fact that faculty members at public universities are funded by taxpayers, creating an expectation of transparency. Since taxpayer funds are utilized, it is only reasonable that the salaries of all faculty and staff are disclosed to taxpayers as a matter of policy. While the published data may not always be up-to-date, it is typically easy to interpret and serves as a valuable tool in ensuring financial transparency (a critical aspect, as the U.S. tax system treats concealed income as a form of tax evasion).

Since American state universities are financed by the state government, most of the funds for running schools come from the state government and are part of the state budget. Therefore, usually in the third week after the start of each semester, the school requires faculty to count the number of students (Census Date Rosters), report this total to the relevant state government departments, and obtain corresponding financial allocations. The student-faculty ratio at U.S. colleges and universities is usually 1:16 at public universities (a slightly lower ratio of 1:10 can be found at private universities). If a university or college has a high student registration rate, it will receive higher government financial allocations and vice versa. As a result, state universities tend to invest heavily in increasing student enrollment in order to obtain more grants and improve school status.

Various definitions of "salary" exist within academic circles, but a widely accepted interpretation characterizes it as follows: "Employees exert efforts to advance their employer's objectives, and in reciprocation, the employer compensates them with a designated salary. Compensation serves as a signal within the organization, communicating to employees what holds value, which work behaviors, attitudes, and competencies the organization promotes, and how policies and procedures govern employee remuneration." It's evident that such a definition relies on a robust market-based economic environment.

The features of the salary system within American colleges and universities underscore the roles of institutional chief executives and establish distinct ranks for faculty professional titles. This salary framework underscores the significance of executive leadership in institutional management while incentivizing faculty to excel in teaching and research, thereby encouraging talent mobility. However, the noticeable disparity between administrative officials and faculty and staff can somewhat dampen enthusiasm among all parties. Nevertheless, the United States adheres to a market-oriented social system that places a premium on individual capabilities and respects individual choices as fundamental values. People have grown accustomed to this distribution model.

Additionally, the presence of comprehensive social insurance systems, coupled with relatively stable price levels, contributes to a generally high standard of living. Consequently, even though disparities in income distribution exist, they typically do not lead to significant societal issues.

In the early years following the establishment of the People's Republic of China, the salary system for domestic university and college faculty and staff primarily adhered to a supply-based model. While some adjustments were made after the period of reform and opening up, it still largely resembled the planned economy concept of a nationwide chess game. There were also evident regional disparities and variations based on disciplines and majors, mirroring patterns seen in other provinces.

During the early stages of the reform and opening up in the 1980s, faculty and staff began to operate under a structural salary system based on job position remuneration. This system consisted of four components: basic salary, job position salary, seniority allowances, and incentive-based pay. However, compared to other sectors of society, university and college faculty salaries remained relatively low, resulting in significant brain drain and professors venturing into entrepreneurial endeavors.

In the late 1980s, the government granted colleges and universities the autonomy to generate revenue, leading to substantial changes in the total amount, structure, and distribution mechanisms of salary within these institutions. Subsequent salary adjustments in the 1990s introduced a professional and technical job grade salary system, which took into account the nature of work, skills, responsibilities, and contributions of academic and technical personnel. The salary structure primarily comprised two components: professional and technical position salaries and allowances, with a fixed portion of 60% and a variable portion of 40%.

Nevertheless, even as the new millennium approached, the monthly salary for an average university or college faculty member remained modest, with little more than 100 yuan per month, barely sufficient to purchase a set of children's encyclopedias (an experience the author personally encountered). After 2000, salaries offered by these institutions experienced the effects of marketization, resulting in a significant salary base increase. While these adjustments factored in currency inflation, they did not entirely eliminate the characteristics of the centrally managed planning system. Consequently, various forms of subsidies were introduced into the salary scale for university and college faculty and staff, encompassing living allowances, one-child allowances, housing allowances, job position stipends, financial supplements, and more.

From a national perspective, substantial disparities exist between prestigious institutions like the 985 universities and 211 universities (state-designated key universities) and their counterparts among ordinary colleges and universities. These disparities stem from differences in government funding, resource allocation, and capacity to attract off-campus financial support, which consequently lead to variations in faculty salaries.

When looking at faculty members individually, discrepancies in income are further exacerbated by the so-called "grey income" generated through various channels within university and college communities. Additionally, there are covert subsidies stemming from research project funding, contributing to income disparities between faculty members with and without active research projects. Loopholes in the utilization of research funds, combined with prevalent issuance of regular invoices for reimbursement, have inadvertently facilitated illicit income sources. Given the relatively modest fixed salaries for university professors, a myriad of hidden income streams have emerged under different guises. Many unpaid service obligations that were initially part of the job description are covertly compensated in this manner. Such practices include payment for reviewing doctoral dissertations and master's theses, accepting monetary gratuities for proposal reviews at conferences, and more (it's important to note that these are illegal income sources in American colleges and universities and run counter to professional ethics).

In recent years, the high salary policy for recruiting overseas talent in various colleges and universities appears to have inadvertently given rise to a dual-track compensation system, which may not be a sustainable long-term strategy. A related survey reveals that "the marketization of university education in China is progressively widening the income gap among professors." The survey notes that the salary gap between the top 10% and bottom 10% of college professors is 5.9 times, and for associate professors, it's 4.5 times. Substantial salary disparities are also evident between well-established universities and municipal colleges. In established universities, the high-salary group with annual incomes ranging from 100,000 to 200,000 yuan comprises 19.6% of faculty members, whereas in municipal colleges, it only represents 9.8%—a nearly 10% difference (based on 2012 data, which is very different now).

It's crucial to emphasize that the primary factor contributing to salary disparities among Chinese university and college faculty is not the basic salary itself but rather the performance (job position) salary, research project income, lecture fees, and bonuses offered by their respective institutions. While these various forms of "grey income" may seem advantageous on an individual level, they also pose challenges for tax collection at the national level, contributing to opacity in the overall faculty salary landscape. This opacity negatively impacts the campus environment, fostering an atmosphere susceptible to corruption.

As the old adage goes, "People can truly appreciate etiquette, honor, and shame only when their basic needs for sustenance and clothing are met." As leaders of social civilization, university and college professors deserve not only respectable salaries but also a standard of living commensurate with their role. In today's market-driven economy, it becomes imperative to reevaluate and reform the salary systems within Chinese colleges and universities. This entails moving beyond the traditional egalitarian approach and introducing competitive mechanisms to fully harness the power of salaries as signals for resource allocation within the market economy.

The success of a university hinges on the collective efforts of its entire faculty. To aspire to the status of a world-class university, providing faculty with decent salaries is a critical step. However, achieving this objective is an ongoing journey that requires substantial efforts and reforms.

Relevant Information for Reference

The salary grading system and evaluation process for professors in Chinese and American universities can exhibit both similarities and differences. Let's explore these aspects:

<u>Similarities in Salary Grading System and Evaluation Process</u>

1. Rank-based System: Both Chinese and American universities often have a rank-based system for professors, with different levels of titles such as assistant professor, associate professor, and full professor. Advancement through these ranks is typically associated with increased salary and higher academic standing.

2. Criteria-Based Evaluation: In both systems, the evaluation of professors for salary adjustments and promotions is typically based on predetermined criteria. These criteria often include research productivity, teaching effectiveness, service contributions, and professional development.

<u>Differences in Salary Grading System and Evaluation Process</u>

1. Salary Structure: Chinese universities often have a more centralized and standardized salary structure, where salary scales are determined at the institutional level or by government regulations. In contrast, American universities may have more variation in salary structures, as they are influenced by factors such as institutional budgets, market competition, and faculty negotiations.

2. Tenure System: American universities often employ a tenure system, which provides job security and long-term employment for eligible professors. Tenure is typically granted after a rigorous evaluation process that assesses a faculty member's research, teaching, and service over

a specified probationary period. Chinese universities do not have a tenure system in the same way, but some professors may still enjoy job stability based on their seniority, qualifications, and institutional policies.

3. Research Emphasis: American universities often place significant emphasis on research productivity when evaluating professors for salary adjustments and promotions. Factors such as publications, grants, citations, and research impact are closely considered. While research is also valued in Chinese universities, the emphasis may vary depending on the institution and academic discipline. In some cases, teaching effectiveness and professional service may carry relatively more weight in the evaluation process.

4. Evaluation Process: The evaluation processes can differ between Chinese and American universities. In Chinese universities, the evaluation process is often more centralized and conducted by internal committees or external experts. These committees assess professors based on their qualifications, research outputs, teaching effectiveness, service contributions, and overall performance. American universities may have a more decentralized evaluation process, with individual departments or committees conducting assessments. External evaluations, such as peer reviews and letters of recommendation, may also be part of the process.

5. Market Factors: Market factors can significantly influence salary levels in American universities as institutions compete to attract and retain top talent. Salaries may vary across disciplines and geographic regions. In Chinese universities, while there can be differentiation in salaries based on seniority and qualifications, market factors may have less direct impact due to the centralized nature of salary structures.

It's important to note that the salary grading system and evaluation processes can vary within both Chinese and American universities. Institutional policies, disciplinary norms, and individual circumstances can influence the specific mechanisms and criteria used for salary adjustments and promotions.

CHAPTER 7

"Multicultural Ecology" in the American University

T
he United States has the largest immigrant population of any other country in the world, with millions of immigrants arriving every year. According to the 2013 report "Changes in Global Migration and Remittance Patterns" published by the Pew Center, the number of immigrants living in the United States doubled in 20 years to 46 million, which accounted for one-fifth of the total number of immigrants in the world at that time. It is estimated that there are foreign immigrants from more than 170 countries living in the United States today. As the origins and numbers of immigrants continue to increase, so does cultural diversity. Sociologist Nathan Glazer once compiled a statistic and found that the main American newspapers only began to use the term multiculturalism in the late 1980s, and the word appeared only 33 times in 1989; it increased to 600 two years later, and by 1994, it appeared 1,500 times the phenomenon of multiculturalism has gradually become an important reality of American society since then.

Multiculturalism, also known as cultural pluralism, is shaped by the diverse racial and national makeup of the American populace. It extends beyond academic discourse and significantly influences various aspects of U.S. domestic policy. College campuses throughout the United States not only embrace the ethos and principles of cultural pluralism but also collectively forge a substantial "multicultural ecosystem." This rich tapestry of multiple ethnicities and cultures is evident across a spectrum of institutions, including prestigious private universities, public universities, state colleges, and even community colleges nationwide. To some extent, the characteristics of this "multicultural ecosystem" can be exemplified by the state university I am affiliated with.

School Governance Principles: Diversity

The first article of a school's Guiding Principles emphasizes something they term as diversity. Diversity means that there is a difference or that the parts of the whole are not the same. Relative to population status, it refers to individuals from different countries, from different ethnic groups, who may possess various skin colors, religious beliefs, belong to various differing social classes, and come from a wide variety of cultural orientations.

Figure 7.1 – Example of a School's Guiding Principals

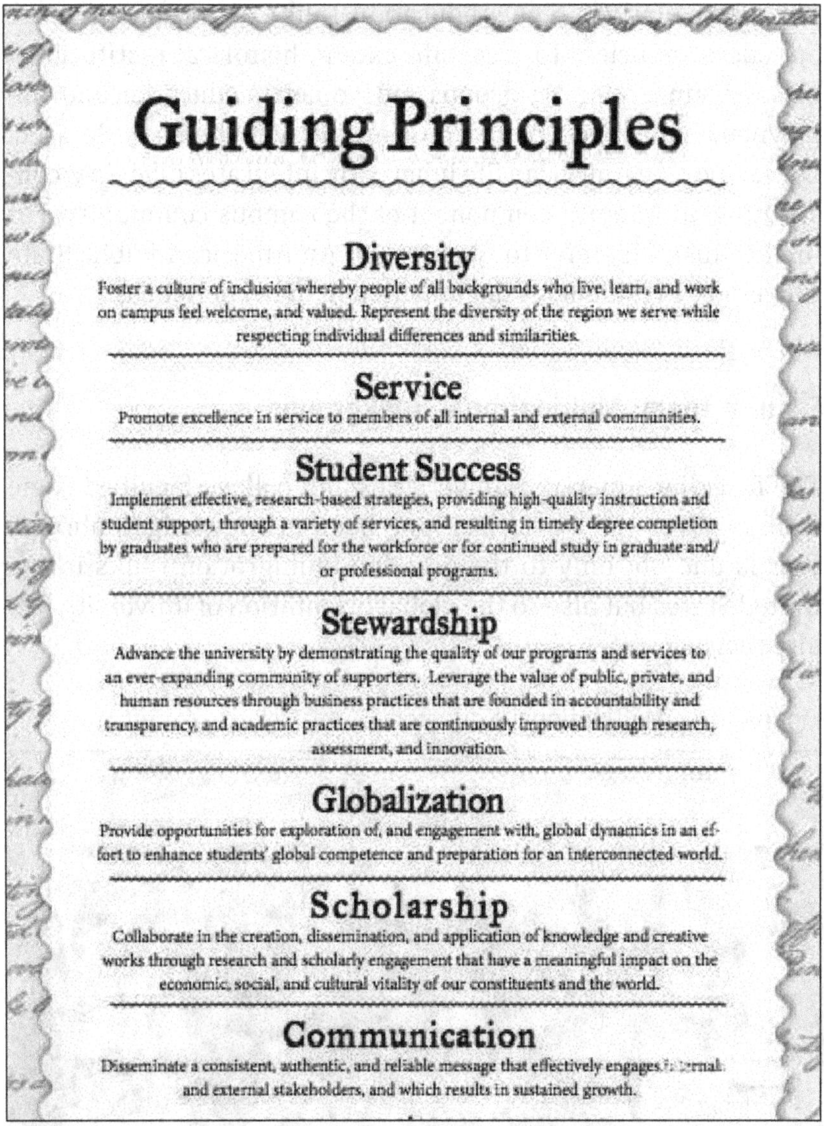

Guiding Principles

Diversity

Foster a culture of inclusion whereby people of all backgrounds who live, learn, and work on campus feel welcome, and valued. Represent the diversity of the region we serve while respecting individual differences and similarities.

Service

Promote excellence in service to members of all internal and external communities.

Student Success

Implement effective, research-based strategies, providing high-quality instruction and student support, through a variety of services, and resulting in timely degree completion by graduates who are prepared for the workforce or for continued study in graduate and/or professional programs.

Stewardship

Advance the university by demonstrating the quality of our programs and services to an ever-expanding community of supporters. Leverage the value of public, private, and human resources through business practices that are founded in accountability and transparency, and academic practices that are continuously improved through research, assessment, and innovation.

Globalization

Provide opportunities for exploration of, and engagement with, global dynamics in an effort to enhance students' global competence and preparation for an interconnected world.

Scholarship

Collaborate in the creation, dissemination, and application of knowledge and creative works through research and scholarly engagement that have a meaningful impact on the economic, social, and cultural vitality of our constituents and the world.

Communication

Disseminate a consistent, authentic, and reliable message that effectively engages internal and external stakeholders, and which results in sustained growth.

Diversity undeniably constitutes a fundamental facet of American university campuses, warranting recognition as a paramount philosophy and governing principle of educational institutions. In the context of the United States, diversity has, to a significant degree, transformed the essence and scope of American education, particularly in higher education, thus exerting an influence on federal policies. To a certain extent, historical institutional biases against minority groups and women in education and employment have been rectified or are actively being addressed. Contemporary American life inherently integrates diversity, constituting an integral component of the campus community. For further insights, refer to Chapter 19: An American Public State University President, as documented in my experiences.

Faculty Team: Multinational Background

The fact that American universities and college faculties come from all over the world has long been acknowledged abroad. This is due not only to the growing immigration ranks in the United States but also to the global orientation of university faculty recruitment.

Figure 7.2 – Multinational Educators

As a case in point, within my liberal arts college, we boast a diverse array of professors hailing from various corners of the globe, spanning Europe, Asia, and Africa. Many of these educators represent the first generation of their families to settle in the

United States, while others belong to the second or third generation. Despite their disparate countries of origin and distinct cultural backgrounds, they maintain a profound mutual respect, coexisting harmoniously and fostering strong camaraderie. This spirit of multicultural unity is prominently evident during our school-wide faculty conferences, which occur several times each year. During these gatherings, professors don their doctoral regalia and convene in a meticulously organized venue to partake in presentations. Speakers, with a blend of gravity and levity, captivate their audience, and the ambiance in the venue oscillates between rapt attention and exuberant applause.

Sociological theory highlights the tendency for individuals in secondary groups to exhibit greater discipline, as they often maintain a degree of anonymity and interpersonal distance. Conversely, in primary groups, where mutual familiarity and friendships prevail, enforcing such norms can prove more challenging. Professors within American campus settings clearly belong to a diverse and heterogeneous secondary group. In contrast, various factors, including historical practices like selective "inbreeding" (where a significant portion of faculty is recruited from the institution's own graduates), make faculty teams in China particularly susceptible to the formation of cliques or factions, thereby accentuating characteristics typical of primary groups.

Curriculum Arrangement: Prepare Students for an Interconnected World

American colleges and universities emphasize that the curriculum should reflect the principle of diversity, and some related disciplines in the liberal arts curriculum should emphasize the global perspective and cross-country comparisons in the curriculum. In recent years, the Quality Enhancement Plan (QEP) proposed by colleges and universities aims to prepare students for participation in an interconnected world by developing their global competitiveness. QEP proposes some meaningful curriculum structures and teaching processes to enhance and improve students' global competitiveness through two programs, the Global Scholar Program (for faculty) and the Global Partnership Program (primarily for students) encourage professors and students to work together to prepare the students for the global workplace after graduation.

Certain courses in literature, history, and philosophy, such as Global Sociology, Foreign Policy, U.S./Ukraine Relations, and non-Western cultures (including histories, literature, philosophy, religion, etc.) are required for university and college students. In addition, some universities, such as the University of California, Berkeley, require students to take two additional courses to improve their knowledge of cultures other than their own in order to graduate. This provision has become a common practice in colleges and universities across the United States, with some schools stipulating that undergraduate students must complete coursework in at least one non-Western culture or history course, and the courses for students' history requirement must include at least one country history other than American or European.

The multiculturalism trend of thought that began to form in the 1990s has already penetrated into all aspects of social life, and the melting pot theory of American society that has been touted in the past seems to be slowly weakening. The wave of globalization since the beginning of this century has further promoted the concept of higher education and the renewal of its curriculum content. Influenced by economic globalization and the expanding global interests of the United States, it is also required to cultivate students with a knowledge of or background in internationalized multiculturalism.

Student Body: Multiracial with Skin Colors

American colleges and universities reflect their multiethnic and multicultural composition in diverse ways. The student body comprises not only the descendants of immigrants but also an increasing influx of international students from across the globe. Consequently, classrooms often see students of various skin colors and cultural backgrounds sharing seats. Beyond the academic setting, students from diverse ethnicities and cultures frequently engage in interactions, forging friendships that can evolve from cordial classmates to intimate partnerships and, in some instances, culminate in interracial and intercultural marriages.

Figure 7.3 – Class Photo

The university's canteen must also be constantly renovated to adapt to the multiethnic and multinational characteristics of the fluctuating student body. Oftentimes, the restaurant provides a buffet (for a discounted fee), and students can choose from a wide variety of international foods to suit their appetites.

Figure 7.4 – Canteen Advertisement

In order to implement the Affirmative Action Plan, the U.S. federal government has established special programs in many universities that deliberately recruit minority students in order to diversify the student body. This concept, among other things, determines whether an institution of higher learning has a particular number of minority students and international students in its student ratio as one of the many criteria utilized to measure the overall quality of any school. According to the 1998 U.S. News & World Report ranking of U.S. universities, the degree of student diversity at the top 25 universities is positively correlated with their academic quality. Asian Americans make up about four percent of the U.S. population this century. Still, the number of Asian-American students, which includes international students, continues to grow at some of the nation's most prestigious universities. The data shows that Asian-American students make up 25% of Columbia University's student body, 24% at Stanford University, 18% at Harvard University, 17% at Yale University, and 16% at Cornell University. One of the most prominent examples of student body diversity is described in the literature. In 1974, white students accounted for 68.6% of the student body at the University of California, Berkeley, but in 1994 it was only 32.4%. Berkeley thus became the first major state university in the United States with a majority of minority students, a situation that seemed to only strengthen Berkeley's already high reputation.

However, in a controversial decision on June 29, 2023, the U.S. Supreme Court ended affirmative action in college and university admissions decisions, making race-conscious college admissions programs that have been used to promote racial diversity illegal. See the details in "Supreme Court guts affirmative action, effectively ending race-conscious admissions" (https://www.npr.org/2023/06/29/1181138066/affirmative-action-supreme-court-decision).

Students Clubs: Multicultural Elements

Because students come from different countries and have their own national traditions, international student associations in American colleges and universities develop unique cultural landscapes based on their populations. My university has student associations for individuals who maintain ties to Africa, the Caribbean, China, Latin America, India, Korea, Nepal, Thailand, Saudi Arabia, and so on. Since American colleges and universities tend to only have the concept of classmates (students who are taking the same course), and lack a unifying concept of a class system, the student associations for these different groups provide their student populations with a greater sense of belonging. These groups can each form their own organizations and activities, with frequent gatherings and individual financial support from the school, all of which undoubtedly contribute to the phenomenon of campus subcultures. There are also various crossover student associations in the mainstream culture, such as Alpha Kappa Delta (AKD), an international honor society for sociology. The purpose of this particular association is to promote the advancement of social science research and sociology while also encouraging and stimulating academic research. AKD has grown to more than 80,000 scholars and has more than 490 branches around the world. It also plays a role in students' self-management and group communication skills.

Figure 7.5 – Cultural Diversity on Campus

Annual Event: Multicultural Festival

An annual Multicultural Festival is usually held on campus in April, and it has become a grand carnival where students from different countries and national and traditional cultures gather together. Each student association prepares their own traditional gifts or small-dishes to share with students, faculty, and staff. At the same time, they don festive costumes and traditional regalia and perform programs with rich ethnic characteristics on stage. There are also special judges from the student and faculty body who score the performances in order to present festival awards.

Figure 7.6 – Multicultural Festival Flyer

Figure 7.7 – Japanese students dressed in traditional kimonos serve their national specialties

Figure 7.8 – Students from mainland China and Taiwan have prepared colorful pendants for everyone, as well as delicious Chinese meals for the whole school to enjoy

Figure 7.9 – Korean students use pen and ink to write names and other words for students who are interested in oriental cultures

Figure 7.10 – The African Student Union organize traditional dance performances

"Gardener" Care: Multilayer Institutional Services and Coordination

The multicultural ecology of the campus needs to be cultivated and maintained, and several specially established institutions at the university level are naturally gardeners, including the International Program Office, International Student and Scholar Services under the Provost International Student and Scholar Services, and the Office of Institutional Diversity and Inclusion directly under the President. These institutions are especially responsible for promoting and developing students' international exchanges and helping international students to solve various problems in study and life; at the same time, they also deal with and coordinate assistance for various practical problems and research projects related to multicultural ecology. These agencies are responsible for inspecting and supervising the strict implementation of relevant legal provisions. For example, as early as 1964, the Civil Rights Act in the United States explicitly prohibits companies with more than 25 employees from discriminatory practices against employees based on the individual's race, religion, color, gender, or immigration background. The 1967 Employee Age Discrimination Act also stipulates that no discrimination in employment shall be leveled at individuals over the age of 40, which provides legal protection for the elderly to obtain and maintain employment before retirement. Therefore, recruiters are not legally allowed to ask applicants their age, gender, race, place of birth, or immigration status during the application process for American colleges and universities. If these questions are asked, an appeal can be made on the grounds that "the real reason for the refusal of employment may be related to discrimination" if the applicant is unsuccessful in obtaining a position of employment. Depriving a person of the right to work for these reasons is illegal, which would create great trouble for the institution.

These institutions are also engaged in related research in campus multicultural ecology. For example, in 2016, the Office of Institutional Diversity and Inclusion conducted a Campus Climate Survey to build a healthy university community, aiming to make building a healthy university community a top priority. The task was to investigate the learning, living, and working conditions and feelings of professors and students from multicultural backgrounds on campus. The survey was to help the university work towards nurturing a campus climate and culture of inclusion whereby people of any background at A&M-Commerce feel comfortable and respected (relative information can be seen at https://www.tamuc.edu/news/university-conducts-learning-living-and-working-climate-survey/).

The multicultural environment within American colleges and universities fosters a conducive atmosphere for faculty and students of diverse nationalities and cultural backgrounds to coexist harmoniously through mutual interaction and integration. In the backdrop of our ever-globalizing world, this multicultural ecology also equips university students with valuable cultural readiness and practical experience during their campus life.

The campus multicultural ecology is emblematic of a societal shift that has gained prominence in American culture since the 1990s. Simultaneously, multiculturalism as an ideology presents a significant challenge to the traditional American thought and value system, prompting Americans to reevaluate the nation's history and envision new futures. As Fei Xiaotong, a distinguished figure in Chinese sociology, asserted, the future's ideal society is one where individuals "...cherish their own uniqueness while respecting the uniqueness of others; when both are celebrated, the world unites." In the United States, a vibrant and more perfect world marked by the harmonious coexistence of diverse cultures appears to be gradually emerging. This phenomenon invites deeper contemplation on how to nurture the current state and future prospects of this multicultural ecology. If this multicultural ecosystem represents the aspiration of people in the era of globalization, can it be replicated? These questions warrant extensive exploration by sociologists.

Relevant Information for Reference

The campus cultural ecology of Chinese and American universities encompasses the social, cultural, and environmental characteristics that shape the overall campus environment. While there are similarities, there are also notable differences between Chinese and American universities. Let's explore these aspects:

Characteristics of Campus Cultural Ecology

1. Diversity: Both Chinese and American universities often have diverse student bodies, faculty, and staff, representing various cultural backgrounds, ethnicities, and perspectives. This diversity contributes to a rich and multicultural campus environment.
2. Academic Excellence: Both Chinese and American universities prioritize academic excellence and strive to create an environment conducive to learning, research, and intellectual growth. They often promote a culture of intellectual curiosity, critical thinking, and academic rigor.
3. Student Engagement: Student engagement is a key aspect of campus cultural ecology. Universities in both systems provide opportunities for students to engage in extracurricular activities, clubs, sports, and community service. These activities foster personal growth, leadership skills, and a sense of community.
4. Campus Facilities: Chinese and American universities typically provide a range of campus facilities to support students' academic and social needs. This includes

libraries, laboratories, research centers, student centers, recreational facilities, and dormitories. The quality and scale of these facilities may vary across institutions.

Similarities in Campus Cultural Ecology

1. Campus Spirit and Traditions: Both Chinese and American universities often have a strong sense of campus spirit and traditions. This can include annual events, sports competitions, homecoming celebrations, graduation ceremonies, and other shared experiences that foster a sense of belonging and pride within the university community.
2. Student Organizations and Clubs: Chinese and American universities have a vibrant student life with a wide array of student organizations and clubs. These groups cater to various interests, hobbies, and academic pursuits, allowing students to explore their passions and connect with like-minded individuals.

Differences in Campus Cultural Ecology

1. Cultural Values: Chinese and American universities reflect the cultural values of their respective countries. Chinese universities may emphasize collectivism, respect for authority, and harmony, while American universities may emphasize individualism, freedom of expression, and diversity of thought.
2. Academic Focus: Chinese universities often have a more structured and examination-oriented academic culture. There may be a greater emphasis on memorization, discipline-specific knowledge, and adherence to established curricula. American universities often prioritize interdisciplinary approaches, critical thinking, creativity, and student-centered learning.

3. Campus Size and Layout: The size and layout of campuses can differ significantly between Chinese and American universities. Chinese universities, particularly larger ones, may have expansive campuses with extensive facilities and residential areas. American universities can vary in size, but they often have more spread-out campuses and a mix of residential and academic buildings.

4. Social Interaction: Cultural norms and social interactions can differ between Chinese and American universities. Chinese universities may place greater importance on hierarchical relationships between faculty and students, while American universities often foster more egalitarian interactions, encouraging open discussions, and faculty-student collaborations.

It's important to note that the characteristics of campus cultural ecology can vary within both Chinese and American universities, as each institution has its own unique culture and values. The comparisons provided here offer a general overview, but individual universities may have distinct cultural ecosystems influenced by their location, history, academic focus, and institutional traditions.

CHAPTER 8

Professors' Office Culture and University Spirit in the American University

---

R egardless of their academic titles, professors within American universities all have their dedicated offices. These spaces serve as indispensable environments for educators to engage in scientific research, lesson preparation, relaxation, and the facilitation of meetings and interviews with students. Stepping into any professor's office offers an immediate glimpse into the unique personality and style of that particular academic.

With years of experience in teaching and research within American higher education institutions, I have had the opportunity to visit numerous college and university campuses, gaining access to the offices of many esteemed professors. What becomes apparent is that these offices serve not only as repositories for books and lesson planning but also as sanctuaries for solitary scientific exploration, providing essential elements like solitude, autonomy, and convenience. Moreover, they foster a distinctive office culture that enriches the spirit of the university. The subsequent section presents a summary of the five facets comprising this "office culture."

Free Space

First of all, the offices are equipped with enough bookshelves to house the necessary books and basic network services, telephones, computers, printers, and other electronic equipment, which are uniformly configured by the university and belong to the school's assets. Consumable supplies, such as printing paper, stationery materials, etc., are freely available in the department office according to each instructor's needs. If there is a problem with the network or computer, a simple call to the department secretary will provide a remedy. Usually, the secretary will contact the school's computer network service department on the same day.

Figure 8.1 – Office Desktop

The office is a free private space for professors and may include items deemed daily necessities, such as microwaves, small refrigerators, coffee machines, or electric kettles. Of course, these items must be configured at the instructor's expense. Year-round central air conditioning in the office maintains a comfortable temperature and provides a quiet place to rest. Chinese professors may have developed the habit of taking naps in China between classes and office hours and, inevitably, will squeeze a folding bed into the office once they are situated at an American college or university. However, American professors typically do not arrange for naps. Since all aspects of the office can be arranged to meet the needs of professors for scientific research and teaching, many professors are willing to spend more time in the office, especially those who live far from the school.

University professors, particularly those in liberal arts, are recognized for their solitary intellectual endeavors, necessitating a tranquil research setting when crafting lessons or pursuing scientific inquiry. During these phases, minimizing passive interactions and communication is essential to maintain a focused research mindset. The secluded privacy offered by individual offices adeptly fulfills this requirement. Consequently, arrangements akin to commercial office spaces or open-plan departments with clusters of cubicles and low dividing walls, designed for extensive worker collaboration, are ill-suited for the unique office requirements of university educators.

Personality Embellishment

Office culture is also reflected in the layout of the office, the knickknacks on the bookshelf, and so on. Professors of different cultural backgrounds will use iconic objects from their cultures to decorate their offices.

Figure 8.2 – Office Design

History professors often post a large number of historical photos on the doors of their offices. An anthropology professor may post anecdotes and cartoons about anthropology on their door. Professors will often also put their recently published articles on a corkboard by their door as soon as possible to share them with colleagues and students.

Figure 8.3 – Office Door Display

Other instructors use the space to reflect their interests outside of the classroom, which can aid in creating a more welcoming environment for the student seeking assistance.

Figure 8.4 – Personalized Office Door

Humorous Post

The posting position outside the office door, also known as the corkboard, reflects the professor's different subject backgrounds and cultural accomplishments. Animated pictures, stickers, posters, and various inspirational quotes on the corkboard are even more exciting. This is also a cork-board culture of university campus offices. It is a small and unique cultural garden for professors worthy of the name.

Figures 8.5 – The Professors Corkboard

Open Door

Another facet of office culture lies in its accessibility. Unless holding administrative positions, professors are not bound to remain confined within their offices. Since courses typically convene only two or three days a week, the office often remains accessible. Colleagues may drop by for casual interactions, yet for more substantial discussions, it is customary to schedule appointments in advance to ensure a private setting. Moreover, as a longstanding unwritten norm in office culture, when a classmate or colleague of the opposite sex enters the office, the door is to be left ajar to safeguard the comfort and boundaries of both the professor and the visitor.

All instructors in American colleges and universities must have regular weekly office hours. It is determined by professors based on their schedule and announced to students. Therefore, in addition to class time, professors need to have several hours a week as office hours to facilitate students and other instructors to meet and talk.

Usually, the department keeps track of all teachers' office hours and lists them in a table for students to reference. During posted office hours, instructors' offices must be open, and students can drop by to ask questions or discuss what is being taught in class with the professor. If there is a conflict between the student's class schedule and the teacher's office hours, the student can make an appointment with the teacher for a mutually agreed-upon time.

All faculty must be in the office during posted office hours, and department chairs sometimes check to see if the schedule is followed. If students cannot locate their professors during office hours, they will report this to the department. Therefore, professors are usually quite serious about keeping their scheduled office hours. Even if they cannot be in the office in an emergency, they need to put a note at the door to explain the situation or call the office secretary, and they will affix a notice to the instructor's door.

De-hierarchical

American colleges and universities communicate salary, benefits, and office arrangements in written offers to prospective instructors. Consequently, on their first day at the institution, instructors are greeted with an office bearing their name and are provided with a corresponding key. Thereafter, this office becomes their personal workspace. Notably, in American universities, offices for assistant professors, associate professors, and full professors exhibit minimal variations in size and functional layout. Some professors maintain the same office for decades, regardless of their evolving academic titles, as the office assignment remains consistent despite changes in rank. The guiding principle for office allocation typically follows a "first come, first served" approach, where office size may vary, but the hardware and amenities offered remain consistent across professional titles.

Moreover, the offices receive daily attention from a dedicated cleaning team. This team possesses master keys granting access to all offices on the floor and meticulously schedules their work during periods when professors are away to minimize disruption. Consequently, the professors' workspaces remain consistently neat and free of blemishes, seldom exhibiting signs of disarray or dust accumulation. Thanks to the unwavering efforts of the cleaning staff, the cleanliness extends beyond individual offices, encompassing hallways and lavatories, culminating in an impeccably maintained and hygienic environment.

The office culture among American university professors forms a vibrant kaleidoscope, offering a window into a collective ambiance characterized by individuality, humor, and a relentless quest for knowledge. Serving as the tangible support provided by the institution, these offices not only foster the academic research ethos among professors but also shape their academic way of life to a considerable degree. It exemplifies the idea that material surroundings can profoundly influence one's intellectual and professional spirit, and this principle finds a compelling manifestation within this context.

During the 1950s and 1960s in China, due to severe space constraints, educators in colleges and universities commonly adhered to a "one person, one desk" practice. This meant that several teachers or an entire teaching and research section would share a single office. Remarkably, this situation persisted into the 1980s. While there has been some marginal improvement, with certain institutions now adopting a policy of providing each full professor with their own room, the ideal of " one room, one person" remains elusive for most colleges and universities. The shared office arrangement has the potential to create disruptions among colleagues and foster the formation of exclusive cliques. The excessive passive communication and interaction stemming from shared spaces can detrimentally affect an individual's ability to concentrate on scientific research and lesson preparation. Consequently, some educators find it necessary to work from home. Young teachers, lacking dedicated on-campus offices, often rush home after classes to continue their lesson planning and research activities. Consequently, the office culture in Chinese universities differs significantly from its American counterpart.

The Chinese government has made substantial investments in colleges and universities, significantly boosting funding. However, some educational institutions have allocated excessive resources to the construction of symbolic campus buildings, aiming to underscore the school's prestige while neglecting the development of adequate office spaces for instructors. This approach appears somewhat misaligned. Even in cases where institutions have strived to achieve the "one room for one professor" standard or at least a ratio of one room for two associate professors, a prevalent occurrence is that of "people inside the office, yet doors remain closed." Professors often maintain a closed-door policy, and there exists no consistent policy mandating fixed office hours to facilitate student-teacher interactions. Consequently, students may feel hesitant to approach their instructors, reluctant to knock on the closed doors seeking assistance. A survey conducted at a Chinese university revealed that "only 40% of instructors specify fixed 'office hours' in their syllabi." Among those who do, only 63.3% actually keep an "open-door" policy within the specified timeframe. While this marks a step towards enhancing instructor availability, it suggests that comprehensive reforms promoting greater accessibility have yet to fully take root.

The essence of university spirit finds its primary expression within the foundational office culture. To instigate meaningful transformations, prioritizing the establishment and upkeep of instructors' offices must assume the foremost position in the planning and development of Chinese colleges and universities. Possessing a dedicated office space should be recognized as an inherent right for all college and university instructors and a fundamental requirement for fostering an enriched environment conducive to teaching and scientific research.

Relevant Information for Reference

The faculty office assignment and office culture in Chinese and American universities can exhibit both similarities and differences. Let's explore these aspects:

<u>Similarities in Faculty Office Assignment and Office Culture</u>

1. Individual Office Spaces: Faculty members in Chinese and American universities are typically provided with individual office spaces. These offices serve as a dedicated workspace where professors can carry out their academic responsibilities, such as research, teaching preparation, and student consultations.
2. Office Hours: Faculty members in both systems often have designated office hours, during which they are available to meet with students for academic advising, mentoring, or discussions. Office hours provide an opportunity for students to seek guidance and engage in academic conversations with their professors.

Differences in Faculty Office Assignment and Office Culture

1. Office Assignment Practices: Chinese universities often adopt a more centralized approach to office assignment, where faculty members are typically allocated offices by the institution. The allocation process considers factors such as rank, seniority, and availability of space. On the other hand, American universities may provide more autonomy to individual departments or faculty members in office assignment decisions. Professors may have the flexibility to choose their office locations within their departments or academic units.

2. Office Culture: The office culture can vary between Chinese and American universities. In Chinese universities, the office environment may be more formal and hierarchical, with greater emphasis on respect for authority and seniority. There may be established protocols for interactions between faculty members, and the office space may be perceived as a place primarily for individual work and less for collaborative activities. In American universities, the office culture may be more informal and collegial, with a focus on open-door policies, collaboration, and interdisciplinary interactions. Faculty members may engage in informal discussions, collaborative projects, and social interactions within the office space.

3. Office Size and Layout: The size and layout of faculty offices can differ between Chinese and American universities. Chinese universities, particularly larger institutions, may allocate more spacious offices with additional furniture, storage, and amenities. American universities may have varying office sizes, ranging from relatively small spaces to larger offices, depending on factors such as rank, availability, and institutional resources.

4. Office Hours and Availability: While office hours are common in both systems, the expectations and practices may differ. In Chinese universities, faculty members may have specific office hour requirements set by the institution or department. In American universities, while faculty members are generally expected to hold office hours, there may be more flexibility in determining the specific schedule and duration based on individual preferences and student needs.

It's important to note that the practices and office culture can vary within Chinese and American universities, as each institution may have its own policies, norms, and expectations. Additionally, individual departments and faculty members can contribute to variations in office assignment practices and office culture within the same university.

CHAPTER 9

The Self-nomination Mechanism in the Acquisition of Administrative Posts

n addition to open recruitment, a significant portion of candidates for administrative positions in American universities emerges from internal recruitment, with self-nomination constituting a notable proportion. Self-nomination exemplifies a democratic ethos to a certain extent and underscores a more people-centric approach.

Figure 9.1 – Self-nomination Snapshots

Administrative management in American universities encompasses various roles, including the president, the executive vice president overseeing academics, vice presidents responsible for scientific research, finance and administration, campus facilities, and others, alongside deans and department heads. The majority of major administrative openings are typically publicly advertised in the United States or globally through online recruitment platforms. After an extensive selection process, a select few proceed to on-campus interviews to determine the final candidates.

Traditionally, the appointment of the university president is carried out by the board of directors. The president is accountable to the board and possesses the authority to oversee and direct all university affairs, in addition to other rights and obligations granted by the board (see Chapter 19: An American Public State University President). Simultaneously, the president may formally delegate their rights and obligations to an individual, specifying the conditions for the exercise of these delegated responsibilities. The appointment of vice presidents is typically made by the Board of Directors upon the recommendation of the president. Vice presidents report directly to the president. Deans of university colleges are usually appointed by the president, while department heads are appointed by the respective college dean.

However, in addition to open recruitment, a considerable selection of candidates for administrative positions in American colleges and universities is generated through internal postings, of which self-nomination accounts for a considerable proportion. For example, the vacancies for these positions in my university are publicly released through the campus recruitment network (Job Path). At the same time, they are also sent to the mailboxes of every faculty and staff member through the campus email system. Some of the positions may allow for external applicants, while some are limited to internal applicants only.

This is a common practice, and I have received dozens of recruiting emails in the last month alone. Here are a few examples of such email messages.

Figures 9.2 - Recruitment Emails

[FSNotify] Position Announcement
fsnotify-bounces@tamuc.edu 发送的 Faculty/Staff Notification List
已发送: Thursday, October 6, 2016 at 9:50 PM
收件人: 'fsnotify@tamuc.edu'
  ATT00001.txt (0.2 KB) 〔预览〕

The following position is posted and accepting applications:

Global Programs Abroad Coordinator

https://jobpath.tamu.edu/postings/101594

[FSNotify] Position Announcement
fsnotify-bounces@tamuc.edu 发送的 Faculty/Staff Notification List
已发送: Thursday, November 3, 2016 at 4:54 PM
收件人: 'fsnotify@tamuc.edu'
  ATT00001.txt (0.2 KB) 〔预览〕

The following position is posted and accepting applications:

Director of Communications

https://jobpath.tamu.edu/postings/102790

Another example is a notice that only recruits from the existing pool of on-campus personnel (Internal Listing only).

Figure 9.3 - Recruitment of a Deputy Director of Agronomy College

[FSNotify] Position Announcement

fsnotify-bounces@tamuc.edu 发送的 Faculty/Staff Notification List

已发送: Monday, November 7, 2016 at 1:28 PM

收件人: 'fsnotify@tamuc.edu'

📎:   ATT00001.txt (0.2 KB) 预览

The following position is posted and accepting applications:

Associate Director - School of Agriculture (50%) (Internal listing only)

https://jobpath.tamu.edu/postings/102684

Administrative vacancies are openly advertised on campus, allowing candidates to apply for these roles through self-nomination based on the specified criteria. Similarly, a significant number of candidates for voluntary service positions within the university are also sourced through self-nomination. Personally, I have engaged in two self-nominated applications for on-campus service roles in recent years. In one instance, when vying for a position on the University Diversity and Inclusion Committee, two professors from the department submitted applications, yet only one vacancy was available. In this scenario, the committee's chairperson conducted separate interviews with both candidates and ultimately selected one to join the committee. In the second case, I sought membership on the university's Faculty Senate Committee. To secure this role, I initiated the self-nomination process, which was followed by a departmental meeting where a vote was conducted, resulting in my final approval for the position.

General administrative positions and voluntary service positions are obtained through open recruitment and self-nomination mechanisms, and positions such as department heads and even associate deans of colleges can be obtained through this self-nomination or personal application process. Here is just one example: in the first half of the year, our liberal arts college recruited an associate dean in charge of student affairs, and the recruitment information was publicly posted on the campus recruitment website. The published information specified the requirements and expectations of this position (subsidy of $5,000 and deduction of one course per semester, etc.). Conditions such as age, gender, race, religion, party affiliation, etc. are absolutely prohibited in such publicly posted job advertisements. The recruitment of administrative positions must also clearly stipulate that it is a 100% (full-time) administrative position, or 50% (part-time) administrative position, etc.

Figure 9.4 –Administrative Position Posting

The following position is currently accepting applications:

Assistant Dean - College of Humanities, Social Sciences and Arts (Internal only)

Apply at: http://jobpath.tamu.edu/postings/97012

Posting Details

Position Information

Position Title	Assistant Dean - College of Humanities, Social Sciences and Arts (Internal only)
Title Code	TAMUC-9124
Posting Title	Assistant Dean - College of Humanities, Social Sciences and Arts (Internal only)
O*Net Occupation Title	Education Administrators, Postsecondary 11-9033.00
FLSA	Exempt
System Member Institution/Agency	TEXAS A&M UNIVERSITY - COMMERCE (TAMUC)
Department	DEAN - CHSSA / 21-131000
Posting Number	S01111FY16
Salary	$5000 total stipend; one course release per Fall and Spring semester
Pay Basis	Annually
Job Open Date	06/08/2016
Job Close Date	07/15/2016

Usually, after receiving the application materials from candidates, the recruitment committee will screen and refine the applicant pool to a smaller selection of candidates and hold an open review meeting, sometimes referred to as an Open Session to collect feedback or faculty review materials. To better understand this process, I participated in an on-the-spot inspection of a public review meeting for the position of Associate Dean. Below is an excerpt from the email notification I received explaining when and where the open session will be held:

Figure 9.5 – Notification of Public Review Meeting

All CHSSA staff and faculty are welcome to attend an open session with Dr. Christopher Gonzalez, candidate for the CHSSA Assistant Dean position. This session will be held on Wednesday Aug. 10th 11-11:30am in the CHSSA conference room, Ag/It suite 222 room 222K.

Attached is the position description and Dr. Gonzalez's vita.

Attached to the email was the resume of candidate Dr. Gonzalez. At the same time, in another email with the same content, the information of another applicant and the time and place of their open session were released:

Figure 9.6 – Notification of Additional Public Review Meeting

All CHSSA staff and faculty are welcome to attend an open session with Dr. Tony DeMars, candidate for the CHSSA Assistant Dean position. This session will be held on Tuesday Aug. 9th 2:30-3pm in the CHSSA conference room, Ag/It suite 222 room 222K.

Attached is the position description and Dr. DeMars vita.

Notifications regarding the open segments of public evaluation meetings are distributed to all university faculty members via email. These meetings are open to all, inviting attendees to listen to candidates' job proposals. Typically, the public deliberation process concludes within an hour, and each participant receives a form for recording their comments, opinions, and votes based on the candidates' job applications and proposals for the positions they are seeking.

During one such evaluation, I actively participated in the assessment of two candidates for the role of associate dean. Ultimately, I selected the candidate whom I believed to be the most qualified. Despite having spent just over two years at the university, my chosen candidate compensated for their relative brevity with an abundance of youthful vigor and determination. At the time, they held the position of assistant professor, a role well-suited for handling student affairs, in my view. In contrast, the other candidate, despite their seniority and several years of university service as an associate professor, did not strike me as a better fit for the position involving student affairs. A few weeks later, when the college announced its choice for vice dean, it coincided with the candidate I had voted for during the evaluation. In light of this, I extended my congratulations to the successful candidate through a heartfelt letter.

Figure 9.7 – Congratulatory Letter

From: ning Sun
Sent: Thursday, September 01, 2016 11:07 AM
To: Christopher Gonzalez
Subject: Congratulations

Good morning, Dr. Christopher Gonzalez,
Congratulations Interim Associate Dean!
Hope you will be successful in your new duty.
Best wishes,
aming

....
aming Sun, Ph.D.
Director of Graduate Studies in Sociology
Professor of Sociology

Figure 9.8 - New Associate Dean Gonzalez's Reply

RE: Congratulations

Christopher Gonzalez

已发送: Thursday, September 1, 2016 at 11:37 AM

收件人: Jiaming Sun

Thank you so much, Dr. Sun! I appreciate your well wishes. They mean a lot.

Cheers,

Chris

Dr. Christopher González | Interim Associate Dean
College of Humanities, Social Sciences, and Arts
Assistant Professor of English
Department of Literature and Languages
Chris.Gonzalez@tamuc.edu

This marks the culmination of the combined open recruitment and self-nomination process for the referenced position. Self-nomination is notably apparent through the active participation and self-recommendation of candidates within the context of open recruitment, mirroring the recruitment of faculty in American universities, albeit with a focus on on-campus applicants (as detailed in Chapter 4: The Process and Characteristics of Faculty Recruitment and Selection in the American University). The fundamental procedure unfolds as follows:

1. Campus-wide dissemination of recruitment information, encompassing specific prerequisites and working conditions.
2. Candidates express their interest in the available position through self-nomination and the submission of pertinent documentation.
3. The recruitment committee undertakes a comprehensive review of application materials, meticulously screening and identifying qualified candidates.

4. Public review meetings are convened to gather feedback and insights.
5. The recruitment committee or the designated executive officer meticulously evaluates the candidates and furnishes qualification reports.
6. Ultimately, the director responsible for recruitment makes the definitive selection from among the candidates.

In Chinese idioms, self-nomination can be equated with self-recommendation, setting it in contrast to the concept of external nomination. Self-nomination manifests in various facets of American university management, encompassing the self-reporting component within the annual performance award, self-nomination for participation in professional committees, and the self-nomination and application process for the appointment of administrative officials. This mechanism for selecting campus administrators within American universities serves as a reflection of several key aspects.

First and foremost, the self-nomination mechanism underscores a sense of self-respect that resonates with the ethos of individualism, a core value in the United States. It embodies the principles of equality, openness, fairness, personal drive, the significance of individual growth, and reverence for individual fulfillment. The embrace of diversity further underscores the foundations of a people-oriented spirit. This concept stands in contrast to the bureaucracy-driven underpinnings of higher education in China, where official nomination consciousness and organizational inspection are lacking, and even external nominations often carry a power-oriented ideology.

Secondly, the self-nomination mechanism reflects candidates' proactive mindset, as well as their heightened self-assessment and elevated self-esteem. Individuals who engage in self-nomination typically exhibit competitive drive and a positive attitude. Their

active participation and self-recommendation during open recruitment signify a commitment to demonstrating their capabilities throughout the selection process, ensuring that the most
suitable talents are identified for potential positions.

Thirdly, self-nomination constitutes an integral element of the
democratic governance framework within educational institutions. It embodies a cultural trait intrinsic to the democratic
process, representing the most foundational and fundamental
aspect of a democratic system. Without self-nomination, discussions around democratic elections, evaluations, and related cultural components become moot, as does the broader institutional
framework of democracy. The cultural essence of this system can
be distilled into key attributes: self-initiation, reverence for individuals and individuality, fairness, openness, and procedural democracy. To a significant extent, the self-nomination mechanism
within colleges and universities mirrors the societal political
landscape, reflecting the status of democracy and equality within
the broader society.

Furthermore, the self-nomination mechanism finds theoretical underpinning in various psychological and organizational
theories. For instance, a humanistic needs theory advanced by
Clayton Alderfer at Yale University in the United States builds
upon Maslow's Hierarchy of Needs by identifying three core
human needs: Existence, Relatedness, and Growth (ERG). Self-
nomination directly aligns with the pursuit of personal growth
and development needs, as it empowers individuals to actively
seek opportunities for advancement. Additionally, the comprehensive incentive model introduced by Potter and Lawlor underscores the importance of employee participation in management
and the presentation of well-reasoned suggestions. This approach
enhances employees' sense of ownership and contributes to a
more engaged and motivated workforce. Another relevant theory
is the Self-Motivation Theory, which posits that self-motivation

represents the pinnacle of incentive-based management within organizations. It signifies the transformation of individuals from passive performers to proactive and enterprising contributors within the organization, reflecting a heightened state of personal growth and development driven by intrinsic motivation.

Historically, the appointment of university administrative officials in China predominantly followed methods such as direct appointments (where superiors made specific appointments), airborne appointments (deployed from higher authorities), equal transfers (exchanging positions within an organization), or internal promotions (advancements from within the same organization). While nominally, these appointments might appear to involve organizational scrutiny, in practice, they often served as a means to cultivate personal networks and alliances. In essence, administrative positions across all levels were largely recommended and appointed by leaders or supervisors. This form of in-group cultivation aimed to safeguard the party's power and prevent it from falling into the hands of other factions or cliques. When issues arose with upper-level officials, it often resembled the Chinese proverb, «when the tree falls, the monkeys scatter.»

In recent years, substantial improvements have been made in this regard, transitioning from an appointment-based system to a selection-based one. Presently, the recruitment of administrative officials incorporates methods such as mass evaluations, campus-wide transparency, and organizational appointments. Despite these changes, there remains room for improvement. For instance, candidate selection is often influenced by organizational departments, and at times, the candidate pool is restricted, or preset criteria (such as the exclusion of non-Chinese Communist Party (CCP) members) limit the diversity of potential candidates. The absence of a self-nomination mechanism, along with age, gender, party affiliation, and excessive organizational scrutiny, further impede the process.

The self-nomination mechanism embodies a facet of procedural democracy, an essential component of democratic governance within colleges and universities. Procedural democracy, working hand in hand with substantive democracy, represents two interdependent aspects of a holistic democratic framework. Substantive democracy asserts the equality of all individuals and the decision-making process based on the will of the majority. In essence, the harmonious integration of procedural and substantive democracy is paramount for achieving the cornerstone of constructing and advancing the culture of higher education institutions.

Relevant Information for Reference

The nomination and appointment mechanisms for administrative positions in Chinese and American universities can exhibit both similarities and differences. Let's explore these aspects:

<u>Similarities in Nomination and Appointment Mechanisms</u>

1. Selection Committees: Both Chinese and American universities often utilize selection committees for nominating and appointing administrative positions. These committees may include representatives from various stakeholders, such as faculty, staff, and sometimes students. They are responsible for reviewing applications, conducting interviews, and making recommendations for appointments.
2. Qualifications and Experience: In both systems, individuals nominated for administrative positions are typically expected to possess relevant qualifications, expertise,

and experience in their respective fields. This ensures they have the necessary knowledge and skills to effectively carry out their administrative responsibilities.

Differences in Nomination and Appointment Mechanisms

1. Centralized vs. Decentralized Systems: Chinese universities often have a more centralized approach to the nomination and appointment of administrative positions. The process is typically coordinated at the institutional or provincial level, with a higher level of control and involvement from central authorities. In contrast, American universities may have a more decentralized approach, with individual departments or units having more autonomy in nominating and appointing administrative leaders.

2. Appointment Authority: In Chinese universities, the appointment authority for administrative positions often lies with higher-level administrative bodies, such as university presidents, executive committees, or government agencies overseeing higher education. In American universities, the appointment authority may vary, with some positions being appointed by the university president, while others may require approval from governing boards or external authorities.

3. Role of Faculty and Stakeholders: In Chinese universities, faculty members and stakeholders often have a consultative role in the nomination and appointment process for administrative positions. They may provide input, participate in interviews or selection committees, and offer recommendations. In American universities, the level of faculty and stakeholder involvement may vary depending on institutional practices and policies.

4. Duration and Term Limits: Chinese universities often have fixed-term appointments for administrative positions with specific duration limits. This helps ensure

regular turnover and opportunities for new leadership. In American universities, administrative positions may have varying durations and term limits, depending on the specific role, institutional policies, and governing board decisions.

5. Political Considerations: In Chinese universities, political considerations and government policies may influence the nomination and appointment of high-level administrative positions. This is particularly true for key leadership positions at the institutional or regional level. In American universities, while political factors can also play a role, there is generally more emphasis on qualifications, experience, and alignment with the institution's mission and values.

It's important to note that the nomination and appointment mechanisms can vary within both Chinese and American universities, as each institution may have its own specific policies, practices, and decision-making structures. Additionally, the level of autonomy, involvement of stakeholders, and transparency in the process can differ between universities within the same system.

CHAPTER 10

Reflections on the Pattern of Difference Sequence Caused by the Half-staff Flag on Campus

L owering the campus flag to half-staff as a tribute to those who have recently passed away has become a longstanding tradition within American colleges and universities. This seemingly small gesture holds notable significance within the campus community, reflecting a deep reverence for human life and the principle of equality.

A recent email from the university administration reads: "On November 4, 2016, the campus flag will be flown at half-staff in memory of student David Calvin, who passed away on October 28, 2016."

Figure 10.1 – University Flag at Half-Staff Email

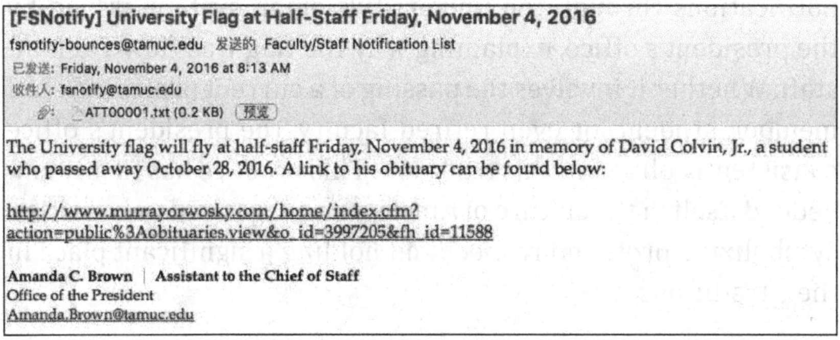

[FSNotify] University Flag at Half-Staff Friday, November 4, 2016
fsnotify-bounces@tamuc.edu 发送的 Faculty/Staff Notification List
已发送: Friday, November 4, 2016 at 8:13 AM
收件人: fsnotify@tamuc.edu
附: ATT00001.txt (0.2 KB) [预览]

The University flag will fly at half-staff Friday, November 4, 2016 in memory of David Colvin, Jr., a student who passed away October 28, 2016. A link to his obituary can be found below:

http://www.murrayorwosky.com/home/index.cfm?
action=public%3Aobituaries.view&o_id=3997205&fh_id=11588

Amanda C. Brown | **Assistant to the Chief of Staff**
Office of the President
Amanda.Brown@tamuc.edu

Figure 10.2 – Student Obituary

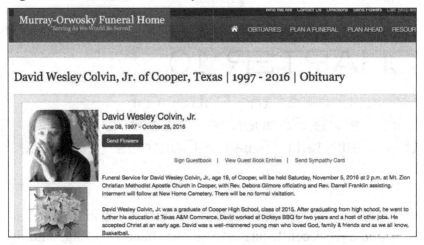

In the United States, the president holds the authority to issue executive orders mandating the nationwide display of the flag at half-staff as a ceremonial gesture or as a sign of reverence and mourning for individuals who have served the U.S. government and other notable figures. During such occasions, all federal government buildings, offices, public schools, and military bases throughout the nation are required to lower their flags to half-staff.

Within American college campuses, it is customary to receive notifications through the university's email system, issued by the president's office, explaining why the flag was flown at half-staff. Whether it involves the passing of a current professor, staff member, student, or even retired faculty, the president's office consistently observes this tradition. This practice has firmly embedded itself in the culture of American colleges and universities, symbolizing profound respect and holding a significant place in their traditions.

First and foremost, it serves as a testament to the value of human life. While it may seem that the tragic passing of a 19-year-old college student in the aforementioned obituary, resulting from a car accident on a distant highway a week prior, falls outside the direct purview of the university, it still warrants acknowledgment. The incident was covered in local newspapers on the day of its occurrence. The university recognizes that it bears no responsibility for events transpiring off-campus, yet it believes that honoring the loss of a young life is a gesture of profound respect.

Secondly, this practice exemplifies the principle of equality for all individuals, regardless of their social standing. It upholds the notion that every person deserves equal respect, aligning with the fundamental belief that all should be treated with fairness and impartiality. This aligns harmoniously with the meaning behind the U.S. president's directive to lower the flag to half-staff, signifying tribute to the departed, irrespective of their societal status. Consequently, whether it is the university president, members of Congress, school principals, professors, or regular students, each receives the same half-staff honor, underscoring the universality of this symbolic gesture.

The practice of flying a flag at half-mast is believed to have originated in 1612 aboard the English steamship Heart's Ease. While exploring the waterways to the Pacific Ocean off the North American north coast, Captain James Hall met a tragic fate. In a heartfelt gesture of respect and condolence for their fallen leader, the ship's crew suggested lowering their flag to half-staff. This poignant display of mourning soon found resonance with other vessels, gaining traction among seafaring communities. Due to its solemn and straightforward nature, this tradition gradually extended its influence to the mainland.

Figure 10.3 –Flags and Student Deaths in the News

It is understood that it is a common practice to fly the flag at half-staff for the deceased on college campuses in the United States, and it is often reported in the newspapers. Moreover, many American colleges and universities have written regulations in this regard. For example, the University of California, Los Angeles (UCLA) school regulations stipulate the basic requirements for flying the flag at half-staff.

Figure 10.4 – Example of School Regulation

> **II. GENERAL POLICY**
>
> The lowering of flags to half-mast at campus locations is done, traditionally, upon the death of certain designated persons, as set forth below.
>
> A. Upon the death of a Federal or State official, or otherwise at the direction of the President of the United States or the Governor of California, the flag of the United States will be lowered to half-mast for the period of mourning announced in the proclamation; the State and University of California flags must also be lowered to half-mast, accordingly, if flown.
>
> B. The UCLA campus follows the practice of honoring any campus employee or elected student government official upon his or her death by lowering to half-mast the University flag only at the Pauley Pavilion location for one day (refer to Section III. below). The first Thursday and Friday of each month are reserved for commemoration of deceased UCLA employees and deceased student officials or others, as the Chancellor deems appropriate, who passed away the previous month.

The provision allows the flag to be flown at half-staff for any faculty member, member of the student body, and other deceased members of the university as a means of expressing condolences for their death. And the first Thursday and Friday of each month are reserved for the mourning of the deceased who passed away in the previous month. It can be seen that flying the flag at half-mast on American campuses to mourn the university faculty, staff, and students is not an anecdotal case but is instead a pattern. However, such an approach is unthinkable for those of us who have long lived in a society with stark hierarchies. Why do American colleges and universities attach so much importance to lowering the flag for the deceased? What is the underlying core value behind this phenomenon?

Undoubtedly, the United States actively promotes the idea of universal equality, as exemplified in the Declaration of Independence of 1776, which originally stated that "all men are created equal." Notably, this wording underwent an alteration after the Declaration of the Rights of Man and Citizen emerged during the French Revolution in 1789, where the term "creation" was replaced with the concept of "birth." This shift emphasizes that equality pertains to one's inherent identity rather than specific natural attributes. In practical terms, equality encompasses equal access to political and legal rights and entails shared societal responsibilities. It stands as a foundational principle in modern society, reflecting a prevailing ethos.

The fundamental principle underpinning the concept of universal equality is closely linked to individualism, which stands as a cornerstone of American values and occupies a central position within American cultural thought. Its profound impact has reverberated throughout the course of American history, significantly shaping its trajectory. Individualism, both as an ideological system and a theoretical construct, is firmly rooted in Western political and social philosophy. Its core tenets encompass the preservation of personal dignity, the prioritization of individual interests, and the promotion of personal striving. These principles have given rise to a range of interconnected ideas, including the recognition of human beings as the bearers of inherent value, the affirmation of an individual's right to self-determination, and the paramount importance placed on personal self-discipline and self-improvement.

Individualism champions a life philosophy centered on the individual, emphasizing that personal advancement is achieved through one's own diligence and continuous effort. It serves as a primary symbol of self-realization and self-worth. In American society, terms such as rights, fairness, justice, integrity, and dignity are frequently invoked, carrying significant emotional and psychological weight. These concepts are intimately tied to the ethos of individualism. As such, a comprehensive analysis and understanding of individualism contribute to a deeper appreciation of contemporary American society.

Figure 10.5 – Individualism Graphic

The philosophical concept of individualism is intricately inter-twined with, and indeed derives strength from, the notion of social equality. In essence, the pursuit and realization of individ-ualism are best safeguarded within an environment of relatively equal social relations. In such a context, personal interests can fully flourish, particularly when underpinned by the bedrock of human rights equality. Consequently, the American social frame-work hinges on a profound respect for the individual, considering it the foundational yardstick for societal behavior.

The principles of freedom and equality embedded in the tapestry of individualist culture determine the dynamics of cooperation within society, establishing the sole avenue through which eq-uitable contracts and their corresponding legal parameters can take root. Such a system design places a paramount emphasis on the welfare of individuals, respecting their rights, safeguarding their freedoms, and upholding equal opportunities for all. In es-sence, it forms a framework of equal rights.

In contrast to the framework of equal rights lies the concept of a "pattern of difference sequence," a term introduced by the es-teemed Chinese sociologist, Fei Xiaotong. The common interpre-tation of his concept characterizes it as an illustration of interper-sonal dynamics, akin to ripples expanding on water, delineating proximity and distance based on one's relationship to oneself. However, this interpretation merely scratches the surface and provides a somewhat one-sided explanation. Mr. Fei Xiaotong's concept delves much deeper than this initial understanding.

First and foremost, Mr. Fei Xiaotong's definition of the "pattern of difference sequence" does not revolve around self-centeredness. In traditional Chinese rural society, the fundamental social unit is the family, not the individual. Consequently, the "pattern of difference sequence" does not pivot around an individual but, at the very least, centers on the family unit. It does not pertain solely to individual relationships but encompasses family groups and, at its broadest, even the entire clan system.

Furthermore, Mr. Fei Xiaotong conducted a comprehensive analysis of China's social structure from a macro perspective, drawing upon community research. He meticulously examined various facets of Chinese society, including rural communities, cultural transmission, family systems, moral values, power dynamics, social norms, and transformations. This research allowed him to construct a comprehensive framework for understanding the structure and foundational attributes of rural society in China. Building on this research foundation, he introduced the concept of the "pattern of difference sequence" to encapsulate the hierarchical nature of Chinese society, steeped in patriarchal values and an orientation toward officialdom. This concept delineates the graded levels of hierarchy, distinguishing between higher and lower status positions.

The traditional Chinese belief in hierarchy, as epitomized by the saying "heaven has ten days, and people have ten grades" (taken from the book "Zuo Zhuan·Zhaogong Seven Years"), permeates various aspects of culture. In this worldview, "corporal punishment does not go up to senior officers, and courtesy does not go down to commoners." Subjects must obey their emperor absolutely, even if he orders them to die. A son must obey his father absolutely, even if his father orders him to die. Respect and humbleness have their specific rankings. Subjects are expected to unconditionally obey their emperor, even in matters of life and death, just as sons must submit unquestioningly to their fathers. This hierarchy is further reflected in specific rankings for respect and humility. These cultural norms persist today, manifesting in practices such as seating arrangements during meetings, where leaders are positioned according to their hierarchy within the context; the central seating of the chief during communal meals; the hierarchy-based placement in group photographs; and varying reimbursement standards for business trips tied to an individual's official rank. These real-life scenarios exemplify the pervasive nature of the "pattern of difference sequence."

Consequently, the "pattern of difference sequence" reveals a deeply ingrained cultural phenomenon and a hierarchical system. It establishes a tiered social structure in which higher tiers enjoy greater privileges while lower tiers possess fewer rights. This arrangement forms a ladder-like social hierarchy that, due to its emphasis on group hierarchy, diminishes individual agency, weakens awareness of rights, and stifles the concept of equality. Consequently, it becomes challenging to foster a collective consciousness and behavioral patterns that prioritize justice, fairness, equal rights, and freedom. In essence, the "pattern of difference sequence" operates as a structural force that has influenced Chinese society throughout its history. Even in the context of contemporary market-driven economic development, its impact remains profound in people's daily lives and activities. In this regard, Mr. Fei's "pattern of difference sequence" not only serves as an encapsulation of traditional Chinese society but also as a representation of objective social dynamics.

In contrast to the "pattern of difference sequence," the pattern of equal rights places a heightened emphasis on the relative equality among members of society. For instance, in the context of an annual academic conference in the United States, leaders typically do not occupy central seats during meetings. The individual speaking on stage assumes the role of speaker without the presence of higher-ranking leaders on the platform. Similarly, at receptions resembling cocktail parties, attendees stand, serve themselves food, and engage in social interactions with little indication of their hierarchical status. These situations seldom reveal the hierarchical positions of the participants.

Another illustration of the pattern of equal rights can be found on American college faculty recruitment websites. Demographic details such as gender, age, and race cannot be publicly indicated as recruitment scoring criteria. This practice is designed to avoid running afoul of federal anti-discrimination laws and to ensure fairness in the recruitment process. In the United States, a foundational societal value is equal rights, and its underlying premise unequivocally asserts that all individuals are equal, regardless of their social status. In this sense, the act of flying the flag at half-staff on university campuses also signifies adherence to the principles of equal rights.

Figure 10.6 – Equal Rights Graphic

American values may not appear overly intricate, yet they are firmly grounded in the bedrock principles of respect for individuals, trust in moral values, and a strong emphasis on the societal legal framework, constituting the very DNA of American culture. Admittedly, this society is not devoid of negative aspects, and its civilization may fall short of the ideal, but the allure of American values permeates every facet of American life. The reverence for individuality, the emphasis on morality, and the commitment to a robust legal system are all indispensable attributes for the vitality of a society. While American society is far from flawless or perfect, its enduring impact on the global stage is undeniable. The underlying catalyst for this influence likely resides in the core concept of equality.

Relevant Information for Reference

In Chinese and American colleges and universities, the hierarchical handling of faculty and student deaths can exhibit both similarities and differences. Let's explore these aspects:

Similarities in Hierarchical Handling

1. Immediate Response: In both Chinese and American universities, there is typically an immediate response to faculty and student deaths. The university administration, faculty, and staff work to ensure the well-being of the campus community and provide necessary support to affected individuals.
2. Communication and Notifications: Chinese and American universities prioritize effective communication and notifications regarding the death of faculty or students. They aim to inform relevant parties, such as family members, colleagues, classmates, and the broader campus community while respecting privacy and confidentiality.

Differences in Hierarchical Handling

1. Cultural Factors: Cultural factors influence how Chinese and American universities handle faculty and student deaths hierarchically. In Chinese universities, traditional hierarchical structures and respect for authority may play a significant role in decision-making and communication. There may be a stronger emphasis on centralized control and coordination from higher-level administrators. While there may still be hierarchical structures in American universities, decision-making may involve a more collaborative approach with input from various stakeholders, including faculty, staff, and students.

2. Notification Processes: In Chinese universities, the responsibility for notifying family members and handling funeral arrangements often falls primarily on university administrators, with a focus on maintaining a respectful and orderly process. In American universities, while university administrators may assist in notification, local law enforcement and medical professionals may have a greater involvement, who take the lead in contacting family members and initiating necessary procedures.

3. Support Services: Chinese universities often provide immediate support to affected individuals and offer centralized resources, such as counseling services, grief support, and memorial events. American universities also provide support services, but there may be more emphasis on individualized support and decentralized resources, such as counseling centers, chaplains, and student affairs offices.

4. Involvement of Government Authorities: In China, government authorities may have a more direct role in the hierarchical handling of faculty and student deaths, particularly in cases that attract significant public attention or involve legal considerations. The government may be involved in the decision-making process and provide guidance or oversight. In the United States, while government authorities may be involved in certain cases, their extent of involvement may vary depending on the nature of the incident, local jurisdiction, and legal requirements.

It's important to note that the hierarchical handling of faculty and student deaths can vary within both Chinese and American universities, as each institution may have its own policies, procedures, and cultural dynamics. The specific circumstances of the incident, the campus culture, and the needs of the affected individuals and their families also play a role in shaping the hierarchical handling process.

CHAPTER 11

How American Universities Incentivize Private Donations

O ver a decade ago, upon completing my Ph.D., I secured a faculty position at a public state university located in Texas. Within the following year, I received an email from a representative of the Alumni Association at my alma mater in Chicago, prompting me to arrange a meeting during their visit to my campus. On the appointed day, the alumni association representative paid a visit to my office, extending a warm handshake while clutching a stack of materials on the other hand. During our conversation, I was introduced to recent developments at my alma mater and informed about the presence of alumni residing near Dallas. They kindly provided me with the "Alumni Newsletter" and other informative materials, alongside guidance on how to reach out if I ever needed assistance. My arrival in Texas had been a friendless venture, making the news they shared all the more heartening and appreciated. Toward the end of our meeting, the representative expressed hope that I might consider making a future donation to support my alma mater. I agreed to this suggestion in a non-committal manner, not giving it too much immediate thought.

Since then, nearly every year, I have received donation requests from my alma mater, both through emails and traditional letters delivered to my physical address. Sometimes, there are even follow-up letters to ensure I've seen their appeals. During my doctoral studies, my alma mater provided me with a full scholarship, covering not only the hefty tuition fees but also a modest monthly stipend that supported my family. Now, in my stable faculty position, I felt a deep-seated obligation to give back to my alma mater. Consequently, I make it a point to periodically contribute to my alma mater as a way to convey my profound gratitude.

Following each donation, my alma mater promptly sends a gracious thank-you letter, complete with a receipt and information emphasizing the tax-deductible nature of my contributions. Subsequently, I engaged in conversations with fellow Chinese professors here, and we shared similar experiences. It became apparent that many of us had analogous narratives. It's hardly surprising, considering that alumni donations serve as more than just a benevolent gesture from former students to their alma mater; they also represent a mutually beneficial endeavor. These contributions enable the alma mater to maintain connections, cultivate relationships with alumni, and extend its influence. Alma maters take immense pride in the remarkable achievements of their alumni, while alumni cherish the ongoing progress of their alma mater. Hence, it feels entirely natural for alumni to support their alma mater through donations.

Figure 11.1 – Harvard University Endowment

Among the funding sources of American universities, donation income is an important source of funding, and both private and public universities attach great importance to it. Of course, due to the different nature of colleges and universities, the proportion of funding sources is also very different. Generally speaking, the main sources of funding are as follows:

1. Federal or State Grants - Whether it is a public or private university or a community college, institutions are able to receive financial grants from the federal or state governments. Due to their nature, public universities receive more funds than private universities. There are two methods of funding for public universities: one is based on a student quota, which mainly solves the problem of school operation funds, including administrative costs; the other is based on special construction or scientific research plans, which usually need to be approved before being dispersed

2. Tuition and Fees - Tuition is the main source of income for American colleges and universities. Compared with private universities, the fees of public universities and community universities are much lower, so the salary of the faculty is relatively low; the tuition fees of private universities are higher, and the salary of faculty is correspondingly higher. Generally speaking, tuition fees account for about half of a school's total revenue. Tuition is usually charged by the academic year, and the institution also charges accommodation and other miscellaneous fees.

3. Endowment income - Endowment income (donations) is an important part of the funding source of American colleges and universities. The amount of donation income varies widely among schools. Private universities claim up to nearly 70% of their funding comes from private donations, and public universities generally claim about 10%. Donation

income includes donations for designated purposes as well as those for non-designated purposes. Designated purposes include student awards, grants, special construction projects, and special scientific research funds.

Figure 11.2 – Largest University Endowments in the United States

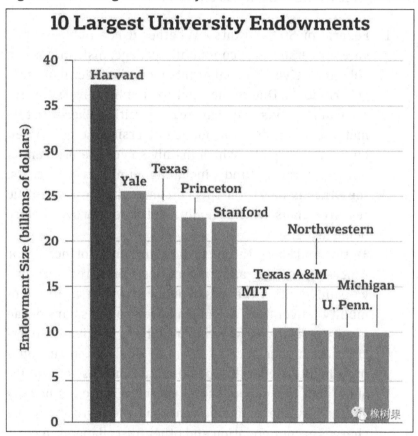

Take my public university as an example. In the second week after the start of each semester, the faculty is required to report the number of students enrolled in the courses (Census Date Rosters). This is for reporting to the state government for funding. Since tuition fees and miscellaneous fees are relatively low in public schools, and they are charged uniformly in accordance with policies and regulations, the development of schools mainly depends on the third type of funding, namely donation income. In other words, if your school's various public relations are well developed, it has a good reputation, and there are many "celebrities" among its alumni, the social donations will also increase accordingly. In such cases, the school gains great potential for development and attracts a greater number of students. This creates a virtuous circle. Because of this, the university president often regards donations or various means of fundraising as one of their important tasks and responsibilities in order to obtain sufficient school funds and focus on strategic vision and long-term development. American university presidents generally do not govern teaching but restrict their focus to major institutional policies, public relations, and fundraising. Teaching is managed by the provost. In order to ensure the implementation of the donation income from the organizational structure, the school has set up an Institutional Advancement department and has a vice president in charge of this work. The purpose of this department is as indicated: "To provide public and private support for the University and the community, to create a personal legacy for donors, and to be remembered by future generations. Our job is to strive to develop resources that match donor interests with university needs and encourage faculty, staff, and alumni to engage with." The Institutional Advancement consists of several parts: Development is responsible for donation matters, donation plans, etc.; Advancement Services is responsible for donor management and contact, financial fund management, etc.; Alumni Relations is responsible for liaising with alumni, annual events, alumni associations, and so on.

The donation income of colleges and universities is largely positively related to the effectiveness of the work of the Alumni Association. Alumni are the backbone of the endowment groups of American universities. The Alumni Association stays in touch with alumni over the years through various means, regularly distributes publications to alumni, conveys information about university planning, goals, development, and changes to donors and the public, often holds Alumni Association events, and invites alumni to come back to the institution. The school conducts discussions, lectures, and gatherings and holds alumni donation activities on a fixed date every year. Therefore, alumni are a huge intangible asset and an important resource for American colleges and universities to enable social and private donations.

Generally speaking, the endowment income of American colleges and universities is mainly raised in two ways:

1. Donation: The transfer of ownership, disposal, or use of property by an individual to the University. Donations can be in the form of currency, land, buildings, artworks, heritage, stocks, building use rights, etc. If the donation is in currency, it is generally designated for a certain activity or special use; these donated properties can generally be directly disposed of or used by the school.

2. Endowment: The nature of the funds obtained by the foundation method is currency or negotiable securities. There are also donations in non-monetary form, which are generally converted into currency or securities in the end; while universities manage funds centrally, conduct fund capital operations, and then use its interest part, and generally do not directly distribute and use the principal; funds are generally composed of the university foundation and are managed and operated in a unified manner.

My state university stipulates that donations can be made one or more times through funds. A Permanent Fund can be established if the total amount of donations exceeds $25,000. Usually endowments are created as a means of paying for sponsored projects after the profits are invested. Endowments are named by the donor and can be named in honor of relatives and friends.

Figure 11.3 – Endowment Appeal on the Institutional Advancement Webpage

VICE PRESIDENT FOR INSTITUTIONAL ADVANCEMENT

Vice President for Institutional Advancement

About Us

The Advancement Division shares one common goal: to inform our alumni and friends of our faculty, alumni and students' success, inspiring each of you to support current and future Lions.

A gift to Texas A&M University-Commerce is an investment in a world-class teaching and research community that embodies the creed of our founder, Professor William L. Mayo.

"Ceaseless industry, fearless investigation, unfettered thought and unselfish service to

All donation income is managed by the school based on the agreement of the particular endowment fund, which stipulates the purpose, form, progress, etc., of the donation.

Donors can make pledges or memos expressing their preferences concerning the utilization of their donation. Each donation has a receipt, which serves as the donor's proof of their contribution to the University and is exempt from personal income tax as a charitable donation. Meanwhile, Advancement Services verifies that all expenditures are in accordance with the donor's wishes.

In addition to giving incentives to alumni and members of the community, my state university also has endowment opportunities for current faculty and staff. For example, "Bridge Builders" is a mechanism for current (or retired faculty) and staff to make various donations/gifts to the University. The term "Bridge Builders" is taken from a favorite poem of the school's founder, Professor Mayo, more than 100 years ago, and it reflects the way faculty and staff contribute to student growth. Generosity means building bridges to connect students and faculty. These donations are also tax deductible.

Figure 11.4 – Employee Giving Program

VICE PRESIDENT FOR INSTITUTIONAL ADVANCEMENT	**BRIDGE BUILDERS**
Vice President for Institutional Advancement	EMPLOYEE GIVING PROGRAM
About Us	Bridge Builders are current faculty and staff who have made financial and in-kind gifts to the university. The term Bridge Builder was taken from a favorite poem of Professor Mayo's and this term embodies what our generous faculty and staff do for our students when they make
Staff	a contribution; building bridges between students and education.
Giving through the Foundation	
Development	Contact Amber Countis at Amber.Countis@tamuc.edu or 903-468-8187 to discuss becoming a Bridge Builder, or to find out about the other ways you can give back to the

The "Brick Garden" project is another form of donation offered to faculty and staff at my university. In this type of donation, the donor can buy a brick paver for the school's Alumni Center, on which can be engraved the donor's name, commemorative words, etc. (see the picture below). Several years ago, I also participated in this project and bought a brick paver for $125. As a direct result of this project, the university has received numerous donations, and individuals and families have had their wishes fulfilled.

Figure 11.5 – Alumni Center Brick Garden

Figure 11.6 – Donated Brick Inscriptions

Figure 11.7 – Brick Garden Informational Webpage

ALUMNI AND FRIENDS	BRICK GARDEN FAQS
Alumni and Friends	**WHERE IS THE BRICK GARDEN LOCATED?**
Make A Gift	Directly behind the Alumni Center. It is connected the Alumni Center back doors
About	to the walking mall beside the Ferguson Social Sciences Building. A map of the
Alumni Association	campus, including the Brick Garden location is available.
Awards	**HOW MUCH IS A SINGLE BRICK?**
News	$125
Events & Programs	
Brick Garden	**WHAT SIZE ARE THE BRICKS BE?**
	All bricks will be a single size, 4"X8".

This type of donation helps to create a sense of community. "Faculty and staff also feel a sense of mission in the development of the University by participating in the activities of the University through donations. Experience as a member of the campus, you play an important role in the development of the

University. Because no matter what kind of work you do on campus, you can indirectly provide unparalleled help to your students." Hence, the difference between faculty and off-campus giving is the involvement of current faculty and staff in giving, which can sometimes have wonderful effects on the donor's personal growth prospects.

There are also large-scale fundraising campaigns within colleges and universities, which are irregular special fundraising programs that stipulate that a certain amount of fundraising must be completed within a certain period of time; periodic fundraising events are held as well. The primary participants in American college education fundraising are enterprises, the wealthy, outstanding alumni, and ordinary citizens.

In the United States, education is a socialized industry with public welfare characteristics. Therefore, it is reasonable to expect the general public to donate to education. American colleges and universities have a long tradition of accepting donations to maintain and improve their schools. In the early days, most universities were founded with private donations, and according to data, among the 264 colleges and universities founded before 1860, private universities accounted for 247, most of which were established by church pastors or private donations. Many private institutions founded prior to the 20th century, including Harvard, Yale, Stanford, John Hopkins, and the University of Chicago, are still well known today and have served as models for the creation of institutions of higher education through private funds and donations. The name of the world-famous Harvard University can be traced back to 1638. John Harvard (1607–1638), a dissenting English minister in Colonial America, donated about 400 volumes of literature and nearly 800 pounds to the establishment of Cambridge College, the first school of higher education in the United States. In order to commemorate Harvard's generosity, the school was renamed Harvard College. In 1718, the British businessman Elihu Yale also donated a great deal of money and materials to the school, which played a huge role in its development. In honor of him, the school came to be called Yale College. Gradually, these precedents of donating to such institutions of education formed an atmosphere that subtly became a tradition within American society itself.

Throughout the development of higher education in America, the trend of social donation has been a constant thread running through and accompanying the growth of colleges and universities. In the 20th century, with an improving American economy and the emergence of a large number of wealthy groups, individuals who are enthusiastic about higher education have generously donated money to help finance the construction of universities. Donations to universities from all walks of life in society include sizable donations from celebrities, both corporate and business tycoons, and outstanding alumni, as well as small and medium-sized donations from small companies, general alumni, and various other people who care about higher education. In addition to personal donations, there are also donations from charitable foundations, such as the Carnegie and Rockefeller Foundations. Today, an endless stream of donations pour into American colleges and universities from around the world.

How American colleges and universities incentivize donations can be summarized with the following:

1. The Leader Personally Takes Command – In American colleges and universities, one of the main responsibilities of the president is to raise funds. Every year, he spends a great deal of time and energy interviewing donors, introducing the school's development goals, and revitalizing the school plan. American college presidents (also known as CEOs) attach a high level of importance to the management of their universities just as if they were operating

companies. They establish the school's own brand and core competitiveness, and they publicize and sell their vision of the institution to students, students' parents, alumni, the public, and to enterprises and other organizations. The difference between universities and companies is that after the product is produced, it is possible for that product to give back to the producer of the product exponentially. Therefore, from the very beginning, the school tends to treat students as the future donors of the school and the school's external publicity and promoters. Treating students kindly plays a key role in the development of the school and the future expectation of their donations. The university president will usually appoint a vice president as well as a whole team of members to work full-time in fund-raising endeavors to ensure that donations are in place.

2. Professional Fund Management – Every university in the United States has special institutions called Institutional Giving Departments, The Philanthropy and Engagement Division, or some similarly titled institution. These institutions are equipped with personnel who are in the work of raising funds for an extended length of time. Usually, the endowment fund's proceeds are determined in part based on the wishes of the donors. If the donor specifies that their donation can only be used for student awards or financial aid or can only fund a certain scholarly field, a certain professional direction, or provide support for individuals from a certain area, then the fund must only be used according to this stipulation of use. The principal of the endowment fund is used for investment, appreciation, and preservation. Fund management is scientifically decided by the Council (or the Board of Directors) in accordance with relevant laws and systems and the actual situation of the foundation and the university, whether it

is used for the development of the university or for investment to add and preserve value.

3. Be Attentive to the Interests of Donors – Donors have
    their own hopes and interests. It is unwise to think of
    the donor as a selfless individual without any personal
    demands, and one must also abandon the idea that if the
    donor has their own self-interest at heart, then it must
    not be justified. The reason why American colleges
    and universities can receive a large number of private
    donations is related to the flexible policies of those
    colleges, such as granting the donor an honorary title
    (honorary doctorate, etc.) or providing the donor with the
    right to name infrastructure (such as a teaching building,
    library, etc.). Private universities may also intentionally
    enroll children of the donor's own family, and private
    university medical schools may elect to provide certain
    preferential health care services for the donor's family.
    In addition, the fundraising strategy of the recipient
    institution will affect the donor's decision-making pro-
    cess. The alumni's learning experience, association
    activities, and other memories gained during their time at
    the university will also affect the donor's future donation
    decisions. Therefore, careful and flexible arrangements
    should be made for donors, especially with respect to
    private universities, which, due to their particularity, can
    take more flexible measures to attract donations in or-
    der to fully meet the material and spiritual benefits of
    individual donors.

4. Tax-free Policy Support - Both the U.S. government and
    public policy greatly support and fully understand the
    behavior of colleges and universities in their quest to gain
    social donations. The government implements a tax-free
    policy for all charitable donors. As a result, the implemen-
    tation of this policy has stimulated donors' enthusiasm,

and companies and private individuals are increasingly willing to support University development. Therefore, a certain amount of personal income tax or corporate income tax can be exempted when donating to university education. While becoming famous, it can be tax-free (donated money can be exempted from taxation), which is the rational choice for many wealthy individuals or large companies, thus creating an opportunity for a relaxed environment for universities to accept social donations. In the design of the individual income tax law, the U.S. government has taken into account this incentive mechanism for social welfare, and has formulated a series of long-term preferential policies for donation initiatives, which have created a virtuous circle of a donation ecological environment for stimulating various donations, which is an important cultural phenomenon in the United States.

Figure 11.8 – U.S. University Endowment Ranking

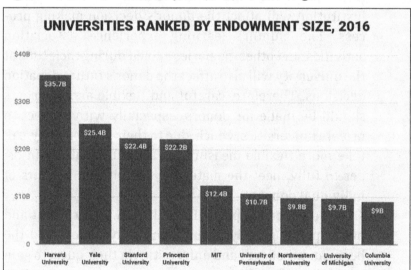

The success of private donation-driven education in American colleges and universities can be attributed to a multifaceted combination of macro-level institutional design, societal ethos, and precise operational strategies. This synergy not only entices both affluent and less affluent individuals within the country to contribute to higher education and various philanthropic causes, but also garners the attention of wealthy donors from abroad. Among these international benefactors are individuals from mainland China and Hong Kong, who find that this system aligns with their philanthropic objectives, maximizing both their personal and material gains as economic entities.

Chinese colleges and universities operated as national institutions primarily funded by the government prior to the economic reforms and opening up of the 1980s. Consequently, there was minimal involvement of private donations in the education sector. In the eyes of the Chinese populace, these universities were government-run entities and esteemed as public assets of the nation. Making social or private contributions to universities was often perceived as potentially detrimental to the reputation of these state-owned educational institutions. This perception was deeply entrenched, partly due to prevailing notions of reliance on government funding for educational advancement and a sense of reluctance regarding private donations. Naturally, this was also influenced by the income disparity among the population. In an era marked by egalitarian ideals, few individuals had disposable income for philanthropy.

The landscape began to shift following the economic reforms of the 1980s. Society's calls for greater involvement in the management of educational institutions grew louder and more pronounced. National policies began advocating for partnerships with social entities in educational endeavors, and the concept of seeking foreign contributions for education gained momentum. During my own tenure at a Chinese university in the 1980s and 1990s, I recall hearing about foreign entrepreneurs, particularly from Hong Kong, investing in projects such as constructing school buildings and endowing libraries on the mainland. Nevertheless, at that time, the concept of widespread donations to universities within local society had not yet taken root.

In recent years, many wealthy individuals have begun to donate to domestic universities in China. According to data from the China Educational Funding Statistical Yearbook, the proportion of social donation income received by Chinese universities from 2012 to 2014 was 0.52% in 2012, 0.53% in 2013 and 0.46% in 2014. Established well-known universities such as Tsinghua University, Zhejiang University, Peking University, Shanghai Jiaotong University, and Fudan University still have the largest source of funding budgeted from government financial appropriation allocation. The proportion of donation income is quite low, accounting for less than 1% of the overall university income. In recent years, Tsinghua University's donation income for one year reached 400 million yuan, the highest in China. On the other side of the ocean, Harvard University in the United States received a single donation of $400 million in that same year, adding a substantial sum to the school's funding of $36.4 billion. Data shows that in 2016, the alumni donations of the University of Electronic Science and Technology of China during the 60th anniversary celebration received a total of nearly 1.7 billion yuan in donations, setting a new record for domestic university donations. The Charity Law of the People's Republic of China came into effect on September 1, 2016, and clearly put forward promotion measures such as tax reduction and financial support, which will undoubtedly bring new donation prospects to education in China.

Furthermore, the government's approach to taxation regarding donations in the education sector necessitates the development of corresponding supporting regulations. Currently, within China's existing tax framework, individual donations remain ineligible for income tax exemptions. The deeply ingrained notion of education's heavy reliance on government funding persists, and a comprehensive ecosystem for donation-driven education has yet to fully take shape. Notably, the leadership within Chinese colleges and universities has not accorded adequate attention to donation efforts, and the institutional infrastructure for this purpose remains imperfect. The absence of dedicated donation channels and a lack of precise management of donation funds underscore the need for substantial improvements.

The success of American colleges and universities in promoting private donation-based education not only underscores their expertise in fundraising and resource management, effectively addressing the challenge of insufficient operational funding, but more significantly, it reflects a profound commitment to educational principles, a communal ethos, and a robust institutional framework. Consequently, for Chinese higher education institutions to truly advance social and private donation-based education, they must undertake fundamental and practical reforms.

Relevant Information for Reference

Comparison of the Scale and Quantity of Private and Non-governmental Donations in Chinese and American Colleges and Universities

As of my knowledge cutoff in September 2021, there's a lack of specific and up-to-date data to provide an accurate comparison of the scale and quantity of private and non-governmental donations in Chinese and American colleges and universities. However, some general trends and factors can provide insight into the comparison.

American Colleges and Universities

1. American universities have a long-established tradition of receiving philanthropic support. Individual donors,

corporations, and foundations contribute to these institutions for a variety of purposes, such as student scholarships,
faculty chairs, research initiatives, and capital projects.

2. As per the Council for Aid to Education's Voluntary
    Support of Education (VSE) survey, in 2020, American
    colleges and universities received a total of $49.5 billion
    in donations. This report also indicated that donations
    from alumni and non-alumni individuals made up over
    half of the total contributions.

Chinese Colleges and Universities

1. Compared to their American counterparts, Chinese uni-
    versities have a much shorter history of receiving private
    and non-governmental donations. This is due to the fact
    that higher education in China was, for a long time, fully
    funded by the government. However, as China's economy
    has grown, so too has the ability of individuals and cor-
    porations to make significant donations.

2. In recent years, there has been a notable increase in
    philanthropy in China, including philanthropic acts to-
    wards higher education. According to a report by the
    21st Century Education Research Institute, donations to
    Chinese universities reached 40.9 billion yuan (about $6.3
    billion) in 2016. The number of donations and the total
    amounts have been increasing, but they're still signifi-
    cantly smaller than those in the U.S.

Factors Influencing Donations

Various factors may influence the scale and quantity of donations
to universities in both countries:

1. In the United States, the culture of philanthropy is deeply
    ingrained, and tax incentives also encourage charitable

giving. Higher education institutions often have large, professional fundraising operations to help generate donations.

2. In China, while the culture of philanthropy is growing, it is not as well-established as in the U.S. The legal and tax structures in China have traditionally not been as favorable to charitable giving, although recent reforms have sought to change this. The fundraising operations at Chinese universities are generally less developed than those in the U.S., which may also impact the scale and quantity of donations.

Please note that the actual figures and comparisons could have changed after 2021 due to various factors, such as changes in economic conditions, legal structures, and societal attitudes towards philanthropy. To get the most accurate and up-to-date information, it is recommended to consult more recent sources or experts in the field.

Footnotes

William Leonidas Mayo

William Leonidas Mayo (1861–1917), founder and first president of East Texas Normal College (now Texas A&M University-Commerce), was born on November 3, 1861, in Prestonburg, Kentucky. He attended Prestonburg Seminary and Cedar Bluff Academy in Tazewell County, Virginia, before entering Central Normal College in Danville, Indiana, where he received his Bachelor of Arts degree in 1883. After graduating, he returned to Virginia to become head of Cedar Bluff Academy. He served there for nearly three years before resigning to spend a season cutting logs to earn money for additional study at Indiana University but the project ended in disaster as a flood washed away his entire season's work. Mayo left for Denver, Colorado, to take a position in the Denver public school system. William Leonidas Mayo's creed was "ceaseless industry, fearless investigation, unfettered thought, and unselfish service to others."

John Harvard

John Harvard (1607–1638) was an English dissenting minister in Colonial America whose deathbed bequest to the school or college founded two years earlier by the Massachusetts Bay Colony was so gratefully received that it was consequently ordered "that the Colledge agreed upon formerly to be built at Cambridge shalbee called Harvard Colledge." Harvard University considers him the most honored of its founders—those whose efforts and contributions in its early days "ensured its permanence"—and a statue in his honor is a prominent feature of Harvard Yard.

Elihu Yale

Elihu Yale (1649 – 1721) was a British-American colonial administrator and philanthropist. Although born in Boston, Massachusetts, he only lived in America as a child, spending the rest of his life in England, Wales, and India. Starting as a clerk, he eventually rose up to the rank of President of the British East India Company settlement in Fort St George, Madras. He later lost that position under charges of corruption for self-dealing and had to pay a fine. In 1699, he returned to Britain with a considerable fortune, around £200,000, mostly made by selling diamonds, and spent his time and wealth on philanthropy and art collecting. He is best remembered as the primary benefactor of Yale College (now Yale University), which was named in his honor, following a sizable donation of books, portraits, and textiles under the request of Rev. Cotton Mather, a Harvard graduate.

CHAPTER 12

The Individualized Campus Ecology
of American College Students
and its Social Consequences

I distinctly recall a conversation I had with some friends, during which we pondered the distinctions between Chinese and American college students. Friend "A" remarked that a significant portion of American college students own private cars, resulting in campuses teeming with automobiles. In contrast, Chinese college students predominantly rely on bicycles, leading to a scattered presence of bikes across campus. Friend "B" chimed in, highlighting that nearly 100% of American on-campus residents enjoy the luxury of single-person rooms, while Chinese university dormitories typically house multiple individuals in a single room. The allure of having one's own car and private bedroom during college is undeniable. However, upon deeper reflection, these distinctions appear to be superficial. What truly sets these student bodies apart? I would like to encapsulate the essence of American college students in one word: individualization. As for the defining traits of Chinese college students, we will delve into that at the conclusion of this chapter.

Figure 12.1 – Campus Parking Lot

In the classes I've taught, the prevalence of American college students owning private cars exceeds a staggering 95%, and in some
cases, even more, depending on the university's location, whether
it be in a city or suburb, which can influence car ownership rates
among students. Part-time employment typically allows students
to accumulate sufficient income to purchase a used vehicle, ranging from $1,000 to $2,000. Whether residing on or off-campus,
students often find themselves needing to commute several days
a week—whether it's for work, visits home, or various other reasons, making car ownership a practical necessity.

For those living on campus, individual dormitory rooms are the
norm, ensuring privacy for each student. Shared spaces like kitch-
ens and living rooms are communal, while bathrooms are typically private. The rationale for these arrangements becomes evident when considering that only couples would share a bedroom.

As students reach the age of 18, a quest for independence and
personal development drives them towards having their own
cars and personal spaces. These accommodations are critical
for meeting their physical and psychological needs during this

formative period. Universities must provide these essential conditions to foster the individualization of college students. This includes ensuring ample parking spaces, providing housing conducive to personal privacy, and enhancing the overall physical environment.

However, it's important to recognize that material environments alone are not sufficient or exhaustive in fostering individualization. The path toward individualization for American college students encompasses not only these material aspects but also the institutional framework and campus culture that shape their educational experience.

Definition of Individualization

In essence, individualization, often synonymous with personalization, serves to distinguish the individual from the collective or broader social group. Delving deeper, we can turn to the renowned German sociologist Ulrich Beck's definition: "Individualization is the outcome of institutionalized individualism and its societal policies." From a sociological perspective, we can succinctly define individualization as the process and path through which individuals who are inherently unique yet part of collectives develop their individuality and personality. Consequently, individualization involves bolstering self-awareness, self-choice, and self-respect, with the ultimate aim of achieving self-reliance, self-reflection, self-esteem, autonomy, and self-enhancement.

It's crucial to note that individualization does not negate the significance of the larger group; in fact, the group plays an indispensable role in the individualization process. The interplay between the individual and the group can be described as follows: individuals gain self-awareness and insights through their interactions within the group, while the group offers a platform for individuals to engage in meaningful communication. Consequently, individuals acquire an understanding of interdependence, mature in their interpersonal relationships, and develop the skills essential for effective teamwork.

Figure 12.2 – German Sociologist Ulrich Beck

Individualized Institutional Design and Campus Ecology

The individualized approach to cultivating college students in the United States is evident not only in its robust material resources but also in its institutional framework, including the credit and grading systems designed to facilitate this process. Unlike the fixed four-year undergraduate system found in many countries, American universities employ a flexible credit-based system. This means that students can graduate upon completing the required number of credits, leading to variations in graduation timelines. Some graduate in three and a half years, while others may take five, six, or more years to earn their degree. Consequently, students entering college at the same time and sharing the same academic year may not necessarily graduate together. Graduation timing becomes contingent on each student's unique academic objectives.

The term "classmates" in American universities, therefore, primarily pertains to students who enroll in the same course during the same semester. It's not uncommon for students within the same class to have limited familiarity with one another after just one semester. This American concept of "class" diverges from the Chinese understanding of the term. In China, a "class" typically refers to a group of students admitted in the same year and expected to graduate in the same year as well. In this context, students tend to have close-knit relationships and know each other well. In American universities, however, students only come into contact with each other when they choose to take the same course together, resulting in more temporary connections as classmates.

Moreover, American universities do not feature faculty representatives akin to the head teachers or instructors commonly found in Chinese universities. Similarly, they lack student officials in roles such as squad leaders or class representatives. This system design is emblematic of a deliberate move toward decentralization and deprioritization of hierarchical structures. Consequently, there are no titles like class cadre, group leader, or class representative, as observed in China's university class systems. In the absence of formalized classes, there are no whole-class meetings or fixed sets of classmates.

Furthermore, the vibrant array of extracurricular activities, such as inter-class competitions and class evaluations, prevalent in Chinese universities, are conspicuously absent on American university campuses. American college students are viewed as independent individuals within the academic environment. While they may voluntarily engage in campus clubs and organizations, their primary role within the university revolves around academic pursuits. There is no discernible hierarchy among students, fostering a sense of egalitarianism.

Notably, during graduation ceremonies in the United States, a unique tradition prevails. Graduates ascend the stage sequentially based on the order in which their names are announced by the emcee. The university president personally presents each graduate with their diploma and shares a handshake. In stark contrast to Chinese university graduation ceremonies, where certificates are often distributed by class units, this American tradition emphasizes the individual recognition of each student. At these ceremonies, the president personally greets and congratulates nearly a thousand graduates, and this practice has become a hallmark of American college graduation ceremonies. Frequently, synchronized video broadcasts of these proceedings reach audiences worldwide. This underscores how the concept of individualization has permeated deeply into the societal consciousness and is reflected in various distinctive customs and practices.

Figure 12.3 – The president personally issues a graduation certificate to each student and shakes their hand

The individualization of American college students is also shaped by the campus environment, which encompasses various normative arrangements within educational institutions. For instance, during their first or second year of college, students have the opportunity to explore subjects of personal interest rather than rushing to declare a specific major. This approach allows students to discover their own passions among the elective courses, creating a broader foundation for designing their majors during their university years.

Another noteworthy practice is the confidential handling of students' test scores. These scores cannot be publicly displayed in lists or linked to identifiable information such as student numbers or other suggestive identifiers. This protocol is firmly entrenched and adhered to as a matter of standard practice. Academic performance assessments are entrusted solely to instructors, with no external interference permitted. Student academic records are maintained as personal files by the faculty and student registration department, safeguarded against unauthorized access. Even a student's parents must obtain the student's consent to access this information, respecting the student's right to personal privacy.

Furthermore, the educational environment upholds the principle that outsiders are not allowed to disrupt classes by calling students out at will. This measure is in place to protect students' rights to receive education uninterrupted. Students enjoy the freedom to select their courses according to their own preferences, and this choice is inviolable, even by their parents or guardians. Additionally, students with disabilities are entitled to special accommodations and confidentiality as stipulated by law, and no one is permitted to interfere with these rights.

The Swiss psychologist Carl Gustav Jung introduced the Theory of Personality Development, emphasizing that "children gradually realize that they are independent individuals" and that "during adolescence, as self-awareness matures, young people must break free from their reliance on their parents." Jung viewed individualization as an intrinsic motivator for individuals seeking self-integrity and balance. A supportive campus ecology plays a pivotal role in facilitating the process of individualization, allowing students to fully unleash their talents and personalities.

Figure 12.4 – The Swiss psychologist Carl Gustav Jung

As the prevailing ethos in American society champions the cultivation of individuality and places a premium on personal orientation, the concept of individualization among college students harmonizes seamlessly with the core principles of freedom, democracy, and equality. This philosophy finds profound expression within the realm of education, encompassing a commitment to respecting students' individual growth, endowing them with comprehensive choice rights, and fostering their unhindered personal development.

In the pursuit of these ideals, educational institutions endeavor to furnish every student with optimal conditions conducive to academic, experiential, and life pursuits. Their aim is to cater to the diverse intellectual interests, hobbies, talents, and future prospects of students. Additionally, institutions strive to enhance the physical and intellectual space available for individual development, ensuring that each student can identify ample opportunities for personal growth, select appropriate learning methodologies, and actively advance their own development. Such a vision embodies the foundational principles and structural framework of an individualized educational system design and campus environment.

Does the individualized training process for American college students exclude the notion of group activities? The answer is unequivocally no. While the pursuit of individualization is paramount, college students, recognizing the importance of holistic growth, naturally gravitate toward group interactions. They seek avenues for communal engagement to explore their unique identities, foster interpersonal connections, and establish friendships both on campus and beyond.

For instance, since American college students are not obliged to reside on campus, they can choose to stay in university dormitories or secure accommodations independently off-campus. This flexibility often leads to diverse groups of students sharing close quarters, each pursuing a different academic discipline—ranging from physics and biology to chemistry, music, history, or politics. When students with compatible personalities engage in frequent interactions, lasting friendships can flourish, transcending the boundaries of majors and extending well beyond their college years.

Beyond dormitory interactions, active engagement in a diverse array of student clubs on campus constitutes another pivotal avenue for fostering student connections. American universities host an array of fraternities, sororities, and various student associations, offering students ample opportunities to satisfy their extracurricular interests, forge group connections, and cultivate their individuality.

Participation in these student groups is entirely voluntary, with some imposing specific entry criteria, such as maintaining a certain grade point average (GPA). Students are welcome to join these groups based on their interests, and no external pressures compel their involvement. Consequently, the sense of belonging within these organizations varies from one individual to another, markedly distinct from the notion of a cohesive class collective.

While some student associations facilitate lasting friendships and establish valuable long-term connections through joint participation, it's evident that group activities on American college campuses hinge on the free choice and enthusiastic participation of individuals.

Figure 12.5 – Concept of Individualism

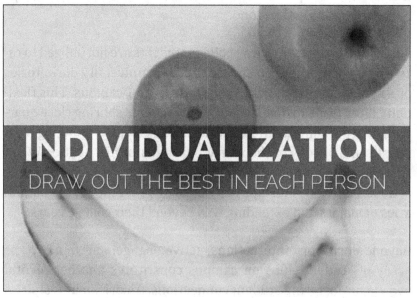

Social Consequences of Individualization

Undoubtedly, the impact of college students' individualization transcends their time in academia, with the implications and societal repercussions of their dedication to specific causes continuing long after graduation. These social consequences can be categorized into direct and indirect effects.

As previously mentioned, American colleges and universities lack the class collective system that is prevalent in Chinese higher education. Consequently, there is no inherent concept of class cohesion, nor do American graduates identify with their former classmates to the same degree as their Chinese counterparts. Statistical analysis of class reunion activities post-graduation may reveal significant disparities between American college graduates and their Chinese peers in this regard. The diminished emphasis on class group identification after graduation among American college students appears to be an established norm. This pattern can be attributed to a fundamental principle ingrained since childhood—the consciousness that lacks recognition of class collectives is clearly shaped and perpetuated by the campus environment in American universities.

Hence, the direct social consequences of individualization primarily encompass a weakening of the group concept, a tendency towards de-authority and de-hierarchy, and challenges in implementing mobilization mechanisms. The mobilization mechanism plays a crucial role in fostering collectivity, often carrying an aura of authority as it leverages the power of exemplary leadership to encourage participation in various movements. Furthermore, authority often derives from collectivism, so wherever collectivism prevails, authority is invariably present.

Another notable social consequence of individualization is the fortification of individual self-awareness and the augmentation of personal responsibility and duty. The substantial volume of philanthropic donations in American society underscores rational behavior stemming from individualization rather than mobilization. According to the 2016 annual philanthropy report released by the Giving USA Foundation, Americans collectively donated an impressive $390 billion that year—an increase of 3% compared to the previous year, marking a record high. To put this into perspective, when contrasted with China, where the number of affluent individuals has risen in recent decades, the total donations in China amount to less than 4% of the donations in the United States.

Within this $390 billion donated in the United States in 2016, individual contributions accounted for over 70%, translating to approximately $282 billion. When calculated based on the current population of 323 million, this translates to a per capita donation of $872, with the majority originating from what one might consider ordinary citizens. A U.S.-based Donor Consultant Foundation once conducted a survey on its official website to inquire about Americans' motivations for donating. The results revealed two primary categories of motivation: emotional, driven by the desire for personal satisfaction, the sense of aligning with societal trends, or the aspiration to be remembered by others; and pragmatic, encompassing a genuine desire to aid others, religious beliefs, and expectations, or the pursuit of tax deductions.

Those who have indulged in American blockbusters may be familiar with the nation's affinity for Hollywood-style tales of individual heroism. By contributing financially, individuals can make a personal decision to become a hero, heightening their sense of self-fulfillment. The roots of this behavior can be traced back to the social effects engendered by individualization.

Returning to the discussion from the outset of this chapter, it's clear that during China's planned economy era before the Cultural

Revolution, the nation's ethos revolved around collectivization. In this period, citizens were encouraged to emulate the example of Comrade Lei Feng and serve as cogs in the revolution's machinery. Conversely, under the conditions of a market economy ushered in by reforms and opening up in the 1980s, Chinese college students exhibited characteristics that can be summarized as a form of weak individualization. This state arose due to the incomplete development of individualization. College students might have aspired to individualization, but they struggled to express this effectively or lacked the mechanisms for its expression.

While educational institutions advocated instilling younger generations with personal awareness and individual responsibility, they also sought to impose certain restraints to ensure compliance with authority. In terms of institutional design, the imperative for individualization was often overlooked in favor of collectivization. Consequently, college students frequently displayed a blend of utilitarianism and conformity in their attitudes and ideologies. This manifestation of weak individualism also manifested as a form of discreet individualism, wherein individuality was concealed beneath a veneer of group dynamics. This approach was perceived as "utilizing the system's resources to achieve personal goals," and historically, the system often favored such talents. Consequently, this dynamic led to the development of a dual personality among college students, as described by Qian Liqun, a retired professor at Peking University.

As early as the late 1700s, Wilhelm von Humboldt, who served as the president of the University of Berlin in Germany, articulated a pivotal idea, "...if there is any institution that needs to shoulder the responsibility for personal development most, it is this one: Education. Education has always been aimed at nurturing the individual." This statement marked the formal inception of personal development as an integral component of the educational system and a clear objective in the establishment of modern universities.

Indeed, the campus functions as a microcosm of society, and the individualized educational journey undertaken by college students serves as a vital opportunity for them to step into the wider world and evolve into self-reliant citizens with a keen eye on the future. The emphasis placed by college students on the notion of personal development signifies not only a conceptual shift but also a substantial project involving the reform of the educational system. In a broader context, the establishment of entrepreneurship within the modern market economy system and the cultivation of academic freedom within universities must find their footing within an individualized framework before they can truly come to fruition.

Relevant Information for Reference

When comparing the phenomenon of individualization among Chinese and American college students, it's crucial to understand the cultural, historical, and socio-economic contexts that influence how individualization manifests in each country.

Cultural Context

1. American Culture: American society, historically and culturally, places a high emphasis on individual rights, freedom, and self-expression. Individualization in American college students may be characterized by a strong desire for personal achievement, independence, and uniqueness. Students are often encouraged to develop their unique talents and interests, pursue their personal goals, and express their individual opinions. This individualistic culture permeates the educational system, where students are often assessed on individual projects and assignments, which encourages independence and personal initiative.

2. Chinese Culture: On the other hand, Chinese society has a Confucian heritage that values harmony, respect for authority, and collective well-being. In this context, individualization can be seen as a balancing act between personal desires and societal expectations. While there is a growing trend towards individualism among Chinese college students, it is often tempered by a sense of responsibility towards family and society. The Chinese educational system traditionally emphasizes teamwork and collective effort, which can be seen as a discouragement to individualization to some extent.

Social Consequences

1. American Society: The strong focus on individualism among American college students can foster innovation, entrepreneurship, and creativity as students are encouraged to think outside the box and challenge the status quo. However, it can also lead to social issues such as isolation, competitiveness, and a lack of community cohesion. Moreover, this emphasis on personal achievement can contribute to high levels of stress and anxiety.

2. Chinese Society: The growing trend towards individualism among Chinese college students can lead to increased personal freedom, self-expression, and a break from traditional norms. It can lead to more diverse interests and ideas, fostering creativity and innovation. However, it can also lead to conflicts between personal desires and familial or societal expectations, which can lead to psychological stress and social tension. The shift towards individualism might also challenge traditional values and social structures, leading to a potential cultural conflict.

Economic Consequences

1. American Economy: The high degree of individualism seen in America can contribute to a dynamic and competitive economy, as individuals are motivated to innovate and start their own businesses. However, it could also lead to economic inequality, as the focus on individual achievement may overshadow societal needs and communal welfare.
2. Chinese Economy: As China continues to develop and globalize, the trend towards individualism could help foster a more innovative and diverse economy. But it could also lead to social inequality, as not all individuals have the same opportunities to express their individuality and pursue personal success.

In summary, while individualization is increasing among college students in both America and China, cultural context significantly shapes how this phenomenon is perceived, as well as its social consequences. Furthermore, as globalization continues, it will be interesting to observe how these trends evolve and intersect with each other.

Footnotes

Ulrich Beck

Ulrich Beck (1944 – 2015) was a German sociologist and one of the most cited social scientists in the world during his lifetime. His work focused on questions of uncontrollability, ignorance, and uncertainty in the modern age, and he coined the terms "risk society" and "second modernity" or "reflexive modernization." He also tried to overturn national perspectives that predominated in sociological investigations with a cosmopolitanism that acknowledges the interconnectedness of the modern world. He was a professor at the University of Munich and also held appointments at the Fondation Maison des Sciences de l'Homme (FMSH) in Paris and at the London School of Economics.

Carl Gustav Jung

Carl Gustav Jung (1875 – 1961) was a Swiss psychiatrist and psychoanalyst who founded analytical psychology. Jung's work has been influential in the fields of psychiatry, anthropology, archaeology, literature, philosophy, psychology, and religious studies. Jung worked as a research scientist at the Burghölzli Psychiatric Hospital in Zurich under Eugen Bleuler. Jung established himself as an influential mind of his time, developing a friendship with Sigmund Freud, the founder of psychoanalysis, conducting a lengthy correspondence, still paramount to their joint vision of human psychology. He is highly regarded as one of the most influential psychologists of all time.

Lei Feng

Lei Feng (1940 – 1962) was a soldier in the People's Liberation Army who was the object of several major propaganda campaigns in China. The most well-known of these campaigns in 1963 promoted the slogan, "Follow the examples of Comrade Lei Feng." Lei was portrayed as a model citizen, and the masses were encouraged to emulate his selflessness, modesty, and devotion to Mao Zedong. The biographic details of Lei Feng's life, and especially his diary, supposedly discovered after his death, are generally believed to be propaganda creations; even the historicity of Lei Feng himself is sometimes questioned. The continuing use of Lei in government propaganda has become a source of cynicism and even derision amongst segments of the Chinese population. Nevertheless, Lei's function as a propaganda icon has survived decades of political change in China.

Qian Liqun

Qian Liqun (1939-) was a professor of Chinese literature at Peking University until his retirement in 2002. He is a leading proponent of May Fourth humanism in post-Mao literary and cultural criticism. The political discrimination and social exclusion that he suffered during the Cultural Revolution motivated his interest in Lu Xun's form of criticism. His key areas of research are modern Chinese literature, with a focus on Lu Xun - the continued relevance of whom he continues to advocate - and the plight of the intellectuals in 20th-century China. Particularly influential in the academic community, were his efforts toward a summation of, and reflection upon, the 20th-century Chinese experience.

CHAPTER 13

The Concept of Whole-Person Development in Student Organizations, Associations, and Educational Ecology

A few years ago, just one day before the conclusion of the spring semester, I received an unexpected email from a student on campus. The subject line read, "Congratulations on Winning the Excellent Teaching Award." Intrigued, I opened the email, which informed me that I had been nominated for this accolade by the student members of the "National Society of Leadership and Success." The award ceremony was slated to take place during the semester's culminating summary and awards event, with the presentation of the certificate being a highlight of the occasion. The student who penned the email, serving as the head of the society branch, explained that they had sought nominations from their fellow members for instructors who had taught during that semester, specifically those who had displayed passion and had inspired students in their pursuit of knowledge – criteria that I, apparently, had met.

Figure 13.1 – Teaching Award Recipients

Initially, I found myself somewhat perplexed by this news. The award and the society were entirely unfamiliar to me, and the email bore the signature "The National Society of Leadership and Success." The organization's name alone piqued my curiosity, prompting me to seek further clarification. Determined to unravel the mystery, I promptly scheduled an appointment to uncover the details.

Figure 13.2 – Award Email Notification

From:	Nijesh Dangol	Sent: Mon 5/1/2017 12
To:	........ngol, Sun	
Cc:	Danielle Davis; Crystal Hardeman	
Subject:	NSLS- EXCELLENCE IN TEACHING AWARD	

Dear . ` Sun,

I am pleased to inform you that you have been nominated by student members of The National Society of Leadership and Success, Sigma Alpha Pi, to receive an award which will be presented at the Society induction and awards ceremony. As the Chapter Manager, I asked members to nominate individuals that teach with heart and passion, and have motivated them in their pursuit of education. You were heartily commended to me as meeting this distinction.

The induction and awards ceremony will be held on Friday, May 5 in Ferguson Auditorium at 7 pm. I hope that you will be   c ⁱ ᵗ we look forward to recognizing you with this honor. Please respond before May 4ᵗʰ to let us know if you will be able to attend.

That evening, after dinner, I made my way to the campus and disembarked from the bus, heading directly to the Ferguson Auditorium. Clutching the invitation letter in hand, I was guided by a student, "Miss Welcome," adorned with a vibrant ribbon stationed at the entrance of the auditorium. Together, we made our way to the front row of the venue. As I settled into my seat, I noticed that the room was brimming with students, with only a few faculty members scattered among them. I exchanged greetings with a professor seated beside me, learning that he had also received an email invitation and had been drawn to the event. Taking a glance around, I spotted a vice provost in the front row and gave him a friendly wave.

The event swiftly commenced as soon as the two hostesses took the stage. To my pleasant surprise, one of them was a student who had attended one of my classes that semester. As the host began her address, I came to understand that this gathering was to celebrate the presentation of their "Excellent Teaching Award" for the semester. Additionally, it featured a summary report of the society's activities, along with an induction ceremony for new members. Each semester's "Excellent Teaching Award" was entirely driven by student nominations, assessed by the society, and ultimately coordinated by the students themselves to host the award ceremony. This contrasted markedly with what we typically understand as the "Excellent Teacher Award," organized by the University's Academic Affairs Office and typically reviewed and ultimately announced by the school's officials. This unique award and its process marked an entirely novel experience for me. It was also the very first time in my life that I had been honored with an "Excellent Teaching Award" bestowed by students. The sensation of receiving such high acclaim and recognition from the education market's own consumers was indescribable.

Following the award ceremony, there was a solemn moment for new student members to take their membership oaths,

culminating in a group photograph. The entire event was master-
fully orchestrated by students, and the atmosphere in the venue
was vibrant and imbued with humor, punctuated by sporadic
cheers from the enthusiastic audience. Strikingly, not a single
school leader graced the stage, and the vice provost remained
seated to the side throughout, abstaining from addressing the
gathering from start to finish.

Figure 13.3 – Award Night Photos

Initially, I hadn't accorded sufficient attention to the numerous
student organizations and societies thriving on our campus.
My awareness was limited to the vague notion that our campus boasted a multitude of such student-led groups, with many
of my students participating in various clubs and associations.
However, following the remarkable award ceremony, my perspective shifted. I found myself compelled to delve into this intriguing
world and decided to embark on a quest for information about

The National Society of Leadership and Success (NSLS), beginning with an online search.

The NSLS proclaims to be the nation's largest leadership honor society, where top students nominated by member schools come together to identify and achieve their goals.

Figure 13.4 –NSLS Logo

The purpose of the NSLS is as follows: "We Build Leaders Who Make a Better World. The Society is an organization that helps people discover and achieve their goals. The Society provides lectures where distinguished speakers from across the country and like-minded, success-focused individuals come together to change lives, inspire, and organize action to improve the world. Founder Gary Tuerack has appeared regularly on national radio and television as a guest on Fox Channel's "Wake Up In The Morning" and many more. He once said: "We are dream supporters - we develop leaders, support people to achieve their dreams, and in their actions make the world a better place."

Figure 13.5 – NSLS Founder Photo

Gary Tuerack

Founder and Chief Visonary

 The National Society of Leadership and Success

橡树果

The NSLS currently has 799 chapters in hundreds of colleges and universities across the country, and there are more than 1.9 million members. They have a news website where members across the country are actively working to become leaders for a better world (https://www.nsls.org/).

Figure 13.6 – NSLS Chapters

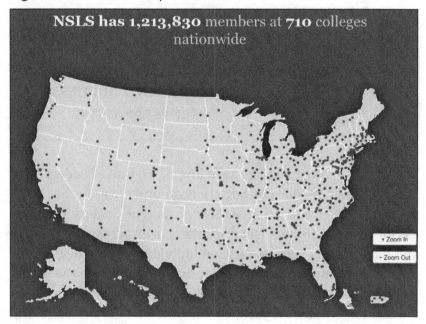

There are literally hundreds of different types of student organizations and societies on American college campuses. According to the data provided by Harvard University, there are nearly a thousand registered and recognized societies, many of which are closely related to a major area of study. Many students participate in societies related to their majors, which can be helpful for the improvement of their professional abilities and future employment opportunities, while taking into account the cultivation of students' service to society as well as their interpersonal communication. Students can freely choose to participate in club activities and take part in organizational work to develop their leadership traits. Of course, foreign students can also form various societies and associations, such as student unions for students from various countries. On my university campus, there are more than 150 different student societies, associations, etc. Each society and community organization has its own logo (emblem) or symbolic pattern to show their differences.

Figure 13.7 – Example of Student Organizations

The nature of each of the societies and associations on campus is different, and there are dozens of categories into which each fit: professional organizations, community engagement, cultural/ social organizations; diversity; fraternities and sororities, governing associations, Greek honor societies, Greek social sororities, honorary societies, leadership development groups, service organizations, special interest groups, sports/recreational organizations, and so forth.

Figure 13.8 – Types and numbers of associations, societies, and organizations on campus

✓ All Categories
  Academic/Professional Organizations (41)
  Community Engagement (1)
  Cultural/Social Organizations (21)
  Departmental (1)
  Development (3)
  Diversity (1)
  Faculty/Staff (1)
  Fraternity & Sorority Life Departmental Umbrella (1)
  Governing Associations (4)
  Greek Honor Societies (1)
  Greek Social Fraternity (10)
  Greek Social Sorority (10)
  Honorary Societies (8)
  Leadership Development (2)
  Other (1)
  Religious Affiliated (11)
  Service Organizations (7)
  Service Umbrella (1)
  Special Interest Group (20)
  Special Program (1)

In addition to the other previously mentioned organizations, there are also business associations that provide students aspiring to pursue careers in finance and medical school with the opportunity to network with celebrities in their specific industries. These associations provide a variety of networking opportunities as well as industry references that can be helpful in facilitating goal achievement. There is usually an annual fee associated with these memberships. There are also organizations that are directly associated with particular religious faiths and denominations. Since the activities of such on-campus societies and associations are purely voluntary, each student decides whether they wish to participate according to their own interests and growth plans, and there are no hard and fast rules regarding participation or attendance. Some societies and associations require members to maintain a certain GPA or average score (such as a GPA of 3.0) to initially join and thereafter maintain their membership. There are also students who never participate in any clubs or associations. Instead, they drive to their workplace after class and participate in another social practice: a part-time job in order to earn money.

On campus, it is also a very simple process for students to start a new club or association. The basic requirements are as follows:

1. Must have and maintain at least six active student members
2. The code of conduct of the members of the organization must comply with the university regulations
3. The organization must have an on-campus official teacher as an advisor
4. The purpose of the activities of the student organization should be in line with the main goals of the university

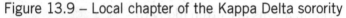

Figure 13.9 – Local chapter of the Kappa Delta sorority

The more typical campus student associations are fraternities and sororities. These are a type of organization that many American college students like to join. Member students participate voluntarily, and new members are selected according to the decisions of existing members. This type of club mainly provides opportunities for socializing, organizes members to play together, party, and is also an outlet for many young people to release their passions. Fraternities and sororities exist widely on college campuses across the United States and have a support network of their members extending beyond graduation. Membership provides access to a wide range of academic support through its support network, hands-on leadership opportunities, community service initiatives, and as a career network assistance for finding a job after graduation to fully assist college students in their personalized campus experience. Family-like bonds are fostered between members of fraternities and sororities, with members often referring to each other as brothers or sisters. Past information indicates that students who participate in fraternity or sorority organizations are often likely to:

1. Achieve better academic performance
2. Be more likely to continue studying until graduation
3. Maintain greater satisfaction with their college experience
4. Be more competitive when looking for jobs and applying to graduate school
5. Develop valuable leadership and interpersonal skills

Fraternities and sororities also have various chapter branches across the country. On my campus, there are currently about 20 branches of four national committees, including the National Pan-Hellenic Council, Incorporated; the College Panhellenic Council; and the Multicultural Greek Council. Some of these offices are located in second-floor suites in the Student Center on campus.

Figure 13.10 – Campus chapter of the Chi Omega fraternity

In terms of the Student Government Association (SGA) at my university, its function is similar to the student union in the universities in China, but it is completely independent to exercise its rights and carry out activities. The mission of the SGA is to empower and provide services and to express needs and rights on behalf of students and the University community. The SGA is composed of senators from various student societies and associations. The main responsibilities of a senator are:

1. Participate in regular Senate meetings
2. Exercise as the leader and organizer of the SGA
3. Comply with the rules and regulations of the SGA's governing documents
4. Act as a liaison for students, various campus organizations, administrative departments, faculty and staff
5. Participate in all meetings that affect the interests of the student body
6. Complete two hours of office time per week throughout the term

Figure 13.11 – Sorority sisters

Do American colleges and universities maintain a completely laissez-faire attitude toward student organizations and associations? The answer is obviously no. The university administrative agency does not directly lead these organizations and associations but conducts its work through a coordinating agency. The university administration has a Student Organization Allocations Committee, which provides funding for student organizations registered on campus each year and encourages various clubs and associations to further improve upon the colorful student' activities taking place on the university campus. This can be somewhat similar to government purchases of public services, not by plans but by needs. These funds are annually approved and distributed by the Student Organization Allocation Committee (SOAC), and all registered student organizations in good standing may apply for funding through SOAC. The amount of funds applied is allocated according to different categories. Funding requests for on-campus activities and travel are primarily for student organizations wishing to request funding for events within the University community or off-campus travel to attend conferences. Amounts of up to $2,000 for on-campus activities can be claimed, including a maximum of $350 per person and $1,400 for off-campus activities. There are also one-time funding applications that apply only to each organization's use of funding for recruitment and marketing efforts. Funds can also be made available for the printing of membership cards, recruitment posters, general organization marketing, the purchase of craft supplies, conference refreshments, organization members' T-shirts, etc.

Educator Lawrence Cremin introduced the concept of Educational Ecology in his 1979 book, "Public Education." He defined it as "a deliberate, systematic, ongoing process of disseminating, inspiring, or acquiring specific knowledge, attitudes, values, skills, or emotions, and any comprehensive outcomes derived from such endeavors." The self-organized activities of American college students within various campus clubs and associations, to a considerable extent, embody the fundamental principles of this educational ecology—namely, the notions of systematicity, equilibrium, and interconnectedness.

The educational philosophy of American universities centers on viewing higher education as a blend of general and elite education. General education emphasizes that each student should be equipped with essential social responsibilities, moral and ethical awareness, and robust physical well-being, thus shaping them into responsible and conscientious citizens. On the other hand, elite education takes the form of distinct schools catering to a range of abilities and interests among students, aiming to maximize each individual's potential and ultimately achieve the goal of personalized student development. The institution places significant emphasis on nurturing students' sense of agency, encouraging them to select their own learning methods based on their unique interests and requirements. This approach fosters a focus on personal growth and the realization of the objective of "comprehensive all-around development."

The concept of holistic personal development derives from humanistic teaching theory and is grounded in the principles of natural human development. Its origins can be traced back to Piaget's cognitive psychology, which places equal importance on students' cognitive and psychological development. This approach underscores the comprehensive growth of individuals and fosters self-reliance and self-actualization among students. In the United States, the values of freedom, democracy, and equality permeate the educational landscape. This ethos promotes respect for students' individual development, granting them the autonomy to make choices and facilitating their free growth. It extends to encouraging students to engage in community service projects, instilling in them a sense of responsibility in learning and practice while enhancing their civic consciousness and social accountability. The learning environment encompasses not only classroom instruction and coursework but also life experiences, community involvement, teamwork, and more.

University life constitutes a pivotal phase of socialization for students. Campus clubs and associations offer students opportunities to hone their skills, nurture their individuality, and engage in social activities beyond the confines of the classroom. Thus, the educational ecosystem of American universities epitomizes its institutional design, which champions students' independent and self-directed pursuits, individual choices, and collaborative group endeavors, rather than conforming to collectivist ideals. Conversely, the process of socialization, from elementary school to university, during adolescence, exemplifies the predominant educational philosophy in the United States – one that emphasizes fostering individualization, teamwork, and leadership skills among students. This approach is not confined to the university system alone; it also permeates the broader societal ideology, highlighting the unique nature of individual growth and the dynamic interplay between individual development and the surrounding environment. However, it's worth noting that the implementation of such a concept may vary across institutions, and student organizations and associations at different universities receive varying degrees of support, resulting in differing levels of effectiveness.

Relevant Information for Reference

Student organizations in universities play a vital role in students' personal development and campus life, serving as an essential aspect of higher education. They offer opportunities for students to explore interests, develop leadership skills, and interact with peers outside of a purely academic setting. While these principles are universal, the specific forms, management methods, and activity content of student organizations can significantly differ between countries, reflecting their unique educational philosophies, cultural values, and societal norms. In comparing Chinese and American universities, several key differences become evident.

Forms of Student Organizations

1. In American universities, student organizations encompass a wide variety of interests. These groups are often divided into academic, athletic, cultural, religious, political, recreational, service, and social organizations, among others. Students are usually free to create their own organizations, subject to university approval, and there's a high level of autonomy in running these organizations.

2. In Chinese universities, student organizations also cover a broad range of fields. However, they are typically more structured and are often related to academic or professional development. These organizations often have a close relationship with university administration or government agencies and are subject to more direct oversight.

Management Methods

1. In American universities, student organizations are typically run by the students themselves. They elect officers, manage their own budgets, plan activities, and make decisions largely independently. Faculty advisors provide guidance but generally do not directly control the organization's activities.
2. Conversely, in Chinese universities, student organizations often have a closer relationship with the administration. They typically have faculty or administrative supervisors who have a more active role in managing the organization. While students still have responsibilities, the level of autonomy is generally less than in American universities.

Activity Content

1. American student organizations' activities range from social events, philanthropic endeavors, sports activities, academic seminars, and political rallies to arts performances and more. These activities generally reflect the far-reaching interests of the student body and promote personal development and social interaction.
2. In Chinese universities, while there are also diverse activities, they tend to be more often academically or professionally oriented. They might include skill-based workshops, industry guest lectures, networking events, or study groups. There is a greater emphasis on activities that contribute to students' professional development and prepare them for their future careers.

In summary, while both American and Chinese universities value student organizations as a key aspect of university life, there are significant differences in their forms, management methods, and activity content. American student organizations tend to be more autonomous, diverse, and student-led, whereas Chinese student organizations tend to be more structured, closely overseen by university administration, and professionally oriented. These differences reflect the countries' respective educational philosophies and cultural values.

Footnotes

Lawrence Cremin

Lawrence A. Cremin (1925 – 1990) was an educational historian and administrator. Cremin received his B.A. and M.A. from City College of New York. His Ph.D. is from Columbia University in 1949. He began teaching at the Teachers College, Columbia University in New York City. In 1961 he became the Frederick A. P. Barnard Professor of Education and a member of Columbia's history department, directing the Teachers College's Institute of Philosophy and Politics of Education in 1965-1974 before becoming the college's 7th president in 1974–1984.

At the Teachers College, Cremin broadened the study of American educational history beyond the school-centered analysis dominant in the 1940s with a more comprehensive approach that examined other agencies and institutions that educated children, integrating the study of education with other historical subfields and comparing education across international boundaries. Cremin won the 1962 Bancroft Prize in American History for his book *The Transformation of the School: Progressivism in American Education, 1876–1957* (1961), which described the anti-intellectual emphasis on non-academic subjects and non-authoritarian teaching methods that occurred as a result of mushrooming enrollment. He was awarded the 1981 Pulitzer Prize for *History for American Education: The National Experience, 1783-1876* (1980).

Jean Piaget

Jean Piaget (1896-1980) was a Swiss psychologist who was the first to make a systematic study of the acquisition of understanding in children. He is thought by many to have been the major figure in 20th-century developmental psychology.

Piaget's early interests were in zoology; as a youth he published an article on his observations of an albino sparrow, and by age 15 his several publications on mollusks had gained him a reputation among European zoologists. At the University of Neuchâtel, he studied zoology and philosophy, receiving his doctorate in the former in 1918. Soon afterward, however, he became interested in psychology, combining his biological training with his interest in epistemology.

In Paris, Piaget devised and administered reading tests to school-children and became interested in the types of errors they made, leading him to explore the reasoning process in these young children. By 1921 he had begun to publish his findings; the same year brought him back to Switzerland, where he was appointed director of the Institut J.J. Rousseau in Geneva. In 1955 he established the International Centre of Genetic Epistemology at Geneva and became its director. His interests included scientific thought, sociology, and experimental psychology. In more than 50 books and monographs over his long career, Piaget continued to develop the theme he had first discovered in Paris, that the mind of the child evolves through a series of set stages to adulthood.

CHAPTER 14

Special Groups on American University Campuses – Students with Disabilities

A merican college campuses boast a diverse and inclusive student body, with individuals hailing from various nationalities and sporting a wide spectrum of skin tones. Additionally, it's not uncommon to encounter students utilizing mobility devices to navigate campus. These students benefit from the Push To Open Door System installed in all university buildings, ensuring that doors automatically swing open upon button activation. Furthermore, to facilitate seamless access for students with mobility devices on staircases, every teaching building on campus features a Handicap Accessible Route System at its entrances and exits. As a result, areas with steps, including teaching facilities, dormitory surroundings, and sidewalks near traffic lights, are equipped with thoughtfully designed ramps integrated into the architectural structure and pathways. I distinctly recall a class I taught a few years back, where a wheelchair-bound student effortlessly wheeled into the front row of the classroom. Thanks to the accessibility amenities mentioned above, he could comfortably commute from home to school and easily participate in classroom activities.

Figure 14.1 – Diploma Presentation

Figure 14.2 – Push-button door opening system and wheelchair access

In U.S. colleges and universities, usually at the beginning of each semester, faculty and instructors will receive a notification email from the school listing the number of students with disabilities in their classes that semester. The email also reminds the recipients that adjustments and proper arrangements may be required in terms of their assignments and examination methods in accordance with the law, including special care such as having a student volunteer take notes for them and delaying examinations when deemed necessary. Clearly, students with disabilities are a special group on college campuses.

American public universities, including all private universities, are required by law to indicate the rights of students with disabilities and the contact information of relevant departments in the syllabus of all courses. For example, all the syllabuses for my courses must list the following content (the unified format and content issued by the university's academic affairs office).

Figure 14.3 – Special care rights and contact details for students with disabilities

Student Requiring Assistance (Students with Disabilities)
The Americans with Disabilities Act (ADA) is a federal anti-discrimination statute that provides comprehensive civil rights protection for persons with disabilities. Among other things, this legislation requires that all students with disabilities be guaranteed a learning environment that provides for reasonable accommodation of their disabilities. If you have a disability requiring an accommodation, please contact:
Office of Student Disability Resources and Services
Texas A&M University-Commerce
Gee Library, Room 132
Phone (903) 886-5150 or (903) 886-5835
Fax (903) 468-8148

This is due to the federal legislative provisions of the United States, ADA, which are guaranteed in the form of legislation. ADA stands for the Americans with Disabilities Act, which was passed by the U.S. Congress in July 1990 and was signed into effect by President Bush, Sr. In 2008, President Bush signed amendments to the Disabled Persons Act, which took effect on January 1, 2009. The Act defines a disabled person as a person who has a documented or perceived physical or psychological abnormality that affects one or more major activities. At the same time, the Act also stipulates the rights that persons with disabilities have, especially in terms of employment, should not be discriminated against.

Figure 14.4 – The website of the Americans with Disabilities Act

All American colleges and universities formulate corresponding regulations and implement them in accordance with this legislation.

Figure 14.5 – School statutes clearly state the provisions

13.01.99.R0.01   Students With Disabilities
Approved September 1, 1996
Revised June 9, 2008
Revised March 8, 2010

This clearly stipulates that after students are enrolled, if they are disabled, they can go to the school's Student Disability Resources and Services Department (SDRS) to apply for specific assistance based on their needs. In any case, the initiative to inform the school of their status as disabled individuals and to apply for assistance rests with the student. That is to say; it is up to students to decide whether they need to apply to this department or not. SDRS, on the other hand, must follow relevant regulations in order to provide corresponding assistance and services to students with disabilities to ensure that students with disabilities will not be discriminated against or receive unfair education because of their disabilities. The specific procedures are: submit a qualified disability diagnosis certificate provided by professional medical personnel, send documents through the website, and fill out the requisite forms. These documents include but are not limited to a professional certificate relevant to the diagnosing physician (i.e., MD, Ph.D., etc.), a definitive diagnostic statement identifying the disability, including severity, a detailed description of the diagnostic criteria and evaluation methods, procedures, tests, and dates. These documents are used by the school's SDRS department to determine if the criteria for students with disabilities have been met.

The definition of disabled students generally includes the following situations:

- Chronic medical conditions such as diabetes, heart problems, cancer, and AIDS
- Emotional and psychological disabilities
- Hearing and visual disabilities
- Neurological disabilities
- Orthopedic and mobility disabilities
- Specific learning disabilities, which include many types of diseases

Figure 14.6 – Disability Accommodation Symbols

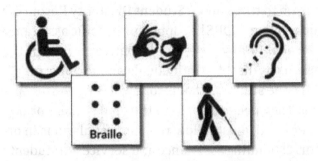

As far as my university is concerned, the data for the fall semester of year 2016 showed that there were 368 students in the school who applied for assistance as disabled students. If the total number of 12,000 students in the whole school is used as the base, this special group only accounts for 3%. These include the following different categories and population distributions:

- Attention-deficit/hyperactivity disorder (ADD/ADHD) (69 people)
- Autism (19 people)
- Blind/Visually Impaired (14 people)
- Deaf/Hard of Hearing (14 people)
- Health Related (66 people)
- Learning Disability (108 people)
- Nervous System Neurological (10 people)
- Psychiatric (58 people)
- Orthopedic (10 people)
- Total (368 people)

It can be seen that students with disabilities do not only refer to deafness, blindness, and other conditions that are physically significantly different from the majority of the population but also include less significant physical diseases and even physical or psychological differences or obstacles that are not as easily identified. For example, the mode in the above statistics is learning

disabilities (108 people in total), and these students are no different from any of the rest of the students on the surface, and their
daily life is no different from other people, and it can be easy to
be ignored. Therefore, a professional physician is required to
give correct identification and provide a certificate of disability
diagnosis.

The SDRS department provides assistance to students with disabilities and creates an accessible learning environment to ensure
that they have equal access to education. SDRS will also make
corresponding adjustments based on each student's individual
needs. Adjustments may include providing assistive devices and
services; arranging priority registration; reducing course load;
arranging alternate courses; providing volunteers to help record
class notes, recording equipment, sign language interpreters, and
so on; extending exam time; serving deaf and hard of hearing
students TTY (Text Phone) device; and providing school computers that support screen reading, voice recognition, or other
hardware and software for conversion. And all of these additional
aids and equipment are provided without an additional charge.

The special services provided by colleges and universities for
students with disabilities can be broadly summarized in the following areas:

Classroom Special Services

Classroom special services offer assistance such as note-taking
on behalf of students with disabilities. I recall a situation from a
few years ago when two disabled students were enrolled in one
of my classes. Prior to each class, they approached me in my office
with forms provided by the SDRS, requesting note-taking support. In response, I reached out to the class and asked if any students were willing to volunteer for this task. Two compassionate

students stepped forward, offering to provide the disabled students with copies of their class notes and guidance as needed. These volunteer students were required to complete a form and submit it to the SDRS office for registration. At the end of the semester, they were compensated for their efforts with labor fees, which are uniformly provided by the federal government in accordance with regulations.

If these students with disabilities choose online courses, SDRS is required to design special PPT courseware for these students (including vision-impaired individuals or others who have specific learning disabilities such as dyslexia). The school has specialized personnel to assist teachers in establishing relevant accessibility tests and inspections on the existing PPT files to ensure that these students can successfully access the content of the course. The SDRS office also has programs that provide course or assignment instruction services, and students with various disabilities and assistance requirements have the opportunity to access this service as long as they apply in advance.

To assist students with vision impairment or specific reading disabilities, SDRS staff will arrange for the technical department to give detailed text descriptions and annotations to the picture materials that do not need to be added under normal circumstances. When questioned, SDRS staff explained that such annotations are designed for visually impaired individuals or students with dyslexia. While working online, anytime their mouse moves over a picture, special software will play the picture text description so that visually impaired students can still access all of the available website content smoothly.

Figure 14.7 – Application Form for Interpretive Services Provided by the Office of Student Resources and Services with Disabilities

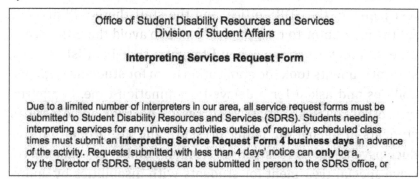

Office of Student Disability Resources and Services
Division of Student Affairs

Interpreting Services Request Form

Due to a limited number of interpreters in our area, all service request forms must be submitted to Student Disability Resources and Services (SDRS). Students needing interpreting services for any university activities outside of regularly scheduled class times must submit an **Interpreting Service Request Form 4 business days** in advance of the activity. Requests submitted with less than 4 days' notice can **only** be a, by the Director of SDRS. Requests can be submitted in person to the SDRS office, or

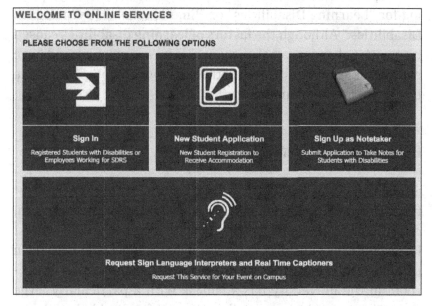

WELCOME TO ONLINE SERVICES

PLEASE CHOOSE FROM THE FOLLOWING OPTIONS

Sign In
Registered Students with Disabilities or Employees Working for SDRS

New Student Application
New Student Registration to Receive Accommodation

Sign Up as Notetaker
Submit Application to Take Notes for Students with Disabilities

Request Sign Language Interpreters and Real Time Captioners
Request This Service for Your Event on Campus

Special Services for Exams

Whether it is midterm exams or final exams, as long as these students need to extend the exam time, the instructor must make corresponding adjustments. If the average student is required to complete the test within an hour, these students have the ability to complete it in an hour and a half or even longer in order to make adjustments based on their specific needs. If the instructor finds it inconvenient to supervise the test, he can send the test paper to the SDRS office, and the staff there will arrange for the invigilator to take the test alone to avoid the influence of others. A few years ago, when I taught a social statistics class, several students took the application form for students with disabilities and asked for a delayed examination time. Compared with other courses, statistics courses are difficult, and American students are generally under pressure and are prone to introduce psychological frustration. A small number of students receive special treatment for students with disabilities by applying for "Learning Disabilities" or "Emotional and Psychological Disabilities." Although the factors of learning disabilities caused by emotional and psychological problems are complex and have considerable ambiguity, the instructors must follow SDRS office documents without ambiguity.

Housing Special Services

Students with disabilities who live on campus also have the right to receive facilities that are more appropriate for their physical condition. For example, the restroom for disabled students must have handrails or grab bars. In fact, many people who have been to American universities have noticed that almost every bathroom in the university has a cubicle with a particularly large area. This is a cubicle specially prepared for disabled students. Students can enter this bathroom directly in a wheelchair.

Figure 14.8 – Wheelchair Accessible Restroom

In addition, the Wheelchair Accessible Route System mentioned above is also one of the prerequisites for students to live on campus. Wherever they are, there will be a ramp to achieve barrier-free access. Some universities are also equipped with wheelchair lifts on campus buses to facilitate students with disabilities to get on and off the bus (wheelchair-accessible fixed route bus system).

Special Services for Meals

The school cafeteria also has special services for students with disabilities. The school canteen is definitely one of the places where people with disabilities are most often seen because students with disabilities also need to eat! The school cafeteria pays special attention to the services for the disabled. Usually, there is a long table in the dining area of the school canteen, which is specifically reserved for them. In addition, there are also certain student volunteers who are responsible for helping these students to bring food to the table and to serve "in place."

Furthermore, during university graduation ceremonies in the United States, special provisions are made to ensure inclusivity for hearing-impaired attendees. A sign language interpreter is present to translate all speeches into sign language, guaranteeing that hearing-impaired individuals are fully included. Although the number of hearing-impaired students or parents in the audience may be relatively small, their needs are given equal consideration.

In accordance with regulations established by American colleges and universities concerning students with disabilities, faculty members are not permitted to question the requirements of students who have been approved by the university's SDRS. Faculty members are also prohibited from refusing to provide reasonable accommodations and appropriate arrangements. However, faculty members do possess the right and responsibility to engage in the decision-making process regarding the nature and extent of adjustments and accommodations that will be made within the curriculum for these students. Students with disabilities are likewise entitled to maintain the privacy of their disability records and test scores.

Simultaneously, university regulations emphasize that the education provided must not compromise academic standards or skip essential components of university-level study due to the presence of students with disabilities in the classroom. Although specific arrangements and adjustments are made for students with disabilities, academic standards and requirements cannot be significantly lowered or altered. For instance, it is possible to extend exam duration without modifying the exam's content or reducing grading expectations.

There is also a provision in the regulations concerning students with disabilities. If a student with a disability believes that they have been discriminated against because of their disability, they can file a complaint. Whenever a student with a disability believes that he or she is experiencing systemic discrimination or harassment based on his or her disability, the student should first seek assistance from the most direct department, such as the SDRS coordinator. If a student is dissatisfied with the coordinator's program, he or she may file a written appeal with the ADA committee. Written complaints must be submitted by the student within thirty working days of the discrimination or harassment.

It can be seen that, in addition to enjoying the same educational environment as other students, disabled students on American university campuses receive special services due to their special requirements, and in some respects, they enjoy privileges that their fellow students do not have, which truly realizes the educational equality.

Figure 14.9 – Students with disabilities enjoy the same fair education as normal students and are not discriminated against

Students with disabilities represent socially disadvantaged groups, and the treatment they receive on college campuses reflects the societal level of civilization. The Americans with Disabilities Act, signed into law on July 26, 1990, has been in effect for over 20 years. During this time, both the U.S. government and society at large have made significant efforts and changes to safeguard the rights and interests of disabled individuals, spanning from infrastructure improvements to employment security. In 2010, President Obama commemorated the 20th anniversary of the act at the White House and issued an executive order to increase the percentage of disabled employees in the federal government. This legislation has compelled society to prioritize the education and employment of disabled individuals.

These protections and associated accessibility standards are not limited to the education system but extend throughout society and the workplace. Data reveals that disabled individuals constitute approximately 12% to 20% of the U.S. population, with roughly 37 million to 57 million individuals facing physical, psychological, and cognitive disabilities. After residing in the United States for an extended period, it becomes evident that American society is actively establishing a barrier-free access framework for disabled individuals. This commitment is reflected in everyday aspects of life, including driving, parking, and building entry, as well as in education, employment opportunities, and government support programs. The ultimate aim is to provide vulnerable members of society with the means to lead dignified lives, marking a significant indicator of overall societal progress and civilization.

China enacted the Law of the People's Republic of China on the Protection of Disabled Persons on May 15, 1991, signaling the nation's legislative commitment to addressing the needs of disabled individuals. Furthermore, China became a signatory to the United Nations (UN) Convention on the Rights of Persons with Disabilities in 2006, though its implementation has faced challenges. Data from the Second National Sampling Survey of Disabled Persons reveals that there are approximately 82.96 million disabled individuals in China, comprising 6.34% of the country's total population. However, disabled individuals are not commonly seen in urban life or on college campuses, with many seemingly living on the periphery of public awareness.

Within the higher education system, instances of refusal due to physical imperfections have unfortunately been prevalent. Furthermore, special services for students with disabilities on college campuses have fallen short in terms of infrastructure, faculty training, and curriculum adjustments. The concept of educational equity and its associated mechanisms remain underdeveloped.

To rectify this situation, the pivotal step is to protect the rights and interests of disabled individuals. This includes establishing and clearly guaranteeing educational fairness in legislation, implementing specific measures, and creating a complaint mechanism accessible to disabled individuals. It is believed that, as other aspects of the country continue to improve, special services and learning conditions for disabled students will gradually see enhancements. Neglecting to serve this special group within the framework of higher education undermines the aspiration of becoming a truly civilized nation.

Relevant Information for Reference

Both China and the United States have specific laws and systems to protect the rights of students with disabilities and to ensure that they have equal access to education. However, the laws and implementation measures vary between the two countries.

United States

In the United States, federal laws such as the Individuals with Disabilities Education Act (IDEA), Section 504 of the Rehabilitation Act of 1973, and the ADA are designed to protect the rights of students with disabilities.

1. IDEA mandates that public schools serve the educational needs of eligible students with disabilities, with the majority of them being served in public schools. Under IDEA, schools are required to provide a Free Appropriate Public Education (FAPE) to all students with disabilities, which includes special education and related services.
2. Section 504 ensures that a child with a disability has equal access to an education and that the education provided is comparable to that given to non-disabled students. This act applies to any program or activity receiving federal financial assistance.
3. ADA extends the concepts of Section 504 beyond just federally funded programs to most places of public accommodation, and it includes private colleges and vocational schools.

The implementation of these laws involves creating an Individualized Education Program (IEP) or 504 Plan designed to meet the unique needs of each child. The program or plan is developed by a team that typically includes teachers, school psychologists, therapists, and the child's parents or caregivers. This ensures that each child with a disability receives appropriate accommodations and modifications to access the general education curriculum.

China

In China, the Law on the Protection of Disabled Persons provides the legal framework for the rights and interests of persons with disabilities, which includes the right to education, regardless of the nature of the disability.

Specifically, the Compulsory Education Law of the People's Republic of China mandates that all children, including those with disabilities, have the right to receive at least nine years of education. This law encourages the integration of students with disabilities into regular classrooms whenever possible.

In 2008, China launched a major initiative to promote inclusive education, which was further boosted by the 13th Five-Year Plan (2016–2020). The initiative and subsequent plan were designed to make general education schools more accessible and accommodating to students with disabilities.

China's implementation measures include the creation of IEPs, similar to those in the U.S., for students with disabilities. The plan outlines the services, accommodations, and support the student will receive. The emphasis is on integrating students with disabilities into general education classrooms whenever possible, with additional resources provided as needed.

Despite these policies, there have been critiques and concerns over the implementation and accessibility of inclusive education in China. It's often reported that facilities, teacher training, and societal attitudes lag behind policy intentions.

Both the U.S. and China face ongoing challenges and critiques regarding their systems. These range from funding and resources to teacher training, parental involvement, and the stigmatization of disability.

CHAPTER 15

Part-time Work after School:
Preliminary Course for College
Students to Integrate into Society

I n the university town where I reside, I frequently encounter
my students working in the nearby supermarket, whether as
cashiers or porters. During the summer months, when my front
yard requires mowing, other college students often drive by and
knock on my door, inquiring if I need assistance with lawn care.
Engaging in part-time work after school is a well-established
practice among college students in the United States.

Figure 15.1 – Student employment, an integration into society

I once conducted a small survey within my class, including a question that asked, "In a typical week, how many hours do you work

at a paid job?" The response options were categorized as follows, along with their respective percentages: no work (21.4%), less than four hours (3.6%), four to eight hours (3.6%), and more than eight hours (71.4%). This survey revealed that approximately one-fifth of the students in my class did not engage in part-time work, while over two-thirds of them worked for more than eight hours per week after their classes.

Figure 15.2 – Small class survey response

In a typical week, how many hours do you work at a paid job?
No job_ 21.4%   Less than 4 hours_3.6%   4 hours to 8 hours_3.6%   More than 8 hours_71.4%

In a typical week, how many hours do you spend for your assignn   ' re course?

This result is consistent with relevant surveys across the United States. A study by the American Council of Education has long shown that 78% of the nearly 20 million undergraduate students in the United States work at least part-time after school. Students who work part-time after school include all ages, genders, races, and ethnicities, regardless of family income, whether they are dependent on their parents, full-time students, or even if they attend private or public schools. Students tend to work an average of 30 hours a week. This ratio has not changed much over the years. Part-time work can be described as one of the typical campus cultures of American college students.

Students' work can be divided into full-time or part-time jobs. If you are working full-time, you can work up to 40 hours per week, and if attending school full-time, undergraduate students must take a minimum of 12 credits per semester, which is about four courses. Therefore, students who work full-time can find it more difficult to maintain their status as full-time students. Half-time or part-time students are subject to many restrictions in applying for scholarships, which will delay their graduation.

Therefore, if college students want to maintain their full-time student status, they must strive to strike a balance between work and study. Among the students I teach, only a few students who are quite smart and have good time management concepts can achieve both, not only participating in full-time work (staggered from class time), but also achieving good academic standings. While most college students remain full-time students, they only participate in part-time work.

Figure 15.3 – The minimum hourly wage for college students in the United States, which began in October 2017, is $10.90 per hour

Minimum Wage Rates		
Minimum Wage Rate	Rates from October 1, 2016 to September 30, 2017	Rates as of October 1, 2017
General Minimum Wage	$11.40 per hour	$11.60 per hour
Student Minimum Wage	$10.70 per hour	$10.90 per hour
Liquor Servers Minimum Wage	$9.90 per hour	$10.10 per hour

Part-time work can also be divided into two types: on-campus part-time work and off-campus part-time work. Undergraduate students have a wide variety of jobs on campus, including working in the campus library, bookstore, coffee shop, computer room, and other similar positions. The graduate students are mostly teaching assistants (TA), research assistants (RA), and so on. It is also generally stipulated that there are 20 hours of part-time work per week. The minimum wage for on-campus work is $10.90 per hour; some can reach $15-20 per hour (there will be appropriate adjustments yearly). Off-campus jobs are varied, from being a cashier in a supermarket, a waiter in a restaurant, or even a security guard in an office building. Salaries vary greatly depending on the type of job the student holds. If a student is a tutor, the hourly salary is generally $10-15, while the Walmart supermarket cashier or bagger has an hourly salary of $9.91; for private lawn and garden maintenance, the hourly salary can be up to $15-20. During the winter and summer vacations, when students do not typically attend classes, they can work full-time. They can generally guarantee an income of $1,500-3,000 USD per month, which is approximately 10,000-20,000 yuan in China.

Figure 15.4 – Different hourly rates at Walmart supermarkets

Walmart ><

| Salary | **Hourly Rate** | Bonus | Benefits | More ▾ |

Wal-Mart Stores, Inc Hourly Rate   Check salary info for your own job »

| Hourly Rate ▾ |

Job	Average	$0		$17
Cashier 575 profiles	$9.91			
Sales Associate 460 profiles	$10.27			
Pharmacy Technician 302 profiles	$13.25			

There are notable distinctions between local college students and international students in the United States when it comes to seeking part-time employment. Local college students have distinct advantages when searching for jobs; they typically require only specific documents, such as a social security card, to apply for employment. In urgent cases, some local college students can even apply for positions online, especially when supermarkets are in dire need of staff. However, international students face a different set of circumstances. Under U.S. government regulations, international students are not obligated to secure a special permit to work on campus, as it is considered legal part-time employment. Nevertheless, they must remain registered as full-time students to maintain their legal status, and their working hours are generally restricted to 20 hours per week, signifying part-time employment. For off-campus work, international students must navigate a more complex process, which includes applying for a work permit and obtaining a social security card before they can legally engage in employment. This application process can be quite intricate and comes with numerous limitations. Due to the limited availability of on-campus job opportunities and the necessity of possessing proper legal documentation for off-campus work, international students face restrictive conditions that can make off-campus employment challenging. However, some international students leverage their unique cultural ties to secure employment. For instance, when there is a Chinese restaurant near the university, some overseas Chinese students may seek assistance from the restaurant owner to secure informal employment. In cases where the restaurant owner is Chinese, they often find a way to hire these students. Additionally, during the academic year, international students can apply for jobs in the United States under the guise of internships. To be eligible, applicants must complete one academic year and then, within a specific timeframe (90 days before graduation to 30 days after graduation), they can submit relevant forms and include a recommendation letter from their school's international student advisor to apply for a work permit.

When my son was in his third or fourth year of university, he had the opportunity to work as a tutor for younger students, which was considered an on-campus part-time job. At the end of the year, the school's finance department would send a tax return form to your home, summarizing your part-time income for the year. Individuals were required to file their tax return before April 15th of the following year. Consequently, through this experience, students gain valuable real-life insights, which are crucial for their future in society and their careers. Engaging in various part-time jobs after classes, students gain a deeper appreciation for the hard work undertaken by their fellow part-time workers. In Chinese culture, tipping at restaurants is not customary, but whenever our family dined out and left a tip, my son consistently insisted on leaving a more generous gratuity.

Figure 15.5 – Part-time Employment

In reality, a substantial number of college students, whether they are local residents in the United States or international students, opt for part-time employment. Some undertake part-time jobs to cover their living expenses or tuition fees, while others aim to accrue work experience and establish a foundation for future job prospects. There are those who engage in part-time work as a means to gain insight into the professional world, comprehend societal dynamics, and expand their social horizons. Regardless of the specific motivations, part-time employment constitutes a significant facet of the lives of American college students. It can be likened to a preliminary course that prepares them for integration into society following graduation. Such part-time work not only delivers immediate economic advantages but also complements and applies the knowledge acquired through their chosen majors. It essentially serves as a form of quasi-vocational training. Additionally, students seize the opportunity to enhance their interpersonal skills, acquire effective time management techniques, and, most importantly, develop a keener understanding of the workforce's demands, which subsequently aids them in making informed decisions about their future career paths.

Figure 15.6 – Small classroom survey where students were asked about the distance from the student's residence to the campus

Where are you living currently?
On campus_28.6%   Less than 15 min. driving distance_28.6%
15 min. to 40 min. driving distance_17.9%   More than 40 min. driving d~ ˙ ˄ ˉ˅

In order to work part-time, students generally need to have their own cars. As mentioned in the beginning of Chapter 12, if you visit American university campuses, you will find that, unlike on Chinese university campuses where bicycles are crowded everywhere, American college students usually have private cars. Therefore, the parking lot on university campuses from Monday to Friday is cramped and overcrowded. Sometimes, students will drive back and forth in the same parking lot, hoping to find a space. In my classroom survey, I asked students how far they lived from campus and provided five options to answer, which resulted in percentages as follows: live on campus (28.6%), live 15 minutes drive away (28.6%), live 15 to 40 minutes drive away (17.9%), live more than 40 minutes drive distance (25%). It can be seen that the majority of college students (71.5%) drive to school for at least 15 minutes. In the absence of public or university-provided sources of transportation in the form of busses or trams, college students must own a car, or they won't be able to attend classes. With a car, they are able to maintain more freedom. College students usually drive to school in a hurry in order to attend class; after class, they drive to the place for their part-time jobs in a hurry as well. After-school work for American college students is indeed a landscape on American university campuses.

Figure 15.7 – Crowded campus parking lot

American universities generally hold a positive stance regarding students engaging in on-campus employment. A significant portion of research funding allocated to professors includes provisions for covering student labor costs associated with their participation in research endeavors. In my own experience, when I applied for research grants at the university, a portion of the funds was earmarked specifically for compensating students who served as RAs, assisting with tasks like literature reviews and organizing survey materials. Once these grants are secured, the funds are exclusively designated for student wages and cannot be utilized for any other purposes. All university departments actively seek opportunities for students to engage in work-study programs. As you traverse the campus, you'll often encounter posters and notices seeking office assistants, research assistants, video producers, and more.

International students typically initiate their job search by consulting with advisors at the International Students Office to inquire about on-campus employment opportunities. If such opportunities are available, international students can partici- pate without the need for a work permit, thus avoiding the risk associated with off-campus employment. Faculty members are generally understanding when individual students encounter challenges such as late assignment submissions or class absences due to their part-time work commitments. These challenges can impact students' rest schedules or their ability to meet assign- ment deadlines. In cases where students engage in off-campus employment, the university cannot intervene, as it is considered a private matter and a matter of personal choice for the stu- dents. If their academic performance falls below the minimum acceptable standards, part-time students have the option to re- take the course in the following semester in an effort to improve their grades, although this may extend their time to graduation. Research has demonstrated that due to the demands of long working hours, college students may require six years or more to complete their studies, impacting their academic progress.

Surveys have also indicated that due to the limited availability of on-campus job opportunities, the majority of part-time students opt for off-campus work, and many of these jobs are unrelated to their respective majors. Although part-time work experience may not be directly aligned with their field of study and might not directly impact future career development, most students do not perceive it as an excessive burden; instead, it is often regarded as an integral aspect of college life. Consequently, American col- lege students, in addition to managing a demanding course load, have an array of other commitments, including part-time jobs, involvement in club activities, and participation in community service, all of which necessitate an investment of their time and effort. Harvard University in the United States is renowned for its "three-one-third" theory, which suggests that students should allocate one-third of their time to coursework, one-third to engage in club activities, and one-third to work part-time after classes. This balanced approach is considered the hallmark of a genuine Harvard student.

Figure 15.8 – After-school employment lays a foundation of self-reliance

Beneath the surface of American college students' after-school employment lies a foundation of self-reliance deeply ingrained in American youth and Western society's cultural tradition of emphasizing individual independence. Influenced by this cultural backdrop, parents are inclined to nurture their children's ability to care for themselves and lead independent lives from an early age. When children enter college, they are regarded as adults and are expected to strive for financial independence from their parents. Continued dependence on parental support may lead to a loss of face among their peers. Consequently, even students from affluent backgrounds often engage in part-time employment. In the United States, once they gain admission to college, children from well-off families frequently endeavor to reduce or eliminate reliance on their parent's financial support, instead opting to earn their own income to cover tuition and living expenses. According to survey data, only 22% of college students have their tuition paid by their parents. In comparison, 41% rely on state grants, 18% take part-time jobs to cover tuition costs, and 16% secure various scholarships to fund their education and living expenses. It is evident that just a fifth of students depend on their parents to finance their education, with nearly half opting for student loans rather than parental financial support. To encourage students' self-sufficiency and independence, the federal student loan program is accessible to all college students, regardless of their family's financial status. Any student can apply for a federal student loan and is responsible for repaying it after graduation. The part-time work undertaken by American college students not only provides valuable work experience and fosters social acumen but also epitomizes the spirit of independence, reflecting the enduring cultural tradition of American society.

Relevant Information for Reference

The experiences of college students in China and the United States vary quite a bit when it comes to working after school, due to cultural, societal, and legal differences between the two countries.

United States

American college students have a long history of working while attending school. The reasons for doing so are varied, including the need to support themselves financially, gain work experience, and pay for their education. Many students take part-time jobs on or off campus. On-campus jobs might include work-study

positions (a form of federal financial aid), research assistant-
ships, or other administrative roles. Off-campus, students might
work in various industries, from food service to retail to internships in their field of study. Several regulations and policies support these students. For example, the Fair Labor Standards Act
(FLSA) establishes minimum wage, overtime pay, recordkeeping,
and youth employment standards affecting employees in the private sector and in federal, state, and local governments. Federal
work-study programs provide part-time jobs for students with
financial need, allowing them to earn money to help pay education expenses.

China

In China, the culture traditionally places a heavy emphasis on
academic achievement. As such, working while studying is less
common, and when it does happen, it's usually in the form of internships, research positions, or part-time jobs during holidays.
The primary reasons Chinese students might work are to gain experience in their chosen field and to improve their employability
after graduation. This contrasts with many American students,
who often work out of financial necessity.

Chinese labor laws apply to these students too, but specific regulations concerning student work are not as developed as in
the U.S. Regulations might vary from one university to another.
Chinese universities, especially the prominent ones, tend to have
stronger ties with industry, and they often help students find
relevant internships and work experience opportunities.

The Chinese government has also established the "3+1" scheme
for some universities. Under this scheme, students study in school
for three years and spend their final year interning in companies.

This program is designed to better equip students with practical skills for the job market.

Comparisons

One of the main differences between the two countries is the driving force behind why students work. In the U.S., it's often out of financial necessity, while in China, it's more for gaining experience and improving employability. Another significant difference lies in the regulatory frameworks: the U.S. has a more developed set of regulations supporting student workers, while China has traditionally less emphasis on student employment outside of internships and work-study programs.

CHAPTER 16
Small Classroom Survey of American College Students' Ideal Partner

The notion of an ideal partner holds significant importance in the realm of love and marriage, serving as a reflection of individuals' choices in these domains while also bearing testament to broader societal ideologies. Marriage, fundamentally, is a social contract, transcending the mere biological union of two individuals to become a profound cultural process characterized by mutual recognition, acceptance, integration, and interplay. It is evident that a successful marriage necessitates more than physical attraction and investment; it calls for a willingness to embrace and acknowledge each other beyond the physical realm, constituting a fundamental prerequisite.

"In the context of marriage, several core elements come into play, encompassing shared interests, congruent political viewpoints, a similar social background, financial stability, mutual respect, accommodation, understanding, tolerance, and harmonious sexual relations. The significance assigned to each of these facets by individuals underscores their unique perspectives on the institution of marriage" (quoted from *Conceptual Generation Difference - Background of Transition Society* (1991-1994)" by Sun Jiaming, Shanghai Social Sciences Publishing House, 1997).

Figure 16.1 – Poem

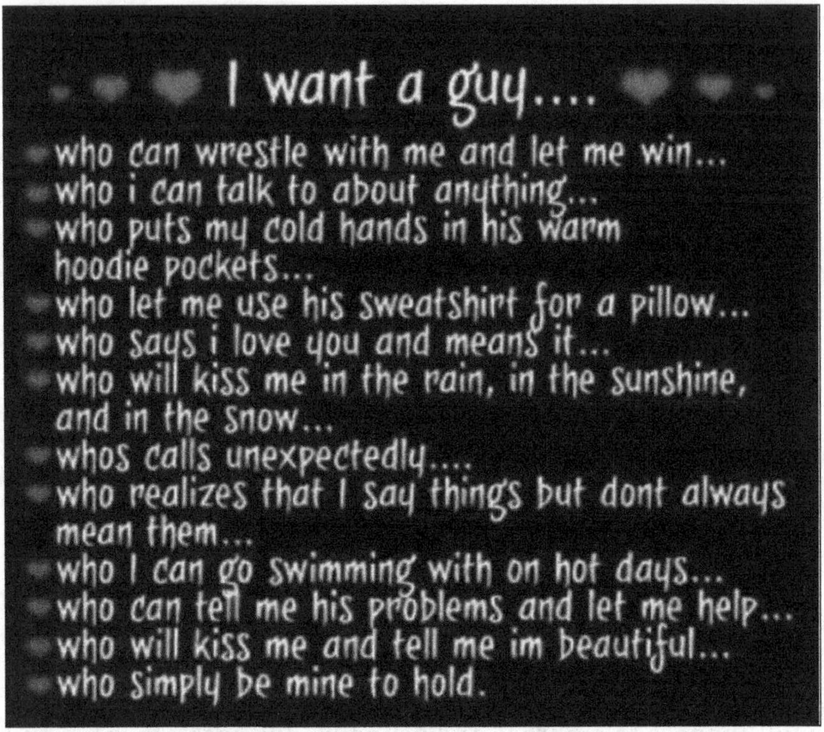

♥ ♥ ♥ I want a guy.... ♥ ♥ ♥
who can wrestle with me and let me win...
who i can talk to about anything...
who puts my cold hands in his warm
hoodie pockets...
who let me use his sweatshirt for a pillow...
who says i love you and means it...
who will kiss me in the rain, in the sunshine,
and in the snow...
whos calls unexpectedly....
who realizes that I say things but dont always
mean them...
who I can go swimming with on hot days...
who can tell me his problems and let me help...
who will kiss me and tell me im beautiful...
who simply be mine to hold.

The concept of marriage and love in American society has undergone tremendous changes. In the 1970s, the United States implemented a law called "legalization of no-fault divorce." The introduction of the law immediately triggered a wave of divorces. In fact, the divorce wave peaked in the 1980s and then gradually declined. The U.S. divorce rate fell to its lowest level in 35 years in 2015. There were only 16.9 divorces per 1,000 married women aged 15 and older in the United States in 2015, the lowest level since 1980 (the rate was 23,000 that year). In 2014, the figure was 17.6 per thousand. The chart below roughly depicts the trends in marriage and divorce rates in American society from 1970 to 2015. The marriage rate (blue line) has fallen sharply, while the divorce rate (red line) has gone out of an inverted V shape, which is a slight convergence in recent years. As can be seen from the figure below, in terms of the ratio of divorce and marriage in 2015, it roughly reached 50% (the marriage rate was 32.3%, and the divorce rate was 16.9%). That number is often misused as the divorce rate in American society.

Figure 16.2 – Trends in marriage and divorce rates in American society from 1970-2015

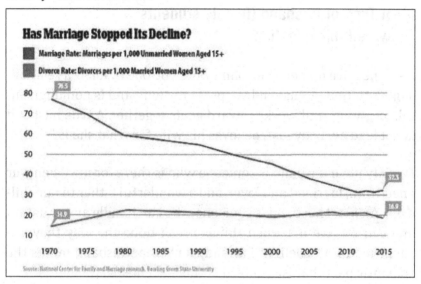

Although the absolute value of the divorce rate in American society is still relatively high, the value placed against premarital sex is more indulgent; premarital pregnancies and single mothers are not uncommon among college students. However, young people's formal marriage relationships are not as casual, demanding, and irresponsible as people think. So, what is the ideal partner for young people?

In my class on social research methods, I once conducted a small survey on the ideal partner. The problem is this:

1. From your point of view, what is the ideal type of husband?
2. From your perspective, what is the ideal type of wife?

Most of the original answering materials in the small survey (without any modification or deletion) are provided to readers here and shared with readers (obviously, the names of the respondents are omitted and are indicated in capital letters. The first letter at the beginning of the paragraph is not in order).

Ideal Type of Husband (female students answered this question):

A – "The pure model of husband would be one that has a relationship with God. A husband supports his wife and is nonjudgmental, forgiving, and works toward goals together. A true husband is not lead away by lust, he loves his wife for what she is."

D – "My ideal husband is someone who is there for me whenever I need him, lo friend and lover, and a wonderful father to our children. An ideal husband is someone who can handle any situation and can forgive me when things aren't done the way they are supposed to be I believe I already have that husband minus the romantic part that is required of the ideal husband."

F – "my ideal type for a husband is someone who is a good listener, trustworthy, loving, compassionate, and shares the same faith I do. Also, he must love children be able to control his anger and get along with my family. He must be educated and have a great sense of humor."

G – "To me, the ideal husband would be a southern gentleman, charming, educated, have the sophistication, attractive, your best friend, lover, and confidant, be the backbone of the family, caring, loves children and family (whether immediate or extend), supportive, humorous, witty, faithful, in other words he would be the person that I am already married to."

H – "My ideal husband would be someone that is a hard worker, smart, good with animals, gets along with my parents, and should be a police officer."

H1 – "An ideal husband would be caring and gentle, kind and generous, have a firm belief in who he is and stands up for what is right, good family ties and strong religious beliefs, and a passion for children, singing, and good food."

I – "My point of view of an ideal husband would include qualities such as: a strong relationship with God, a love for children and people in general, a generous personality, a sports fan(preferably volleyball, basketball, and football), passionate about the mental and physical health of his family good to his parents, a shoulder to lean on, a good communicator, romantic, mysterious strong, truthful, confident, educated on what is going on in this world, willing to give back to his community, and willing to tell people of all creeds about the goodness of the Lord."

J – " The ideal husband for me is a guy that knows how to respect women and shows that he knows how. He should take care of his family at all cost and be faithful to his wife. He should also be a God-fearing man, who has the word at heart."

K – "I grew up watching that television show Home Improvement. Ya know, the one starring Tim the "Tool Man" Taylor. Anyways, I guess the "ideals" of a perfect husband have rubbed off on what I would consider the perfect man. Those qualities would include: Being handy around the house, Ability to work on cars, Strong, Funny, Faithful, Successful and able to take care of his family, Loving."

L – "From my point of view and ideal husband should have faith in God. He must also be loyal and have respect for themselves so they can be respectful of others. He must be a loving and caring person. Must also be responsible and have the ambition to be successful in life. He must also want person. children."

M – "My ideal husband would be: fun-loving, honest, caring, kind, Courageous, protective of our family, want children, enjoy helping others, not afraid to speak his mind about his beliefs and emotions, ambitious, hardworking, very family oriented with both of our families, faithful, humorous, attractive, my best friend, someone I never tire of being with, an animal lover."

N – "my ideal type of husband would love God and attend church regularly with family, love unconditionally, put children before all others and want to spend time with them and wife of course, but would also have separate interests that could enjoy also. Hardworking, honest, loving. Someone who is strong both mentally and physically."

O – "From my point of view, an ideal husband would have such qualities including: faith relationship with Christ, passion for ministry, love of people, patience, honesty, integrity, humor, ability to compromise, ability to be the leader of the family, good father, an interest in culture and travel, ability to forgive, romantic and a heart for service."

P – "My pure model of an Ideal Husband is one that has a personal and close relationship with God. One who respects his wife at all times. my husband to take care of his body can be him to do this by not smoking and working out, like me.I want my husband to know how to do things around the house, such a cooking and cleaning. I also want him to have some type of education."

T – "A pure and ideal type model for a husband for me does not really exist because the ideal man does not exist. We all have flaws and being perfect is not obtainable. I look for qualities such as honesty, integrity and his belief in God to determine my ideal man."

U – "In my opinion, an ideal type husband is 1st and foremost, a man that loves God and puts him 1st in everything that he does. A man that loves and cares for his family under any circumstances one who listens, is kind-hearted, and willing to make sacrifices for his companion/family. An ideal husband would be a man who is hard-working, trustworthy, reliable, and one who strives for success in everything he does..."

X – "The ideal type of a husband is: Honest and has integrity, Hard-working, Intelligent and Educated, Attractive, Well maintained and clean, Budgets and invests money well, Loves sports, but not too much, open to the idea of not having his own children but helping less fortunate ones, Mature but likes to have fun, Respects the wife and her career, Has a good relationship with the family."

A1 – "From my point of view, an ideal husband is someone who is faithful, loyal, loving, attentive and good looking (sorry if there is no attraction, it's not gonna work), good with children, thoughtful, loves God, family oriented, good in bed, and puts me before himself."

B1 – "In my opinion, the ideal husband would be one who is honest, hardworking, attractive, confident but not cocky, funny, sweet, caring, and who loves the outdoors, supports his wife in all that she does, loves his children, and loves animals. I think that when it comes to choosing a partner for life it should be one that has all of the qualities that you love and one or two that you can learn to live with because that's what keeps it interesting."

C1 – "The Ideal husband for me is someone who not only respects me but also the people I am around. I also that there should be complete Trust and Love in the relationship. There should also be a love of God."

D1 – "My ideal type of husband is a MAN that puts God first, DOESN'T CHEAT, good with kids, loving, kind-hearted and most of all a good friend because without friendship you can never be a husband."

Figure 16.3 – Ideal type of partner

Ideal Type of Wife (male students answer this question):

Y – "My ideal type of a wife is someone that is first a God fearing woman that is saved. Someone that is submissive to her man, and puts her man first, over everyone else except all mighty God. Someone that is not into materialistic things."

Z – "From my perspective, an ideal type of wife would be attractive (because, honestly, it has to start at attraction), have a good sense of humor, be fun to be around, be well-educated and have strong convictions and morals, relaxed (not uptight), and be caring (and have the traits of a good future mother)."

V – "my ideal wife would be someone that has a strong faith in God, she would be open and honest, gets along with her family and my family, doesn't hate all my friends, has a good sense of humor and can put up with my goofy butt, down to earth, likes to travel and be active, cares about how she looks to a degree, and has some of the same interests that I do, whether it's in music, sports (football, hockey, NASCAR) or whatever."

Q – "From my point of view, an ideal type of wife is educated, intelligent, goal-oriented, independent, honest, funny, and outgoing. However, ideal types are usually dependent on current cultural values and may differ cross-culturally depending on the era and the society."

R – "My ideal wife would have the following characteristics; Sense of Humor, Nurturing, Loyalty, Affectionate, Educated, Ambitious, Family, and Service-oriented, Physically Healthy. And above all my best friend, lover and soul mate."

S – "My ideal type of a wife would be a woman who is compassionate and humble but someone who expects the same amount of respect she gives. She has a good sense of humor and better taste than I. She is a dreamer but believes actions speak louder than words. She is smart, loyal and believes that love conquers all."

E – "An ideal wife for me would be compassionate, loving, mindful, not attached to too many material possessions, and probably the most important of all, have a sense of humor."

B – "My idea of a perfect wife is one who does not only respect you as their mate, but is also your best friend, the person whom you confide everything and the person who loves you not for your good qualities, but cherishes you for your flaws Example: my grandparents prior to my grandfather's passing were married for 60 years and never had a single fight."

C – "The perfect or ideal wife would be a woman that has the body of Jessica Alba, the cooking skills of Rachael Ray, and can get ready (dress, makeup, and hair in 10 minutes or less, but still look awesome. Actually, I've already got the perfect wife who loves me for who I am, who is an excellent mother, who is hot, and who loves to cook! She is one of smartest people I know but has a terrible judgment (she married me) Nam so lucky for her flaw."

Figure 16.4 – Ideal type of husband meme

Based on the data of this small-scale informal survey, it can be roughly concluded that the ideal partner of the surveyed group of American college students includes the physical, spiritual, social, and ability levels - the PSSC (Physical, Spiritual, Social, Capable) four dimensions:

Physical: Healthy, Charming, Attractive, Strong, Affectionate

Spiritual: Faithful, Loving, Loyalty, Close Relation to God, Honest, Integrity

Social: Enjoy Helping Others, Nurturing, Romantic, Compassionate, Responsibility

Capable: Educated, Handy around the House, Able to Work on a Car, Smart and Learner

This small classroom survey is not intended as a representative sample but rather serves as a point of reference for readers interested in this topic. Nevertheless, its findings provide insight into one facet of American young college students' perspectives on marriage and love. The formation of these views is undeniably intertwined with the prevailing popular culture within American society.

In contrast to the contemporary and utilitarian tendencies often observed among young people in China, the attitudes of young Americans toward marriage appear relatively straightforward and conservative, significantly shaped by religious beliefs. This stands in stark contrast to the ever-evolving landscape of marital values in China, humorously captured in a limerick that satirizes the shifting norms over the decades: "Married to a soldier in the 1950s, a model in the 1960s, a cadre in the 1970s, a manager in the 1980s, and a foreigner in the 1990s." While this may be a broad generalization, it nevertheless reflects the impulsive mindset of Chinese youth, molded by changing social currents and their evolving perceptions of marriage and love, all while mirroring the broader shifts in societal and cultural dynamics.

Relevant Information for Reference

These observations might vary greatly depending on the specific cultural, socio-economic, and individual factors of the student populations in question.

Views on the Ideal Partner

Chinese students: In general, Chinese society traditionally emphasizes qualities like financial stability, responsibility, and family-oriented values. Chinese students, influenced by these cultural norms, may thus lean towards partners who can provide stability and are serious about their responsibilities. Traditional Chinese culture also values harmony, so the ability to get along with one's family may be another important quality.

American students: American culture tends to emphasize traits like emotional compatibility, shared interests, and personal attraction. American students often value independence, shared ambitions, mutual respect, and clear communication. The concept of falling in love is a dominant theme in the idea of an ideal partner in America, and there is often a focus on finding someone with shared hobbies, interests, or lifestyles.

Views on Marriage

Chinese students: Marriage traditionally has strong societal and familial pressure in China. Many students may feel that getting married is not just a personal decision but also involves their family's expectations. In recent years, however, urban Chinese youth have been showing signs of moving away from this traditional pressure, instead focusing more on personal satisfaction and career development before marriage.

American students: Views on marriage among American college students can vary widely. Some students might prioritize career development or personal growth before considering marriage, while others may view marriage as a key life goal. There's often a cultural emphasis on marrying for love and personal fulfillment.

It's important to note that these are general observations and there can be significant variation within each culture. Additionally, both cultures have been seeing shifts in these traditional views with modernization, globalization, and increased emphasis on individual choice and personal happiness.

Footnotes

Jiaming Sun

Jiaming Sun, Sociology Professor, Department of Sociology and Criminal Justice, Texas A&M University-Commerce, USA. Quoted from "Conceptual Generation Difference - Background of Transition Society (1991-1994)" by Sun Jiaming, Shanghai Social Sciences Publishing House, 1997.

Jessica Alba

Jessica Alba is an American film and television actor. In 1993, Jessica starred in her screen debut "Camp Crazy." In 2001, Jessica won the 58th Golden Globe Award for Best Drama Series Actress nominee.

Rachael Ray

Rachel Ray is an American television host, businesswoman, celebrity chef, and author. She has hosted Daily Talk and Lifestyle and three Food Network series.

CHAPTER 17

Virtual Courses Respond to the Covid-19 Pandemic in American Universities

D uring the spring break in early March 2020, the entire campus suddenly received a notice that due to the global pandemic, all courses after the spring break would be taught online. President Mark Rudin said in an email to all faculty and staff on March 14, 2020.

Figure 17.1 – Email from the University President to Faculty and Staff

March 14, 2020

Dear Lion Family:

It goes without saying that the current COVID-19 pandemic has disrupted our society in many different ways. It is also safe to say that it seems the only certainty is that each of us now faces a tremendous amount of uncertainty in our lives. One thing I can say for sure – our university is staying the course and will transition to fully online classes beginning Monday, March 16, 2020, until further notice.

From that moment, the university officially launched a fully online (100%) virtual class plan under the emergency mechanism to completely block the possibility of the raging virus spreading through person-to-person contact at the university.

Virtual does not mean unreal. In the Merriam-Webster English Dictionary, virtual is explained in many ways, including:

- Occurring or existing primarily online
- Not physically existing as such but made by software to appear to do so
- Carried out, accessed, or stored by means of a computer, especially over a network

Figure 17.2 – Online Learning Course

In simple terms, virtual courses, also known as online courses, are conducted over the Internet without consuming physical educational resources or energy. They closely emulate the features and functions of traditional in-class teaching. The concept of virtual learning is relatively recent, rooted in the advancements of electronic computer technology. The first web-based higher education courses emerged in the United States in 1995. The precursor to virtual courses can be traced back to Teleuniversity. The United Kingdom's Open University, established in the 1960s, stands as the world's pioneering successful distance teaching institution, founded on the belief that communication technology could extend high-quality degree education to individuals who might otherwise lack access to college. In the United States, distance learning in higher education was initiated to better serve farmers, ranchers, and skilled workers in certain states, ultimately leading to the development of a dual-mode educational approach, blending on-campus and distance learning.

Due to the rapid development of computers and the increasing expansion of local area networks, as well as the broader use of the Internet, great progress has been made in virtual libraries, virtual laboratories, virtual campuses, and virtual teaching. The basic teaching and evaluation techniques associated with virtual learning have unique advantages, which provide more possibilities for the continued generation and development of virtual courses. Take the University of Phoenix, which was founded in 1976, as an example. In 1978, it was recognized by the North Central Association of Colleges and Universities in the United States. Still, today, because of its online availability, it has 110 campuses and learning centers, which are distributed across more than 20 states in the U.S., Puerto Rico, and Canada. It has more than 100,000 students currently enrolled in degree plans, making it the largest private university in the United States. In 1989, the University of Phoenix launched the first computer-based teaching system, namely the online teaching plan, which gradually developed into the University of Phoenix's online campus (Virtual Campus or Virtual University). The Internet has become an important teaching base for universities. In 1995, John Tiffin and Lalita Rajasingham's book *Finding the Virtual Classroom: Education in the Information Society* (London and New York, Routledge) further promoted the development of virtual courses. Many colleges and universities across the United States currently offer such online programs partially or fully online. An estimated 4,500 such institutions have a total enrollment of at least millions.

Figure 17.3 – University of Phoenix logo

Texas A&M University has been offering partial online courses (hybrid/blended courses) in various majors and departments for several years, and in some cases, full degree online program courses. Students who want to earn a degree but need to maintain a flexible schedule can choose an online program to complete their degree. This is an invaluable ability for such students who wish to continue their education.

Online courses leverage computers and the internet to facilitate virtual interactions among instructors and students, as well as among students themselves. These courses offer a flexible alternative for students who cannot attend on-campus classes due to geographical distance or scheduling conflicts, allowing them to learn at their own pace and location. Consequently, enrolled students come from various geographical regions, including different states and even countries, in addition to local participants. Despite this diversity, the course objectives and content remain consistent with those of traditional classroom settings.

In online courses, students take on greater responsibility for their learning outcomes, with instructors adopting the roles of facilitators and mentors rather than traditional lecturers. Instead of in-person lectures, professors disseminate information through online course materials and internet-accessible learning activities. The presentation of course material may vary depending on the instructor's preferences and design choices. Additionally, professors actively engage with students by seeking feedback on the class as students complete weekly assignments, fostering a collaborative and interactive learning environment.

For example, here are the midterm exam score statistics displayed on the hybrid courses webpage.

Figure 17.4 – Interactive Learning Environment

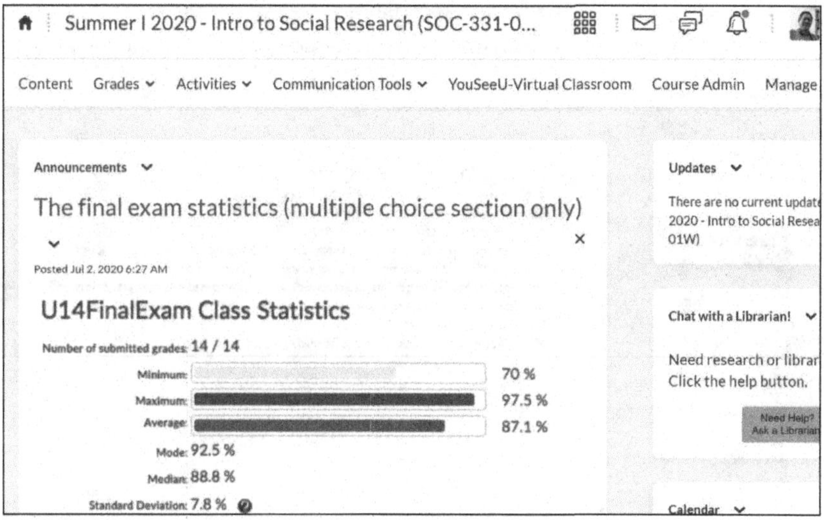

This is an introductory page to the weekly synopsis of an online course, including the main course content for the week, student assignments, requirements, the due dates, grading criteria, and more. Among them are course explanations (video or audio recording), quizzes, weekly feedback, etc.

Figure 17.5 – Weekly Online Course Communication

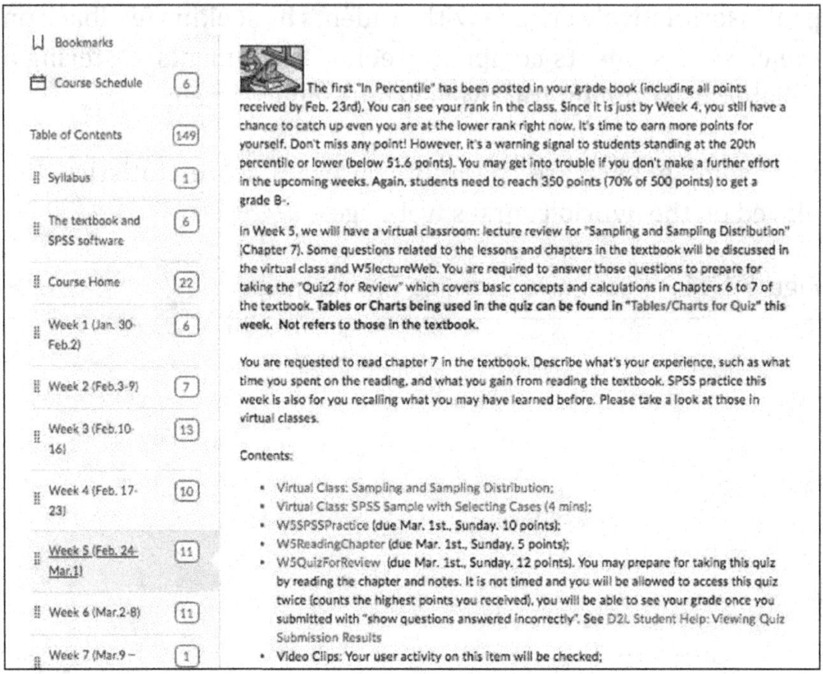
Bookmarks
Course Schedule 6
Table of Contents 149
Syllabus 1
The textbook and SPSS software 6
Course Home 22
Week 1 (Jan. 30-Feb.2) 6
Week 2 (Feb.3-9) 7
Week 3 (Feb.10-16) 13
Week 4 (Feb. 17-23) 10
Week 5 (Feb. 24-Mar.1) 11
Week 6 (Mar.2-8) 11
Week 7 (Mar.9 – 1
The first "In Percentile" has been posted in your grade book (including all points received by Feb. 23rd). You can see your rank in the class. Since it is just by Week 4, you still have a chance to catch up even you are at the lower rank right now. It's time to earn more points for yourself. Don't miss any point! However, it's a warning signal to students standing at the 20th percentile or lower (below 51.6 points). You may get into trouble if you don't make a further effort in the upcoming weeks. Again, students need to reach 350 points (70% of 500 points) to get a grade B-.
In Week 5, we will have a virtual classroom: lecture review for "Sampling and Sampling Distribution" (Chapter 7). Some questions related to the lessons and chapters in the textbook will be discussed in the virtual class and W5lectureWeb. You are required to answer those questions to prepare for taking the "Quiz2 for Review" which covers basic concepts and calculations in Chapters 6 to 7 of the textbook. Tables or Charts being used in the quiz can be found in "Tables/Charts for Quiz" this week. Not refers to those in the textbook.
You are requested to read chapter 7 in the textbook. Describe what's your experience, such as what time you spent on the reading, and what you gain from reading the textbook. SPSS practice this week is also for you recalling what you may have learned before. Please take a look at those in virtual classes.
Contents:
Virtual Class: Sampling and Sampling Distribution;
Virtual Class: SPSS Sample with Selecting Cases (4 mins);
W5SPSSPractice (due Mar. 1st., Sunday. 10 points);
W5ReadingChapter (due Mar. 1st., Sunday. 5 points);
W5QuizForReview (due Mar. 1st., Sunday. 12 points). You may prepare for taking this quiz by reading the chapter and notes. It is not timed and you will be allowed to access this quiz twice (counts the highest points you received), you will be able to see your grade once you submitted with "show questions answered incorrectly". See D2L Student Help: Viewing Quiz Submission Results
Video Clips: Your user activity on this item will be checked;

Figure 17.6 – Weekly Online Course Assignments

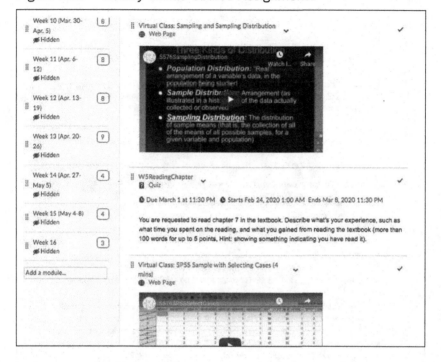

Figure 17.7 – Weekly Online Course Assignment and Quiz

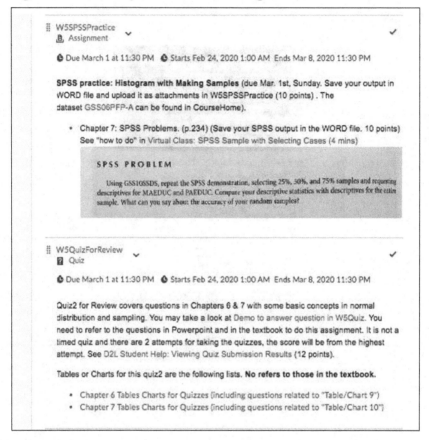

Sometimes, online classes also offer virtual lectures or meetings in synchronized ways that require students to access the internet at a specified time, and students and the instructors can interact online through real-time conversations or video conferences. When students are online, they will automatically sign in, and they can communicate and discuss topics with each other through the platform, such as VoiceThread or Zoom via D2L (Design to Learn). On these platforms, students can also raise their hands to speak or ask questions via video. Such online classroom meetings allow access either by way of a computer, tablet, or mobile phone.

Figure 17.8 – Online Course Lectures and Meetings

As mentioned above, the online classroom provides mobile phone access for students who are unable to access a computer at a specific time but who still wish to participate in real-time interaction. The screenshot below is the mobile page of an online classroom. Its frame and content are basically the same as those displayed on the computer but in a slightly altered format.

Figure 17.9 – Online Classroom as Mobile Phone Page

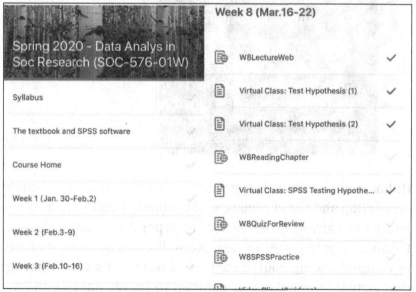

You can watch course videos, participate in course discussions, take quizzes, and view your grade book on your mobile phone, just as you can on a computer or tablet. The section below shows a course video that students can click on to view.

Figure 17.10 – Course Video on Mobile Phone

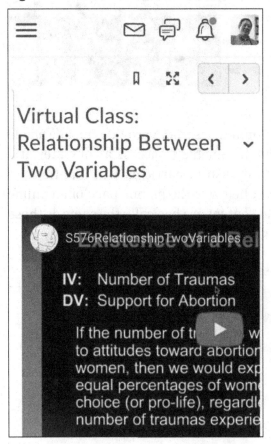

Online courses offer numerous advantages, including flexible scheduling and the elimination of commute time. They also enhance the learning experience by incorporating multimedia materials such as hypertext, video, and audio, which can aid students in comprehending course content. However, it's worth noting that virtual interactions, as opposed to traditional face-to-face methods, may not be suitable for all students. Some individuals thrive in classroom settings with in-person interactions, while others may struggle with time management outside of a structured classroom environment.

Research has demonstrated that online students can achieve the same level of learning as their traditional in-class counterparts. In fact, many students find online instruction more effective because it promotes active learning rather than passive reception of information. It's important to mention that online courses may require specific software downloads and adherence to computer system requirements, as well as the maintenance of a reliable internet connection. Depending on the course, professors may impose additional technical and software prerequisites, such as SPSS (IBM's Statistical Package for the Social Sciences), for students taking research methods and statistics courses. As network technology continues to advance, the future of online courses holds promise for even faster and more robust development.

Following a period of experience in online course instruction, it became evident that students exhibit a preference for asynchronous teaching and discussion formats over synchronous alternatives. Put simply, students lean toward participating in online lectures or discussions at their convenience, which fosters a sense of freedom and willingness to engage. Conversely, synchronous class schedules frequently encounter issues such as significant student absences or lateness, likely due to individual timetable conflicts. This attendance inconsistency can notably compromise the overall teaching quality. In light of these challenges, the utilization of the VoiceThread platform emerges as a viable solution to address this dilemma.

Indeed, VoiceThread's asynchronous online discussion and teaching methods align well with the individual needs of American college students.

VoiceThread serves as a versatile asynchronous online discussion and teaching tool, enabling users to generate presentations and foster discussions via voice, video, and text. While it possesses the potential to enhance student engagement in online learning settings, the extent to which it caters to the specific needs of American college students hinges on a variety of factors:

1. Flexibility: Asynchronous discussions through VoiceThread can offer flexibility to students who may have other commitments or prefer to engage with course materials at their own pace. This flexibility can better accommodate the individual schedules and learning styles of American college students.

2. Accessibility: VoiceThread supports various multimedia formats, making it accessible to students with different learning preferences and needs. It allows for the integration of visuals, audio, and video, which can enhance engagement and understanding for students with diverse learning styles.

3. Collaboration: VoiceThread facilitates collaborative learning by enabling students to interact with one another and the instructor asynchronously. Students can provide feedback, ask questions, and engage in discussions at a time that is convenient to them. This collaborative aspect can foster critical thinking, communication skills, and a sense of community among online college students.

4. Diverse Perspectives: VoiceThread can promote the sharing of diverse perspectives among college students. It allows students to contribute their thoughts and ideas through various media, enabling a richer and more inclusive learning experience. This can be particularly beneficial for students who may be hesitant to participate in traditional face-to-face discussions.

It's essential to recognize that students' individual requirements and preferences can vary significantly. While some students thrive in asynchronous learning environments, others may favor real-time interactions and immediate feedback. Moreover, the effectiveness of tools like VoiceThread, or any teaching method for that matter, is contingent on factors such as the course content, the instructor's facilitation skills, and the overarching learning objectives.

Educators should embrace a diverse range of instructional methods and technologies to cater to the unique needs of their students. Combining both synchronous and asynchronous approaches, coupled with ongoing assessment and feedback mechanisms, can provide a comprehensive and adaptable learning experience for a diverse student body.

While online teaching and learning have had a longstanding presence in the United States, the unforeseen impact of the COVID-19 pandemic in recent years has accelerated their development significantly. Online teaching platforms and advanced technological teaching tools have gained prominence and become more readily accessible. On the one hand, these advancements offer professors a wider array of online teaching methods and tools, enhancing the online learning experience for students. However, it's crucial to acknowledge that disparities in American society, stemming from the digital divide and disparities in internet access, result in varying attitudes and performance in online learning among students. Consequently, the outcomes and grades of online learning differ. With ongoing societal development and technological progress, this situation is likely to evolve over time.

Relevant Information for Reference

When comparing the respective strengths and weaknesses of online teaching in China and the United States, it's important to consider various factors, including infrastructure, resources, cultural differences, and educational systems. Here are some general points to consider:

Online Teaching in China

<u>Strengths</u>:

1. Technological Infrastructure: China has made significant investments in its digital infrastructure, including widespread internet access and advanced technology, facilitating online teaching.
2. Large Market and Demand: China has a massive population, which translates to a large market for online education platforms and courses. There is a high demand for online teaching in various subjects.
3. E-learning Platforms: China has a thriving online education ecosystem with well-established platforms that offer diverse courses and resources, catering to different learning needs.
4. Integration of Technology: Chinese online teaching often integrates advanced technologies such as artificial intelligence (AI), virtual reality (VR), and augmented reality (AR) to enhance the learning experience.

<u>Weaknesses</u>:

1. Internet Restrictions: China has strict internet censorship policies, known as the Great Firewall, which can limit access to certain websites and content, including some educational resources and platforms.
2. Educational Equality: There may be disparities in access to online education resources, particularly in rural areas or among disadvantaged populations, leading to unequal educational opportunities.

3. Heavy Workload: Online teaching in China can sometimes lead to a heavier workload for teachers, as they may need to manage large class sizes and handle administrative tasks associated with online platforms.

4. Lack of Personal Interaction: Online teaching can reduce the level of personal interaction and face-to-face communication between students and teachers, potentially impacting engagement and motivation.

Online Teaching in the United States

Strengths:

1. Technological Infrastructure: The United States generally has robust internet infrastructure, which allows for smooth online teaching experiences and supports the use of various digital tools.

2. Flexibility and Accessibility: Online teaching offers flexibility, allowing students to access educational content from anywhere at any time. It can be particularly beneficial for students with physical disabilities, full-time jobs, or those in remote areas.

3. Innovation and Resources: The U.S. has a strong emphasis on educational technology and innovation, with a wide range of resources, including learning management systems, online libraries, and educational apps.

4. Teacher Training and Professional Development: Many U.S. educational institutions provide training and support for teachers transitioning to online teaching, ensuring they are equipped with the necessary skills and strategies.

Weaknesses:

1. Digital Divide: Despite significant progress, there is still a digital divide in the United States, with some students lacking access to reliable internet connections or appropriate devices, thus hindering their participation in online learning.
2. Educational Equity: Socioeconomic disparities can impact access to online education resources, with disadvantaged students facing challenges in terms of internet access, technology availability, and support systems.
3. Student Engagement: Online teaching requires proactive efforts to keep students engaged, as there can be distractions and a lack of immediate feedback or personal interaction.
4. Teacher-Student Relationship: Building and maintaining strong teacher-student relationships can be more challenging in online settings, as face-to-face interactions and nonverbal cues may be limited.

It's worth noting that the strengths and weaknesses listed above are general observations and may vary across different regions and educational institutions within both China and the United States.

CHAPTER 18

A Comparison between China and America in Graduate Research Proposal Writing

A graduate research proposal, as the name implies, serves as a meticulously designed research plan intended for future execution. It stands as a testament to the comprehensive competence of graduate students within their respective professional domains, encompassing aspects such as theoretical proficiency, conceptual acumen, literature review expertise, and adeptness in research methodologies, among others. In essence, a well-crafted research proposal should elucidate three fundamental dimensions: the "WHAT," "WHY," and "HOW" of the proposed research endeavor. This entails a clear articulation of what will be studied, an elucidation of the rationale behind the chosen research topic (including a justification for its necessity), and a detailed exposition of the research methodology to be employed. It is incumbent upon students to meticulously expound upon these three facets within their research proposals.

Drawing from my personal involvement in numerous proposal presentations conducted by master's students and doctoral candidates in American universities, coupled with extensive experience in similar presentations among graduate students in China, I have identified certain valuable insights that I would like to share with you.

Figure 18.1 – Graduate Student in China

First, let's consider the choice of research topics in graduate proposals. In China, graduate students often gravitate towards expansive and attention-grabbing subjects. Examples of such topics include titles like "On Occupational Acquisition from the Perspective of Interpersonal Network," "Social Class and Diet Structure," and "Community Social Capital and Educational Acquisition." While these topics may capture broad themes, they sometimes run the risk of superficial treatment due to their sheer magnitude. In contrast, American student presentations often reflect a more pragmatic approach with deeper objectives, as seen in topics like "The Effect of After-School Cartoons on Childhood Development," "Parental Involvement in Education and Student Academic Success," and "Geographic Influence on Women's Age at Time of First Marriage." It's evident that the choice of research topic and its broad or narrow scope directly influences the research design.

Secondly, let's delve into the structure of research proposals. A well-structured proposal typically comprises several standard sections: an introduction, hypothesis, literature review, methods, expected results, and, ideally, a section addressing the research limitations.

Graduate students in China typically possess a strong foundation in theory, commencing their studies by delving into both classical and contemporary theoretical frameworks. This emphasis on theory provides a robust theoretical underpinning. However, in some cases, these proposals tend to overly rely on theory while neglecting the essential literature review component. An excessive focus on classical theories, without consulting current research literature, can result in a disconnect from real-world applicability.

Figure 18.2 – Graduate Student Presentation

While the theoretical component of a proposal holds significance, it gains depth and relevance when seamlessly integrated with the literature review. The literature review serves the purpose of consolidating existing research findings within the field and pinpointing avenues for innovation within one's own research direction. Therefore, it stands as a pivotal element within the proposal.

Conducting a comprehensive literature review equips graduate students with insights into the facets of the field that have been explored, the evolution of existing theories, established conclusions, and areas ripe for further investigation. Regrettably, in some research proposals authored by Chinese graduate students, there's a tendency to overly prioritize the introduction of theoretical frameworks. This can create an impression that these theories lack a logical connection to the forthcoming research, potentially leaving readers to accept these theories as factual without substantial supporting evidence. To foster credibility, theories must find their place within the context of the literature review. In practical terms, American professors often encourage students to embark on a literature review after elucidating their intended research direction. This approach allows theories to be introduced and substantiated within the broader scholarly landscape.

A notable aspect of the research proposals by Chinese graduate students is the limited emphasis placed on the research hypothesis (assumptions) section. Typically, following the conventional structure of research proposals, research hypotheses are positioned at the outset, allowing readers to immediately grasp the researcher's intent and emphasizing the research's significance. In essence, the research hypotheses should be introduced after addressing the "WHAT" and "WHY" of the study.

Figure 18.3 – Multiple graduate students' research proposal presentation

However, in the case of research proposals crafted by Chinese graduate students, these research hypotheses are often relegated to the closing section, appearing somewhat redundant and disconnected. This practice hinders the logical coherence of the proposals. It's imperative to recognize that research hypotheses serve as guiding principles, steering the research's trajectory rather than mere ornamental additions. The pitfall of reinventing the wheel should be vigilantly avoided during the research design phase. Revisiting well-established common-sense issues or conclusions that have been extensively validated by previous studies as research hypotheses can be cumbersome and unnecessary.

For instance, hypotheses like "educational conditions in rural areas are inferior to those in urban areas, thereby constraining students' growth potential" require no research endeavor to reach self-evident conclusions. Additionally, the formulation of hypotheses should steer clear of tautology, where an assumption appears valid but reiterates the same idea. For instance, statements like "Those who oppose gun control laws do so due to a negative attitude toward gun control regulations" or "Members of the Ku Klux Klan harbor antipathy toward Black individuals because of their strong prejudice against them" represent tauto-logical constructs. Such hypotheses invariably yield affirmative conclusions, as they merely rephrase the same concept using different wording. In this regard, Chinese students would benefit from enhanced training to refine their skills in hypothesis development within the research domain.

The pivotal segment of a research proposal is undeniably the research methodology, akin to an architect meticulously crafting a blueprint for a building. Every facet of the structure-to-be must be meticulously outlined, encompassing site selection, materials, architectural specifications, utilities such as water, electricity, and heating systems, and more. This comprehensive design provides the engineering team with a clear roadmap to construct the building. Therefore, the more meticulous and detailed this section, the more accessible it becomes for anyone seeking to follow the research journey.

In American universities, when graduate students undertake the task of composing research proposals, the research methodology section typically constitutes 20%-30% of the entire document. However, my experience with university review processes in China reveals a stark contrast, with the research methodology section often accounting for a mere 10% of the total paper or even less, often comprising only a brief paragraph of text. This discrepancy underscores the differing degrees of emphasis placed on the description of research methods by instructors in these contexts.

In essence, the research methodology should provide a comprehensive elucidation of the groundwork to be executed and outline the means and methodologies for data and information acquisition. For instance, in the context of conducting research on sensitive topics like sexuality, it is essential to clarify the research location, methods for identifying and engaging participants, and the specific inquiries to be posed. In the case of quantitative research, a well-detailed sampling plan should be provided, along with a delineation of the sample frame, a distinction between random and non-random sampling approaches, an explanation of the questionnaire distribution process, a draft questionnaire, and a timeline detailing when interviews and surveys will be administered, among other considerations.

Furthermore, there are valuable points of comparison and reference regarding the organization and coordination of the review process for graduate research proposals and presentations. For instance, it is a standard practice for all research proposals to be distributed to the mailboxes of participating professors (reviewers) several days prior to the review meeting or presentation. This ensures that reviewers have ample time to peruse the proposals in advance, allowing them to formulate pertinent questions. This practice becomes even more crucial when multiple graduate students' research proposals are reviewed simultaneously. Simultaneously, adhering to the submission deadline for research proposals to the evaluator's mailbox prevents last-minute revisions by students just before the review meeting.

Figure 18.4 – A review meeting for graduate students' research proposals

The substantial disparities observed in the selection of research topics among graduate students from Chinese and American universities may be attributed to the varying training mechanisms in place and the contrasting thinking patterns rooted in Eastern and Western cultures. In Chinese universities, graduate student training often aligns closely with their supervisor's research project. When a supervisor secures a research project, the graduate students under their tutelage may be required to participate in that project. Consequently, graduate students' research proposal topics often revolve around themes designated by their supervisor, leaving them with limited autonomy in topic selection. This curtails their enthusiasm for the chosen research topic, ultimately impacting the overall design of their research proposals, particularly the formulation of research hypotheses.

Furthermore, the cognitive tendencies inherent to Eastern and Western cultures exert a notable influence on the selection of research topics and the elaboration of hypotheses. Eastern cultures tend to approach matters from a broad and macro perspective before delving into specific details. In contrast, Western culture often commences with micro-level specifics and subsequently expands to encompass the broader and macro aspects. This inclination manifests in language expression as well, exemplified by the contrast in addressing envelopes. In China, addresses on envelopes follow a sequence from the general to the specific, beginning with the country, followed by the city, street name, and concluding with the recipient's name. Conversely, Western addressing starts with the specific recipient, followed by the street, city, and ultimately the country. This divergence underscores how thinking patterns give rise to distinctions in language and culture, or vice versa, reflecting the influence of cultural traits.

In summary, graduate education in Chinese universities has made significant strides compared to previous years, and the standardization of research proposals is gradually taking shape. Acknowledging the existing issues and shortcomings provides the pathway to progress and success in the field.

Relevant Information for Reference

Comparison of similarities and differences between China and the United States in the graduate enrollment process, training mechanism, examination subjects, and degree settings.

Graduate Enrollment Process

China and the United States have an application-based system, but the specific procedures differ. In China, students typically need to participate in a national entrance examination called the National Postgraduate Entrance Examination (NPEE) or university-specific exams for selection. In the United States, students are usually required to submit application materials, including a personal statement, recommendation letters, transcripts, and standardized test scores (such as GRE, GMAT, etc.), and may also need to attend interviews.

Training Mechanism

There are significant differences in the training mechanism between China and the United States. In China, graduate students often join a research group led by an advisor, closely collaborate with the advisor, and work on research projects assigned by the advisor. In the United States, there is a greater emphasis on independence and autonomy. Students usually have more freedom to choose their research direction and engage in discussions with their advisors to explore research questions.

Examination Subjects

The graduate entrance examination in China typically includes two parts: a comprehensive general knowledge test and a subject-specific test. The comprehensive general knowledge test covers subjects like political theory, foreign language, and mathematics, while the subject-specific test assesses the applicant's knowledge in their chosen field of study. In the United States, the graduate entrance exams are more flexible and vary depending on the school and program. Generally, they include standardized tests (such as GRE, GMAT, etc.) and academic proficiency tests (such as TOEFL, IELTS, etc.).

Degree Settings

China usually offers two main graduate degrees: Master's and Ph.D., with longer program durations. The United States has a wider range of degree options, including Master's, Ph.D., and professional degrees such as MBA, MFA, etc., with relatively shorter program durations.

It's important to note that the specific details of graduate education in China and the United States can vary across institutions and programs. The descriptions provided above are general comparisons.

CHAPTER 19

President of an American Public State University

D r. Dan Jones serves as the president of a prominent, traditional American southern state university boasting several distinctive characteristics. With a robust student body of 13,000, encompassing doctoral, master's, and undergraduate students, the university earns its "large" label. Its comprehensiveness shines through its diverse array of academic departments, encompassing literature, history, philosophy, mathematics, physics, and chemistry. This venerable institution also has a storied history dating back to its establishment in 1889, boasting 134 years of educational excellence as of 2023.

Figure 19.1 – Dr. Dan Jones, University President

Presidential Traditions

One week prior to the commencement of each spring and fall semester, the university hosts a campus-wide assembly for faculty
and staff. In this important gathering, President Jones presides
and extends invitations to key figures, including the provost, the
vice president overseeing student affairs, and the vice president
managing the budget and infrastructure. Together, they take the
stage to introduce the upcoming semester to both faculty and
staff members. The assembly provides a comprehensive overview of the university's overarching work plan, primary objectives, budget details, infrastructure developments, freshman
enrollment statistics, and a warm welcome to the institution's
new faculty and staff.

Figure 19.2 – Annual Presidential Welcome

On the inaugural day of admission for incoming freshmen in both
the spring and fall semesters, a heartwarming tradition unfolds

just before the students assemble at the auditorium for their new semester's opening ceremony. President Dan Jones orchestrates a touching gesture: he calls upon every faculty member to form a corridor along the pathway leading to the auditorium, with each of them proudly holding a small flag. This remarkable display is coupled with a spirited band performance, creating a welcoming atmosphere that immediately envelops the newcomers. It's a powerful tradition that fosters a profound sense of connection and camaraderie between faculty and students. President Jones, accompanied by his wife, personally joins in to extend their warm greetings to the incoming students, adding a personal touch to this cherished tradition.

Figure 19.3 – New Student Welcome

Twice a year, in both the spring and fall, our university witnesses the culmination of student achievements as they embark on their post-graduate journeys. Given the substantial number of graduates, these commencement ceremonies are thoughtfully organized in multiple segments. The primary aim is to afford each graduate a precious moment of personal connection with the university's president.

In a heartfelt gesture, President Jones takes it upon himself to individually bestow degree certificates upon every graduate and commemorate the occasion with a photograph. It's worth noting that in the Chinese context, college graduation ceremonies typically involve a symbolic presentation of diplomas to student representatives on stage rather than directly to each graduate. This grand tradition of ours, where each student receives their certificate and a personal photograph with the president, is an experience that imprints itself deeply upon the lives of our graduates. It's a testament to the significance we place on celebrating the achievements of our students as they take their next steps into the world beyond academia.

Figure 19.4 – President Awards Diplomas at Graduation Ceremony

At the conclusion of each fall semester, as the festive Christmas season ushers in a spirit of celebration, our university's president hosts an eagerly anticipated event known as the "President's Holiday Reception." This special gathering is marked by a

delightful array of sumptuous buffets, exhilarating raffles, and a distinguished ceremony honoring and rewarding our esteemed faculty and staff. It's an occasion that resonates with everyone, including myself, as I've had the privilege of winning on two occasions.

The event unfolds with the president and his wife gracing the entrance of the venue, warmly welcoming every attending faculty member with handshakes and distributing door prize tickets. The President's Holiday Reception typically unfolds in three distinct segments. Initially, attendees enjoy a delectable meal from the buffet, fostering connections and engaging in conversations. Following this, various departments recognize the outstanding achievements of their staff members from the previous year, with the president presenting certificates and capturing group photographs to commemorate the moment.

The climax of the evening revolves around a thrilling lottery drawing. Here, the president's wife (and occasionally the president's daughter) draws a random ticket from a lottery box, passing it to the president himself, who presides over the announcement of the winning ticket. The suspense mounts as the number is matched, and the lucky recipient ascends the stage to claim their prize. These coveted prizes encompass a diverse range, from a 48-inch color TV, tablets, and frozen turkeys to valuable gift cards. Notably, the funding for this extravagant gathering is generously provided by the president's special fund, which may include contributions from gifts received by the president throughout the years from various events and well-wishers. The President's Holiday Reception thus stands as a testament to our institution's commitment to fostering a sense of community and recognition among its dedicated faculty and staff.

Figure 19.5 – President's Holiday Reception

Selecting a President

Dr. Dan Jones assumed the role of university president following a rigorous selection process overseen by a dedicated committee. In 2008, as the ten-year tenure of Senior President Keith D. McFarland drew to a close and retirement loomed, our institution established a selection committee. This committee embarked on a nationwide search to identify promising candidates. They meticulously reviewed numerous applications, ultimately inviting the top three contenders to our campus for comprehensive interviews. I had the privilege of participating in this pivotal interview process.

The interviews served as a platform for candidates to expound on their philosophies of university management, share personal experiences, and articulate their vision for governance. During these sessions, faculty members engaged the candidates with questions, seeking insights into their perspectives. I, for instance, queried a candidate about the "globalization of education" and found their response quite satisfactory, as they demonstrated a genuine interest in global engagement.

Following the interviews, participating faculty members completed feedback questionnaires, which were then submitted to the selection committee. Subsequently, the selection committee meticulously assessed all the materials at their disposal. The culmination of this process involved a decisive vote by the university system's board of regents. Upon receiving the board's appointment, the selected candidate assumed the role of university president, embodying the highest authority within the institution and serving as its chief executive officer. This meticulous and thorough selection process led to Dr. Dan Jones's appointment as our university president in 2008, a testament to his qualifications and vision for our institution's future.

President Dan Jones brings a wealth of experience in university administration to his role. His journey in academic leadership began in 1985 and continued until 2002, during which time he held pivotal positions such as Dean of a University College, Interim Dean for Student Affairs, Associate Dean of the Faculty of Humanities and Social Sciences, and Acting Chair of the English Department at a university in the Southern United States. Since then, he has continued to excel in academic leadership, serving as a University Provost at various institutions and also as Vice Chancellor for Academic Affairs before his election as president of our university in 2008. Notably, his academic expertise lies in the field of English, and he continues to contribute to academia as an English professor.

In terms of compensation, when President Jones initially assumed office, the standard annual salary for the university president was approximately $260,000. However, as our university has expanded and student enrollment has increased, his annual salary was adjusted to $320,000 in 2017. In accordance with university tradition, the president resides in the university-provided President's House, situated in a tranquil neighborhood just a brief drive from the campus. This residence boasts a vast lawn area, complete with barbeque facilities and ample space for outdoor activities, capable of accommodating hundreds of individuals. Additionally, the driveway can comfortably host dozens of cars simultaneously. President Jones often utilizes this splendid area for university-related outdoor gatherings and events. I have fond memories of attending two such events at the President's House, one being a meeting of newly tenured faculty members and the other organized by the Chinese Student Union, which took place on the expansive lawn and offered Chinese students a unique opportunity to visit the president's residence.

Dr. Dan Jones was a president known for his approachability and disciplined leadership. I vividly recall a particular incident after one spring commencement ceremony. As lunchtime approached, professors dispersed to nearby campus restaurants or formed small groups of three to five. What struck me as extraordinary was the sight of President Jones, who had just hours earlier presided over the ceremony on the stage, standing alone in line at a restaurant. I couldn't help but observe that when he placed his carry-out order, there was no entourage accompanying him. This contrasted starkly with the expectations in China, where it's customary for the president's office to arrange a working lunch or some form of a roundtable gathering after a campus assembly. However, here in the United States, such moments are considered routine, and it prompted me to wonder if a similar scenario could ever unfold on a Chinese university campus. The reality is that it would be entirely implausible. Admittedly, it might appear somewhat modest in the treatment of a university president. Yet, it's crucial to acknowledge that American colleges and universities strictly adhere to stringent regulations governing fund usage, ensuring that no school funds are allocated for such meals.

In addition to his down-to-earth demeanor, President Dan Jones maintained a presence on Facebook, much like any other professor. He frequently shared snapshots of his enjoyable holiday activities and family reunions on this platform. These posts underscored his multifaceted personality and revealed his sense of humor, further endearing him to the university community.

Figure 19.6 – Image Screenshot from his Facebook profile

18 Likes

↪ Share

Dan Jones with Jalinna James Jones at ◉ ⌄
Cooper Lake State Park - Texas Parks and

Whenever our paths crossed on campus, President Jones would warmly address me by name, gracing me with a genuine smile. In that particular year, I had the privilege of publishing a new book titled *Global Connectivity and Local Transformation*. Upon its inclusion in the university's newsletter, President Jones personally extended his congratulations by sending a thoughtful greeting card to my mailbox, acknowledging my academic achievements.

An annual tradition that never failed to brighten my birthday involved receiving a customary greeting card from him, which appeared without fail in the department office mailbox (a tradition extended to every tenured professor). During those years, I had the distinct honor of being recognized with both teaching achievement and scientific research awards. On both occasions, President Jones personally presented the medals and, in a heartwarming gesture, took photographs with each recipient. These actions beautifully exemplified the president's profound respect for every professor, fostering a sense of appreciation and camaraderie within the university community.

Figure 19.7 – Annual Greeting Card

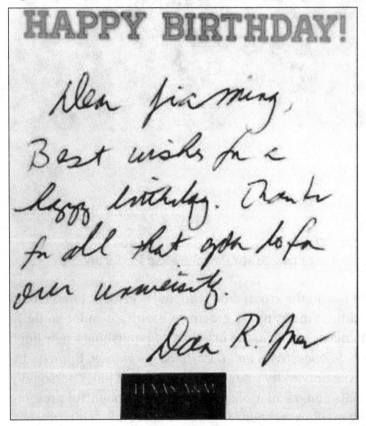

Figure 19.8 – Teaching Achievement and Scientific Research Award Presented by President

In the United States, the president's office best reflects the status and dignity of the top administrator and is also a symbol of the university's authority. The president's office consists of many suites; the most utilized entrance is the office of the president's daily affairs director. However, there are also offices of the heads of some functional departments on the side, and his own office is the innermost location and is both spacious and elegant.

Figure 19.9 – The President's Office (from an online source)

Across an aisle, there is a president's meeting room that can accommodate 20-30 people, and on the wall on one side of the conference room are standard photos of all presidents from previous
years, including the current president and his wife. This display
of portraits is to show respect to past and current leaders and
thank them for their contributions to the development of the
university. Usually, the president's conference room is also used
as a meeting place for the Faculty Senate. As a re-elected faculty
senator (the second round, for three years each), I come here
every month for meetings.

Figure 19.10 – Historical Photo Display

Figure 19.11 – University Presidents

Figure 19.12 – Faculty Senator Meeting in the President's Conference Room

I remember that when the previous president, Dr. Keith McFarlane, retired and the new president, Dan Jones, held a grand commemorative event and presented him with gifts. The president invited all faculty members to participate and provided a sumptuous dinner. A few years later, on March 22, 2013, the new science building was completed, and the previous president's name was officially given to it to honor him: the Keith D. McFarland Science Building. This was to commemorate and recognize the achievements of President McFarland in the expansion of campus facilities and the growth of academic programs during his leadership. This is the highest lifetime honor given to Dr. Keith MacFarlane, the previous president.

Figure 19.13 – Naming Ceremony Invitation

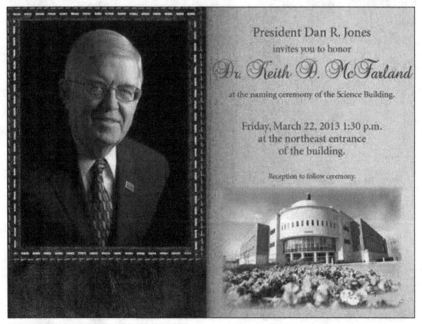

President Dan R. Jones
invites you to honor

Dr. Keith D. McFarland

at the naming ceremony of the Science Building.

Friday, March 22, 2013 1:30 p.m.
at the northeast entrance
of the building.

Reception to follow ceremony.

Figure 19.14 – Keith D. McFarland Science Building

Presidential Standards

In the United States, university presidents are selected and held accountable by the university board of directors or board of regents. Consequently, the president is vested with the authority to oversee and manage all university affairs, guided by rights and obligations conferred by the board of directors. Essentially, the president serves as the campus's primary executive, akin to the role of the president of the United States for the country. In contrast to some Chinese universities, where an additional entity like the party committee may impose constraints on the president's authority, American university presidents typically operate without such limitations.

The university president also serves as a symbolic figurehead for the institution. Many decisions do not necessitate direct presidential involvement. Various administrative departments and colleges autonomously exercise their powers within their defined scope of authority. They are not obligated to seek presidential consent or approval for their actions but rather adhere to established regulations in making and implementing decisions. When required, the president can formally delegate specific rights and responsibilities to individuals, specifying the conditions under which these entrusted powers should be exercised. Vice presidents may be appointed or added as needed, with their roles and responsibilities clearly defined. Such appointments typically receive approval from the Board of Directors based on the president's recommendation. Vice presidents report to and work under the president's guidance.

Additionally, deans of university colleges are generally appointed by the president, while department heads are typically chosen by the respective college deans. Upon assuming office, President Dan Jones made notable changes, including replacing two vice presidents, adding a new vice president, and adjusting the leadership of various colleges within the university. These strategic decisions are made to align the university with the evolving needs and goals of the institution and its community.

The American university system operates within a framework of comprehensive rules and regulations, with precise definitions and continuous updates. The university administration adheres rigorously to these regulations, ensuring their strict enforcement. Consequently, faculty members receive ongoing training that outlines expected behaviors throughout the year. These training sessions are predominantly conducted online, and successful completion entails passing an assessment to obtain an online certificate of completion. Similar regulations apply to department heads and other departmental leaders, including conflict-of-interest guidelines.

For instance, the process of faculty promotion and tenure is meticulously governed. Decisions are made by a provisional election committee comprising representatives from various departments and colleges. Department chairs and deans refrain from voting directly but contribute by crafting recommendation letters based on the committee's decisions. In cases of disagreement, known as a "one-vote veto," detailed reasons are provided, and the candidates are officially notified in writing. If unsatisfied with the outcome, candidates have the right to appeal. This well-established procedure has become routine, minimizing controversies.

In the decision-making process of U.S. university presidents, input is first solicited from various functional departments, followed by extensive discussions within the Dean's Council and Faculty Senate. These deliberations lead to informed decisions that are thoroughly evaluated before the execution of implementation plans is announced. These announcements are typically disseminated via email from the president's office, bypassing the need for intermediaries within colleges and departments. Many of these emails pertain to developing, revising, and disseminating pertinent regulations. These regulations span a broad spectrum, encompassing matters such as faculty and staff benefits, promotions, and overtime allowances. Below, you will find excerpts from two emails that we received.

Figure 19.15 – Amendment notice of the regulations on overtime (code 31.01.09)

University Community,

Revisions to System Regulation *31.01.09. Overtime*, were approved by the Chancellor, effective December 3, 2015. Below is a brief summary of the revisions.

- This regulation was updated into the current regulation template and various sections were updated as needed to adhere to current state and federal laws governing eligibility and compensation for overtime worked.

- Minor editorial revisions were made to provide consistency and clarity, and other changes were made to conform to system style guidelines.

Please distribute the revised system regulation among your staff as you deem appropriate.

Figure 19.16 – Notice of amendments to the regulations on public information (code 61.01.02) and record-keeping (code 61.99.01)

University Community,

Minor revisions to System Regulations *61.01.02, Public Information*, and *61.99.01, Retention of State Records*, were approved by the Chancellor, effective October 14 and 19, 2015, respectively. Below is a brief summary of the revisions.

- These regulations were due for their five-year certifications and no substantive changes were needed.

- In keeping with system style guidelines, statutory references were deleted within the body of the regulations, but retained within the **Related Statutes** section.

- Minor editorial revisions were made to provide consistency and clarity, and other changes were made to conform to system style guidelines.

Please distribute the revised system regulations among your staff as you deem appropriate.

According to the Education Act of the U.S. state government, the president of the university is the chief executive of the university and has the management and decision-making power of university affairs. The president of the university is the executor of the school's development strategy, various major affairs, teaching management, discipline construction, scientific research, and other work. Therefore, the president is the coordinator of important relationships inside and outside the university, the innovator of the university's strategic development, and the main raiser of funds for the operation of the university.

President Dan Jones' main focus can be seen from the items listed on his webpage:

- President's Biography
- President and Staff
- Faculty Senate
- Budget Review and Development Council
- Strategic Enrollment Management Committee
- Addresses & Presentations
- Community Updates

- The Pride Alumni Magazine
- Sam Rayburn
- Documents and Reports
- Living, Learning, and Working Climate Survey

The web page mentions Sam Rayburn. Sam Rayburn is an alumnus of the university. After graduation, he worked for the Texas Congressional District 4 for a long time and was later elected as the Speaker of the U.S. House of Representatives. Sam Rayburn was also one of the founders of the university in its early years and died in 1961. When the university was building a new Student Center, a statue of Sam Rayburn was erected in front of it to commemorate him as an outstanding alumnus.

Figure 19.17 – Sam Rayburn Statue

American university presidents have their own school governance philosophy, university vision, and guiding principles.

President Dan Jones' philosophy of school governance (university values):

- Integrity Integrity
- Innovation Innovation
- Imagination

President Dan Jones' university vision:

- The university will provide traditional and non-traditional learning opportunities through existing and new programs for students, faculty, and staff to set high expectations and goals
- The university will provide all individuals with a sense of community by fostering an environment that best meets the needs of study, career, and personal development
- The University will be a place for students, faculty, staff, and the community to work together and pursue excellence

Guiding Principles of President Dan Jones: Diversity, Service Orientation, Student Success, Optimal Management, Global Readiness, Academic Attainment, and Effective Communication.

Figure 19.18 – Guiding Principals

Guiding Principles

Diversity

Foster a culture of inclusion whereby people of all backgrounds who live, learn, and work on campus feel welcome, and valued. Represent the diversity of the region we serve while respecting individual differences and similarities.

Service

Promote excellence in service to members of all internal and external communities.

Student Success

Implement effective, research-based strategies, providing high-quality instruction and student support, through a variety of services, and resulting in timely degree completion by graduates who are prepared for the workforce or for continued study in graduate and/or professional programs.

Stewardship

Advance the university by demonstrating the quality of our programs and services to an ever-expanding community of supporters. Leverage the value of public, private, and human resources through business practices that are founded in accountability and transparency, and academic practices that are continuously improved through research, assessment, and innovation.

Globalization

Provide opportunities for exploration of, and engagement with, global dynamics in an effort to enhance students' global competence and preparation for an interconnected world.

Scholarship

Collaborate in the creation, dissemination, and application of knowledge and creative works through research and scholarly engagement that have a meaningful impact on the economic, social, and cultural vitality of our constituents and the world.

Communication

Disseminate a consistent, authentic, and reliable message that effectively engages internal and external stakeholders, and which results in sustained growth.

Dan Jones epitomizes a university president, leading a prestigious, expansive, and time-honored state institution. As the university's foremost executive officer, President Dan Jones serves as both its leader and guiding spirit. His philosophy and unwavering work ethic are evident at every turn of the administrative process, leaving an indelible imprint of his values on the institution's essence. This harmonious synergy between leadership and institution is a testament to the effectiveness of a well-structured system and a finely-tuned administrative environment. Isn't it fitting to extend our heartfelt appreciation for such an exceptional president and the remarkable institutional framework that sustains our university's success?

A memorial note for President Dr. Dan R Jones

Dan Richard Jones, Ph.D. (1953-2016) served as the university's president since 2008. Before that, Jones had been Provost and Vice President of Academic Affairs at Texas A&M International University in Laredo, where he served from 2003-08. Additionally, Jones had been an administrator and instructor from 1985-2002 at the University of Houston-Downtown, where he had also served as Professor of English. Before that, Jones had been an instructor at Casper College in Casper, Wyoming, from 1982-85.

During Jones' tenure at A&M-Commerce, university enrollment increased dramatically, including topping the 10,000 mark in 2010. Enrollment for the 2015-16 academic year began at 12,302. Texas Governor Rick Perry recognized Jones' innovation in creating the state's first competency-based degree program in 2013. Under Jones' leadership, the university created a Bachelor of Science in Nursing program in 2012, among many other projects fueled by his vision and energy. A&M-Commerce opened a campus in Rockwall, Texas, and two new residential halls on the main campus. Many other successful building projects marked Jones' tenure at A&M-Commerce. They contributed to Jones' vision and tireless efforts to beautify the Commerce campus and create an inviting, traditional environment to promote scholarship, research, interpersonal fellowship, and recreation. The

Sam Rayburn Student Center opened in 2009 and was expanded in 2014. The university's Music Building was opened in 2011, and a new Nursing Building is in development. Jones oversaw a revival of the university's athletics programs and facilities and was proud to be a Lion.

Jones received a B.A. in English from the University of Texas, where he graduated with highest honors and special honors in 1975. Jones earned a B.J. in Magazine Journalism, with highest honors, from the University of Texas that same year. Jones earned an M.A. in English from Rice University in 1978 before completing an M.A. in American Studies from the University of Iowa in Iowa City, Iowa, in 1982 and a Ph.D. in American Studies, also from Iowa, in 1984.

Relevant Information for Reference

The processes for appointing university presidents in China and the United States differ due to variations in their respective education systems and governance structures. Here's an overview of how university presidents are typically produced in each country and how their roles may differ across universities:

China

1. Selection Process: In China, the appointment of university presidents is usually overseen by government agencies, particularly the Ministry of Education. The selection process typically involves a combination of political considerations, academic qualifications, and administrative experience. The government, university faculty, and party committees play significant roles in decision-making.

2. Government Influence: The Chinese government exercises considerable influence over university presidents, as they are expected to align their policies with national priorities and adhere to ideological guidelines set by the Communist Party. This influence often extends to academic and research activities as well.

3. Administrative Focus: Chinese university presidents are typically responsible for overseeing the administrative operations of their institutions. They play a crucial role in managing financial matters, campus infrastructure development, faculty recruitment, and student affairs. Academic decisions, curriculum development, and research direction are often influenced by the government and party committees.

United States

1. Selection Process: In the United States, the selection of university presidents varies across institutions but generally involves a more decentralized process. Typically, the Board of Trustees or Regents, composed of members from the university community, alumni, and external stakeholders, is responsible for appointing a president. This process often includes candidate searches, interviews, and consultations with faculty, staff, students, and community representatives.

2. Autonomy and Academic Freedom: U.S. university presidents generally have more autonomy and academic freedom compared to their counterparts in China. They have the authority to make decisions related to academic programs, research priorities, faculty hiring and tenure, and campus policies. However, presidents are still accountable to the board or governing body overseeing the university.

3. Fundraising and External Relations: University presidents in the United States often have a significant focus on fundraising and external relations. They play a crucial role in securing financial resources through donations, grants, and partnerships with external organizations. They are also responsible for cultivating relationships with alumni, community leaders, and government officials to support the university's mission and goals.

It's important to note that university presidents' specific roles and remits can vary across institutions within each country. Factors such as the size of the university, its mission (e.g., research-focused, liberal arts, etc.), public or private status, and regional context can all influence the scope of responsibilities and decision-making authority held by university presidents.

EPILOGUE

This book is a collection of articles based on the author's WeChat public account published over the years. These articles were written during the author's campus life in the United States, reflecting the author's firsthand experiences and encounters with different cultural environments in the East and West. The author uses a comparative approach to depict various aspects of real American university campus life. Undoubtedly, the text embodies the author's crystallized observations and reflections on every detail of campus life.

Each article in the book stands alone, yet they come together to form a coherent whole. These articles encompass the author's observations and experiences in American higher education institutions over the decades and serve as an examination and reflection on the characteristics of Western cultural genes by investigating various systems. The significance lies in scrutinizing phenomena and things and in comparison and reflection, revealing more objective patterns and their essence through such comparisons. The author strives to maintain a value-neutral principle in writing, even avoiding political elements in commenting on specific phenomena.

To facilitate readers' understanding, each article is accompanied by illustrations, and some articles include statistical charts to provide readers with a more intuitive and concrete understanding of the realities. Relevant reference materials are directly inserted into the text to offer readers guidance. The language is accessible and straightforward, suitable for individuals from various cultural backgrounds and professions. It is particularly noteworthy for sociologists, cultural researchers, and educators. Due to limitations in on-site investigations, the content discussed in the articles may not comprehensively cover all aspects of university life.

It is essential to note that the discussions in this book are based on the author's observations and dissections of individual cases, and conclusions of a general or overall nature should be left to the reader's discretion.

ABOUT THE AUTHOR

Dr. Jiaming Sun is a professor in the Department of Sociology and Criminal Justice at Texas A&M University-Commerce. Before joining the University, he was a faculty member at Fudan University in China. His influential Chinese book, "Generation Gaps: the Background of Transition Period 1991-1994," is widely cited in studies of social change and cultural transition. The English version "China's Generation Gap" was released by Routledge Publishing in 2018. His book "Chinese Globalization: A Profile of People-Based Global Connections in China" delves into the explicit effects of global connectivity on local culture and society in post-reform mainland China. His book based on empirical data, "Personal Global Connectivity and Local Transformation," examines changing behaviors and value orientations among Shanghai residents influenced by globalization. Dr. Sun has also contributed numerous book papers on globalization, urban residential life, cultural studies, and youth issues in China, Taiwan, Singapore, the United States, and the United Kingdom over the last four decades.

Printed in the United States
by Baker & Taylor Publisher Services

Printed in the United States
by Baker & Taylor Publisher Services